AF505555

FRANK STELLA'S STARS | A SURVEY

SEPTEMBER 21, 2020 TO MAY 9, 2021

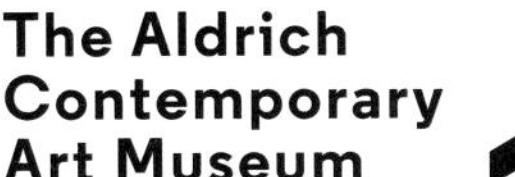

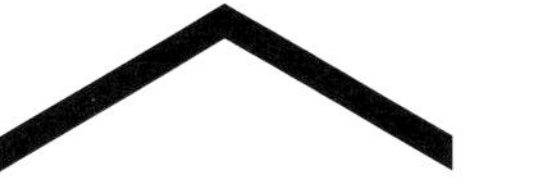

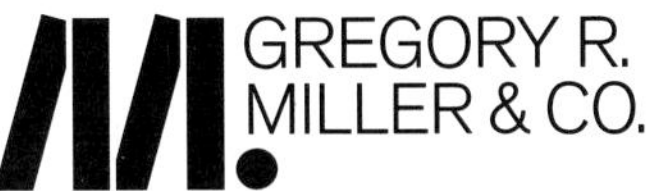

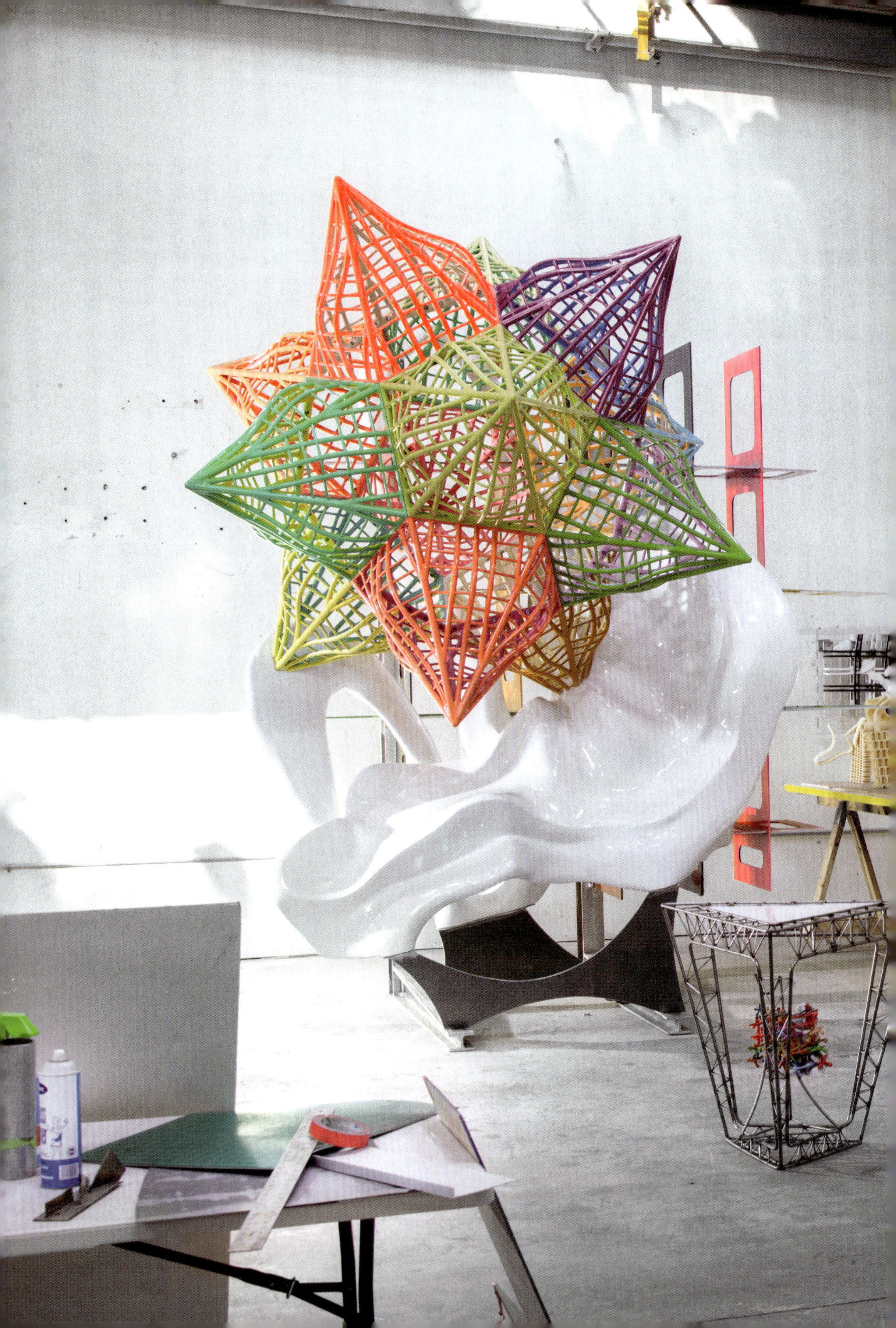

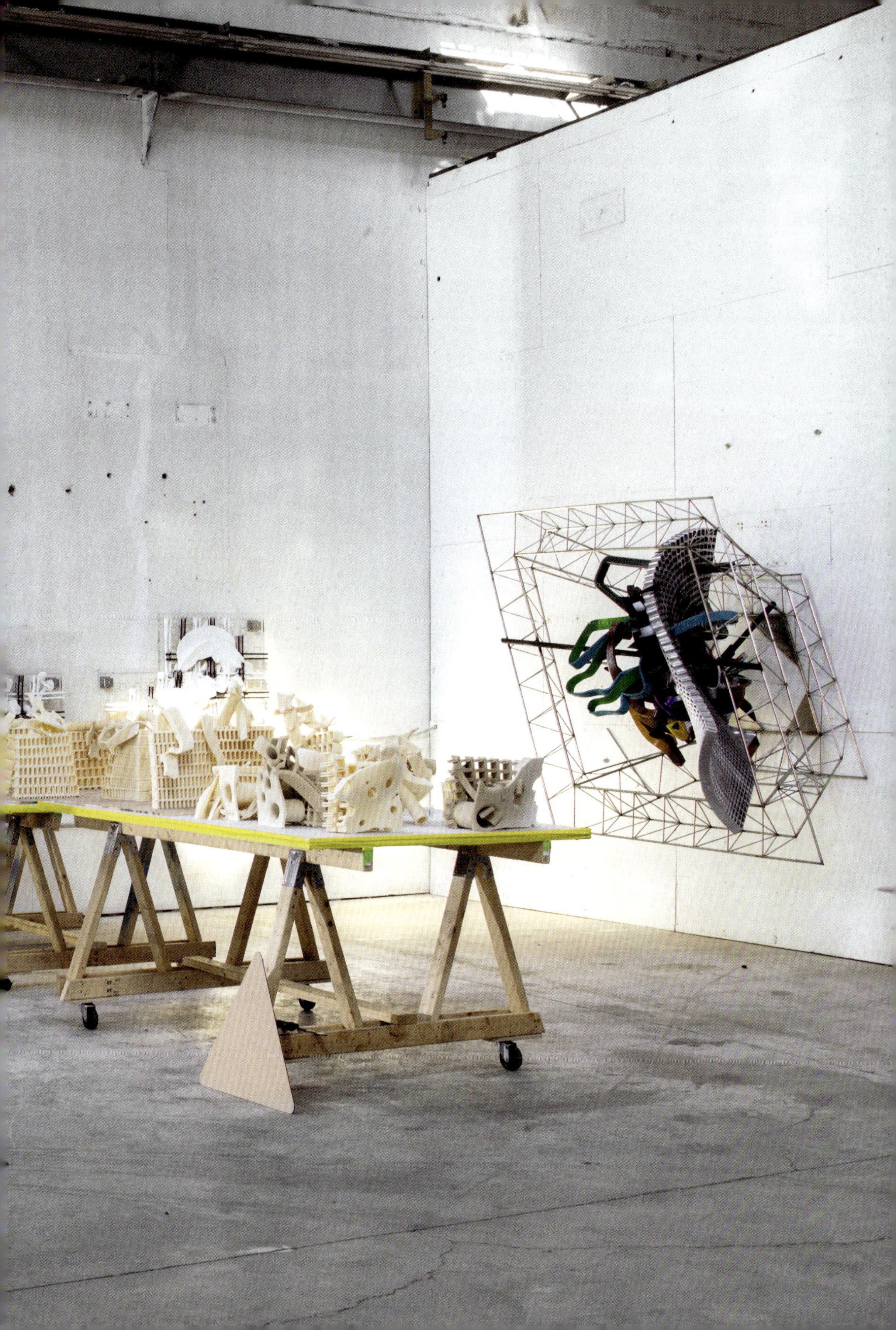

Front cover: *Fat Puffed Star Model*, 2016
(FS2016.043) **Back cover:** *Star of Persia*,
1967 (FS67.178)

TABLE OF CONTENTS

FOREWORD

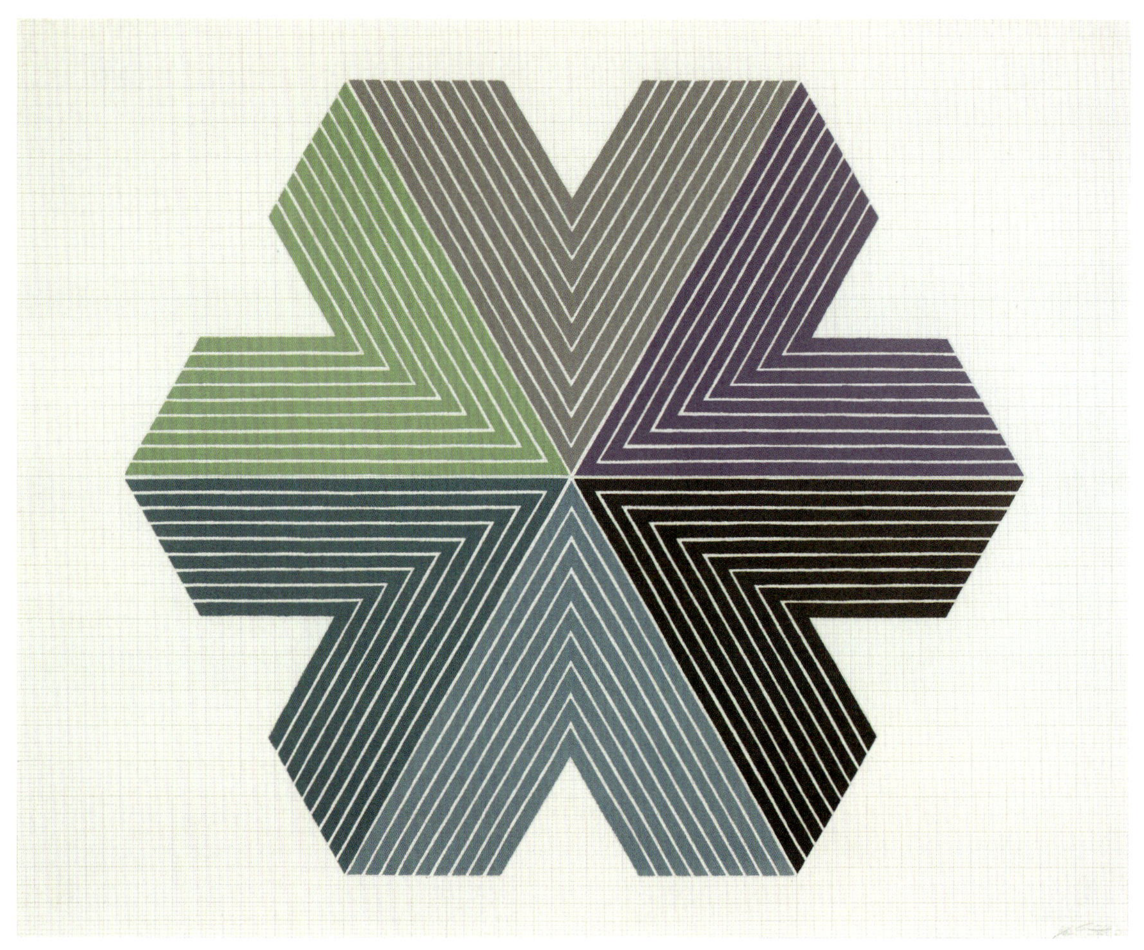

(FIG.1) *Star of Persia II*, 1967 (FS67.111) (Axsom/Kolb 2)

FOREWORD

The Marriage of Reason and Squalor, II, 1959, is the earliest of Frank Stella's works in the collection of the Museum of Modern Art, New York. The painting was acquired for MoMA through the Larry Aldrich Foundation Fund, thus beginning a sixty-year relationship between the artist and the museum that Larry founded five years later, The Aldrich.

Frank Stella's Stars, A Survey considers the enduring nature of a singular form—the star—in the artist's extraordinary career. The works in the show span the early 1960s to the present day, shifting in scale and dimension yet always returning to the star.

Just as Stella has returned again and again to this shape, The Aldrich has returned again and again to his work. Noted for our engagement with emerging and under-recognized artists, the Museum has also developed deep and long-lasting relationships with specific artists whose work we have engaged with over time, highlighting new developments or examining previously unexplored terrain. Since our founding in 1964, Frank Stella has participated in fifteen exhibitions at the Museum. Stella's exhibition history with The Aldrich includes participation in shows such as *Cool Art* (1967), *The Minimal Tradition* (1979), and *Intermedia: Between Painting and Sculpture* (1984). In fact, *Frank Stella's Stars, A Survey* will feature two works that were first presented at The Aldrich in 1969 (*Star of Persia I* and *II*). The present survey, however, marks the first time that The Aldrich has devoted an entire exhibition to the artist's work.

Frank Stella's Stars is the result of a collaboration between my colleagues Richard Klein, Exhibitions

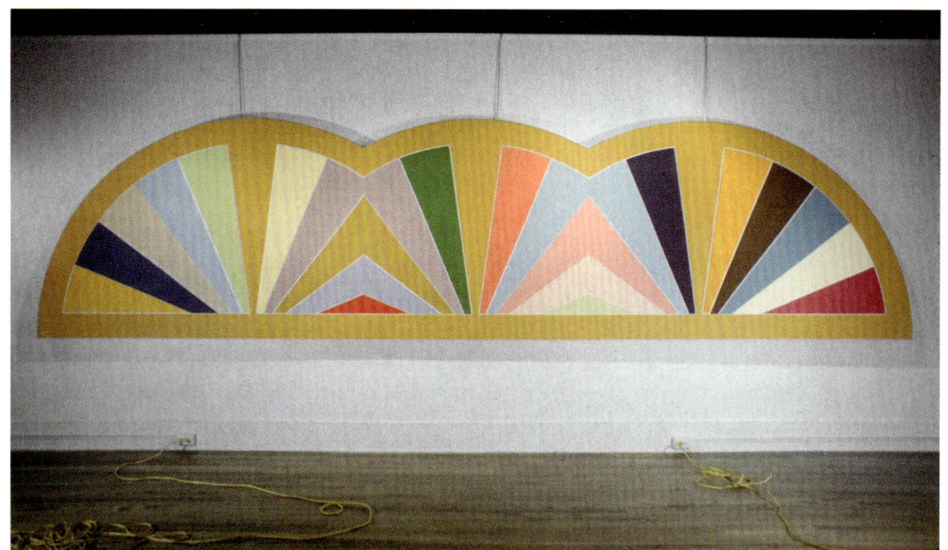

(FIG.2) Frank Stella, *Manteneia III*, 1968. *Highlights of the 1967–1968 Art Season* (installation view), The Aldrich Contemporary Art Museum, 1968

Director, and Amy Smith-Stewart, Senior Curator. What began as a visit to Stella's studio to see new sculpture evolved into this groundbreaking and surprising exhibition, which asks us to consider the artist's work in a new way. Richard and Amy's partnership on this project, and the Museum's program, are great examples of what makes The Aldrich such a dynamic institution.

In addition to the show's co-curators, many other people contributed to its success. Thanks are due to the generous supporters whose philanthropy was essential in bringing this ambitious undertaking to life: the Anne S. Richardson Fund, the Speyer Family Foundation, Martin Margulies, Diana Bowes and Jim Torrey, Linda and Michael Dugan, and Patricia and Lawrence Kemp. Thanks are also due to the Mnuchin Gallery, the Pizzuti Collection, and Jordan D. Schnitzer, who have lent several important works in the show. The Aldrich is fortunate to co-publish this book with Gregory R. Miller & Co., to whom we are grateful for their continued support and partnership. The Marianne Boesky Gallery has provided The Aldrich with tremendous assistance during the planning of this show, and we are grateful to Marianne, Savannah Downs, and Sara Putterman for their ongoing enthusiasm, along with Kristen

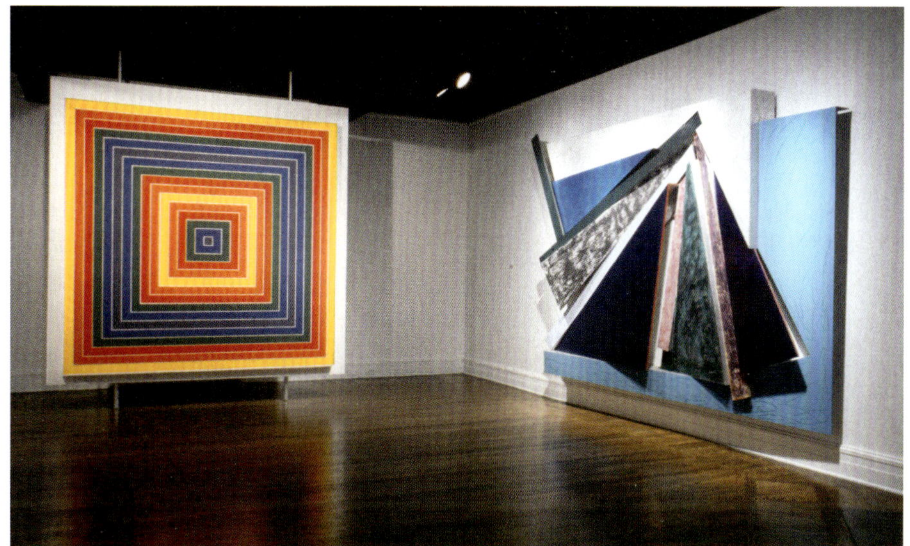

(FIG.3) Frank Stella, *Louisana Lottery Co.,* 1962 (left), *Botafogo I,* 1975 (right). *Changes* (installation view), The Aldrich Contemporary Art Museum, 1983

Becker and Ricky Manne, who have been integral to the exhibition's development. The many members of Stella's studio have also been a tremendous help, including Igal Kapstan, David Lukowski, Dominic Nurre, Paula Pelosi, Veronika Schmid, and Allison Martone Scribner. Thank you also to Robert Van Winkle, Arturo Martinez, and Michele Otero of R.V.W. Sculpture Arrangement, Ltd.

I also wish to thank members of the Museum's staff for their hard work on the exhibition, including Namulen Bayarsaihan, Director of Education; Emily Devoe, Head of Marketing and Communications; Gretchen Kraus, Design Director; and Bruce Smith, Director of Development. In addition, a big thanks goes to the members of our Curatorial Department who have been hard at work with Richard and Amy on this show: Mary Kenealy, Registrar; Chris Manning, Head of Exhibitions and Facilities; and Caitlin Monachino, Curatorial Assistant.

And lastly, our greatest thanks go to the artist, who has trusted The Aldrich at so many points to consider his work, and who has opened his practice to us once again.

Cybele Maylone, Executive Director

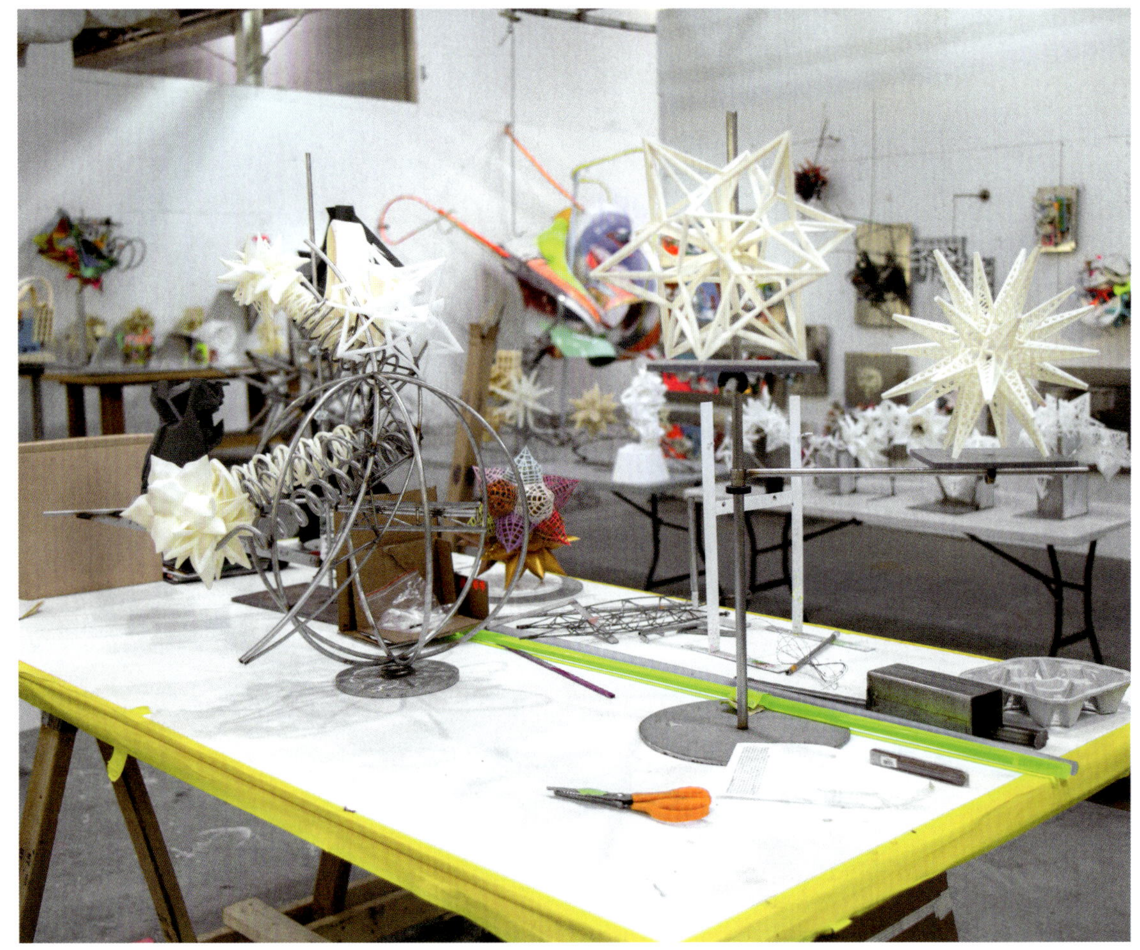

(FIG.4) Frank Stella's Studio, Rock Tavern, NY

ALL THE STARS, *AN INTRO*

Abstraction has the freedom to be large without magnification, the ability to be small without miniaturization. In a sense abstraction gains its freedom, its unfettered expandability, its own working space by eluding the spatial dictates of the real and the ideal image.—Frank Stella.[1]

We are all in the gutter but some of us are looking at the stars.—Oscar Wilde[2]

Inside The Aldrich's Project Space is one of the largest sculptures in the exhibition. With its twelve puffed-up rays stretching twenty-one feet in all directions, Frank Stella's *Fat 12 Point Carbon Fiber Star*, 2016 (fig.5), dominates the room's perimeter like an intergalactic weapon. Its spectral core absorbs the viewer—a dramatic force that harkens back to the shadowy reductive presence of Stella's earliest breakout body of work, the *Black Paintings*, 1958–60 (fig.6), which catapulted him to instant stardom.

Stella has spent his career stretching abstraction to the outer limits. Skirting the line between painting and sculpture, he is a prolific experimenter. To describe his studio production as ambitious would be a glaring understatement. With a career spanning more than sixty years, with work straddling every category—paintings, drawings, prints, sculptures, objects, and public art—Stella's output is estimated in the many hundreds. This survey focuses on *one* enduring motif within a steadily advancing vocabulary: the *star*. Under the spotlight for the first time, this subject is on display in twenty-five works that orbit the Museum. Sited on the grounds and the first-floor galleries, the exhibition tracks the star's

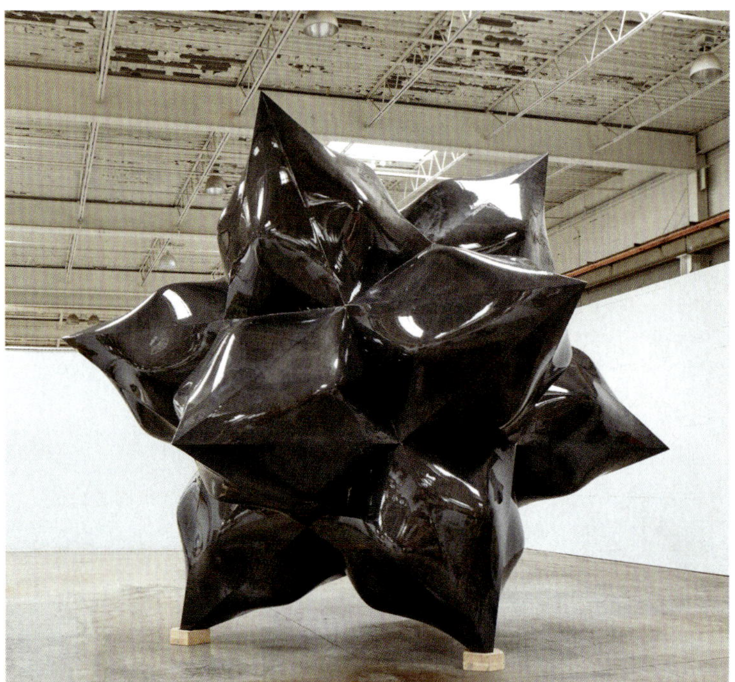

(FIG.5) *Fat 12 Point Carbon Fiber Star, 2016 (FS2016.033)*

origins in Stella's drawing and lithography, and in a significant painting from the 1960s, to its latest incarnations in sculpture, wall reliefs, and painted objects from the 2010s.

A singular element that intersects the realms of the real and the abstract, the star emerged as a motif during Stella's first decade in New York, as he was exhibiting his groundbreaking striped and shaped paintings, and then vanished. It resurfaced many decades later at a moment when Stella was wrestling with a dimensional abstraction that was ricocheting out from the surface. Today, the star is a knotty fixture, the *lead* in scores of works from tabletop objects to towering sculptures.

The star is also a notable signifier, as its arrival and reappearance correlate with the convergence of what have been deemed competing concerns in his long career. Advancing from a planar shape to an

(FIG. 6) *Die Fahne hoch!*, 1959 (Rubin 35)

object in space, the stars seem to emphatically
express Stella's conviction that "abstraction has
to move; it has to extend itself."[3] Signaling a pivot
from the wall to the ground and embracing more
over less, the stars erupt from the pictorial surface,
extending their accentuated edges with a defiance
that confronts the space of the viewer from all sides.
The star's formal evolution attests to Stella's wrangle
with the physical and illusory limits of reduction
and representation, wall and object. Aided today
by new virtual technologies, a sketch becomes a
digital schematic that generates a 3-D object, to be
manipulated and replicated ad infinitum. Stella riffs
on this flawless shape with its perfect proportions
and gleaming allure without entirely obliterating its
identifiable structural features. It is only corruptible
up to a point, its distinctness separating it from his
other abstract subjects. Whether stand-alone stars
or multiple star systems conjoined with his signature
monikers—smoke rings, spiral cuts, soft grids

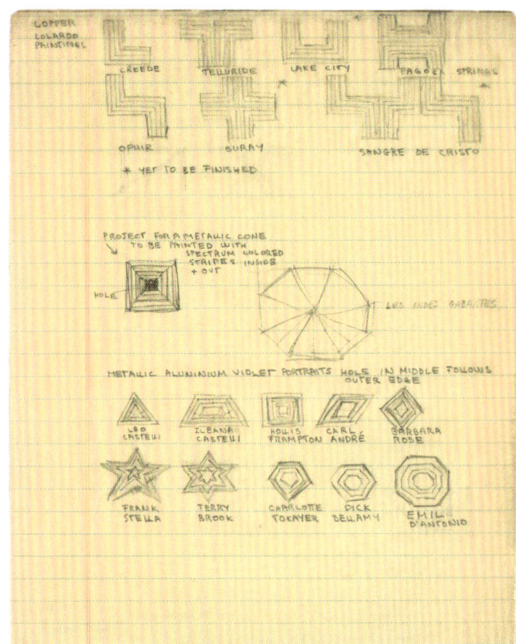

(FIG. 7) Untitled (list of "Copper Paintings," 1960–61, and "Purple Paintings," 1961), 1961

(which he calls marshmallows), sails, and waves— together they flash an abstraction that is chronically in motion.

Scaled to the table or the open air, Stella's star sculptures and objects also flaunt an omnivorous attitude. Compressing the digital and the hand-finished in the pursuit of maximum spatial tension, this is a process that involves multiple hubs of activity. The stars transport us: we imagine how disparate elements shift, how parts are assembled, how shapes are selected, how paint is applied, how sections are rearranged. The works parade an outsized material resourcefulness that collapses analogue and twenty-first-century technologies: RPT (rapid prototype technology) plastics, teak, aluminum, stainless steel, birch plywood, fiberglass, carbon fiber, and more. With their automotive neon hues, shimmering and natural finishes, the stars, big and small, flex and project a spatial dynamism that intimates a potential maneuverability—as if they were built to perform.

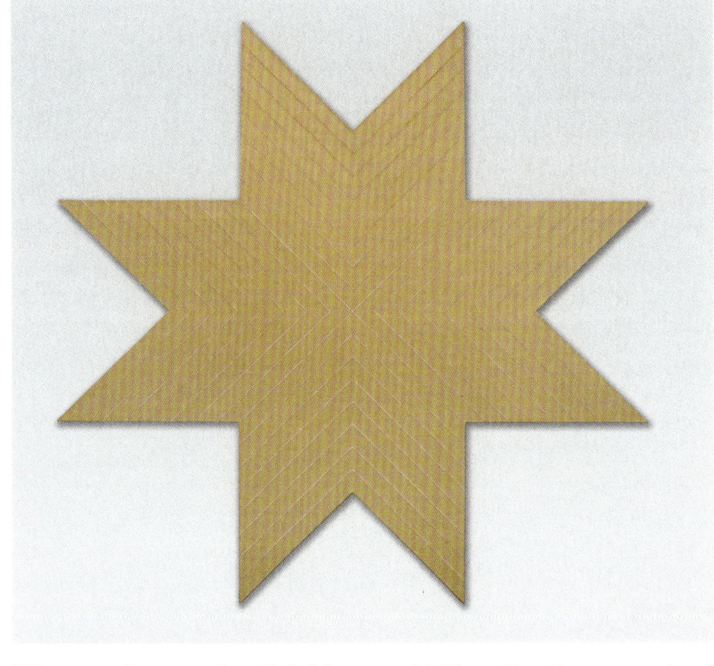

(FIG.8) *Plant City*, 1963 (Rubin 211)

Throughout the 1960s and 70s, Stella regularly made preparatory sketches for his paintings, plotting out ideas in pencil or ink on graph paper and making visual notations on notebook pages or even stationery. The very first star appears in the drawing *Untitled (list of "Copper Paintings," 1960–61, and "Purple Paintings," 1961)* (fig.7), made on yellow lined paper in 1961. The work illustrates plans for two important series: the *Copper Paintings*, titled after towns in Colorado's San Juan Mountains, and the *Purple Paintings*, named after friends in his creative circle. The *Purple Paintings* are portraits depicting Leo Castelli as a triangle; Hollis Frampton, a square; Carl Andre, a rhombus, and so forth. The intentions behind his choices are anyone's guess, but the shape he selected for himself, a star (the painting was never made), exhibits a jocularity not evident in other works from that period. Stella chose a violet metallic paint, diverging from the prior *Black, Aluminum*, and *Copper Paintings*. He referred to the color as "very vulgar,"[4] but also said "that [this] is where I became really committed to color in a funny kind of way—one in which I couldn't avoid it."[5]

In the summer of 1963, Stella was invited by Dartmouth College to be an artist-in-residence. During this period, he stretched the edges of his canvases even further, creating two eight-pointed, star-shaped paintings, each measuring eight feet by eight feet and each named after a Florida city. Stella swapped metallic paints for anti-corrosive industrial primers, using zinc chromate[6] for *Plant City* (fig.8) and a radiant red lead for *Port Tampa City*. With surfaces that appear almost radioactive, Stella formed a star "by joining ... [four] chevron-shaped areas of stripes."[7] Their star shape has been attributed to a 1961 visit he made to Frank Lloyd Wright's historic Anne Pfeiffer Chapel on the Florida State University campus, which vaunts a central tower with a pattern of stacked geometric designs.[8]

In 1967, following his *Notched V* series, 1964–65, Stella made *Star of Persia*, 1967, a pencil drawing on graph paper of a six-sided star that appears more terrestrial than the spiky, hard-edged *Dartmouth* stars. This time he joined six chevrons. Stressing their motion, he described them as "flying wedges."[9] This shape rematerialized in a series of lithographs made with master printer Kenneth Tyler for Gemini G.E.L. in Los Angeles. Experimenting with metallic inks on English Vellum Graph paper, Stella completed a suite of three prints: *Star of Persia I* and *Star of Persia II* (fig.1) (titled after British clipper ships), and the *Irving Blum Memorial Edition* (a tongue-in-cheek homage to the legendary art dealer). These works were exhibited at The Aldrich in the 1969 exhibition, *Young Artists from the Collection of Charles Cowles*. The title *Star of Persia* also names the *Allium christophii*, a showy onion with star-shaped flowers native to Iran. Stella traveled there in 1963, where he would have also encountered Persian monuments ornamented with interlocking star polygons. The six color choices for each, warm tones for *I* and cool tones for *II*, highlight the modular V-shaped elements, underscoring each unit and delineating its boundaries. The colorful inks are superimposed on a silvery base, slightly lifting the image off the vellum.[10] With articulated petals resembling a pinwheel, its shape suggests an object that could twirl.

The *Star of Persia* prints, the *Star of Persia* drawing, and *Port Tampa City* are exhibited in proximity to two recent sculptures, *K.159*, 2013, and *K.359*, 2014 (fig.20), from the *Scarlatti Sonata Kirkpatrick* series (all the works in this series are titled after the 500 keyboard sonatas composed by Giuseppe Domenico Scarlatti). *K.159* is presented on a stainless steel table, amplifying its supernatural presence. It flaunts a collision of four stars with individualized personalities, each on repeat at a different volume and tempo throughout the exhibition: a swollen twelve-point solid in a reflective silver; two open stars sprayed yellow, blue, and green; and a star form familiarly used in a game of jacks, with flat, rounded ends in bronzes and blues. *K.159*, like many of Stella's tabletop objects, has also been sized up, engineered in mirror-polished aluminum and matte carbon fiber. It is a behemoth of interstellar wreckage. Another major sculpture in the Museum's Erna D. Leir Gallery, *Nessus and Dejanira*, 2017, cites a Greek myth in which a centaur, known as Nessus, abducts a beautiful Caledonian princess called Dejanira. Substituting a reflection for plane geometry, a larger-than-life lattice star in glossy pastels—a possible Dejanira abstracted—is encircled by a silky white ripple, an emblematic Stella smoke ring and a probable fill-in for Nessus. Clamped in place by an interlocking metal grid in corresponding soft hues, it stands out from the wall, viewable at all angles.

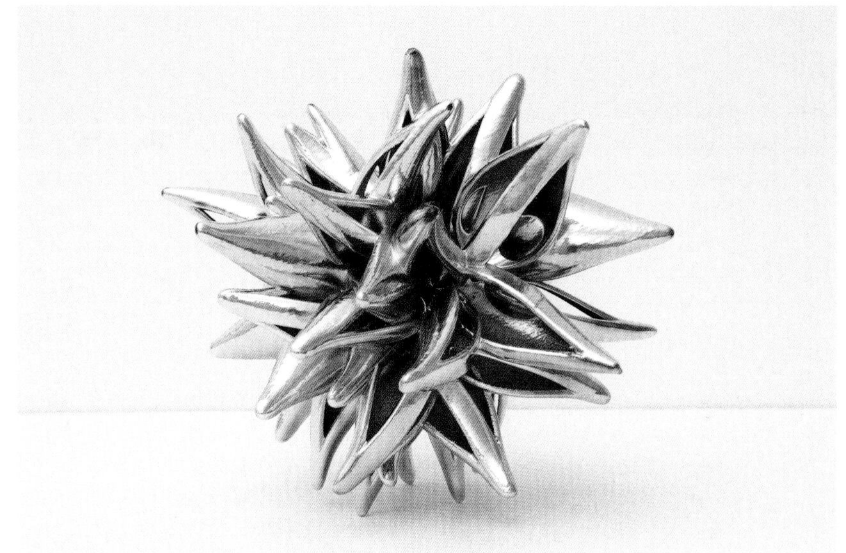

Using additive procedures, sometimes Stella incorporates found objects or makes 3-D copies of them, which he combines with other computer-generated parts translated from his drawings. These works reveal an indiscriminate attitude toward sourcing, deftly fusing the pedestrian and the refined to demonstrate a wit that resists boundaries. This is apparent in two of four sculptural reliefs from 2016 installed along the Museum's Ramp Gallery: *Shoe Piece on Stainless Background* and *Bell Piece on Stainless Background*. Presenting animated, botanical star clusters fastened to stainless steel grounds, these reliefs include recognizable elements, doubles for stellar attributes: the shell of a desk lamp to imply an electric luminosity, and an athlete's cleat signifying a star's fantastic velocity.

In a small gallery on the first floor, a collection of more intimately scaled objects, ranging from the continental to the cosmic, are displayed on sawhorse tables built to imitate those found inside Stella's cavernous studio (fig.4). There, dozens of objects, maquettes for bigger ideas, are side by side with the natural specimens he collects: a log

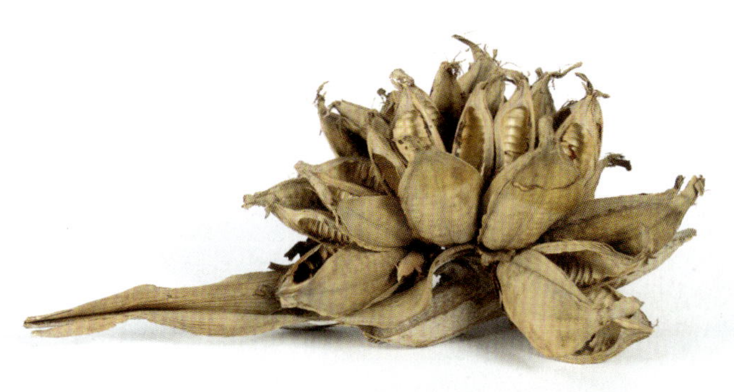

(FIG.10) Natural pod star (FS2019.064)

chiseled by a beaver, a tangled bundle of sticks and natural debris, and a dried pod star (fig.10). Within the installation, the petrified seedpod is set against his *Maquette for Star*, 2017 (fig.9), a computer-generated model sprayed a burnished silver. Some objects are displayed on turntables that rotate, such as the eleven-inch-tall prototype of *Fat 12 Point Carbon Fiber Star*, 2016, coated in a leathery matte black. Its sharp endpoints are fitted with tiny white protective slippers: a functional feature that counterbalances its divine status, making it appear more mortal.

Visible from the Project Space and installed on a grassy expanse in the The Aldrich's Sculpture Garden is the twelve-sided *Jasper's Split Star*, 2017 (fig.12). Six of its open trusses are spray-painted pale shades of gray, purple, and blue; the others are in solid aluminum. Formally, it harkens back to a painting Stella made in 1962, *Jasper's Dilemma* (fig.11). In this tribute to his contemporary, Jasper Johns, a pair of concentric squares—one in primary colors, the other in gray tones, each divided by intersecting lines—forms four triangular quadrants

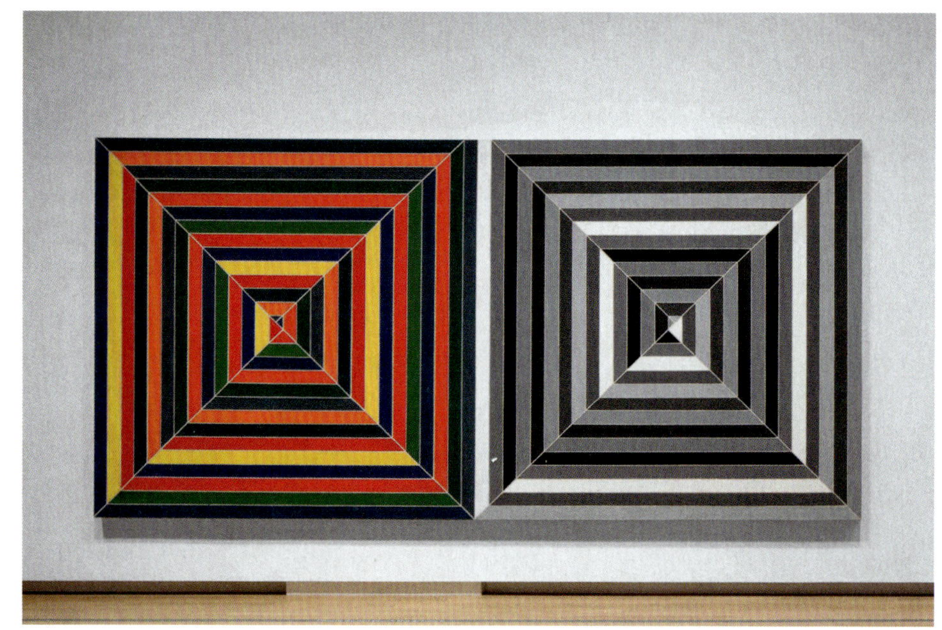

that project out from the canvas. More than fifty years later, this illusionism has mutated into the titanic dodecagon, *Jasper's Split Star*.

The star is characterized in this survey as a breakthrough element. From a simple, planar shape to an ornamented, spatial object, its manifestation reveals stylistic continuity amid decisive variation. Stella's stars personify a built abstraction that is insistently hyperkinetic, unremittingly on the move.

Amy Smith-Stewart, Senior Curator

(FIG.12) *Jasper's Split Star*, 2017 (FS2017.007)

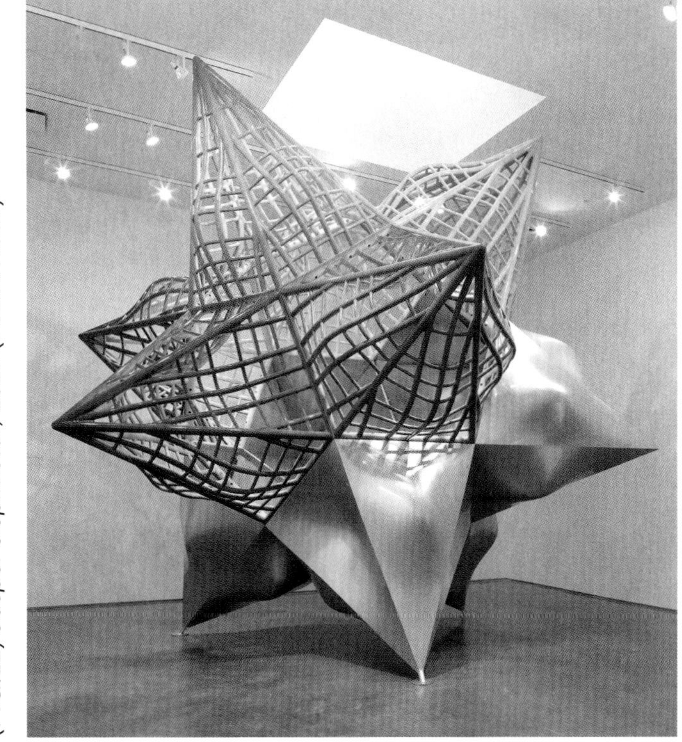

1. Frank Stella, *Working Space* (Cambridge, MA: Harvard University Press, 1986), 167.
2. Oscar Wilde, *Lady Windermere's Fan: A Play about a Good Woman* (London: E. Mathews and J. Lane, 1893), 92.
3. Stella, 143.
4. William S. Rubin, *Frank Stella* (New York: Museum of Modern Art, 1970), 82.
5. Ibid., 89.
6. According to Wikipedia, zinc chromate coating was formulated by the auto industry in the 1920s: https://en.wikipedia.org/wiki/Zinc_chromate.
7. Rubin, 92.
8. Erica F. Battle, in *Philadelphia Museum of Art Handbook* (Philadelphia: Philadelphia Museum of Art, 2014), 365.
9. Rubin, 97.
10. Richard H. Axsom, *Frank Stella Prints: A Catalogue Raisonné* (Portland, OR: Jordan Schnitzer Family Foundation, 2016), 54.

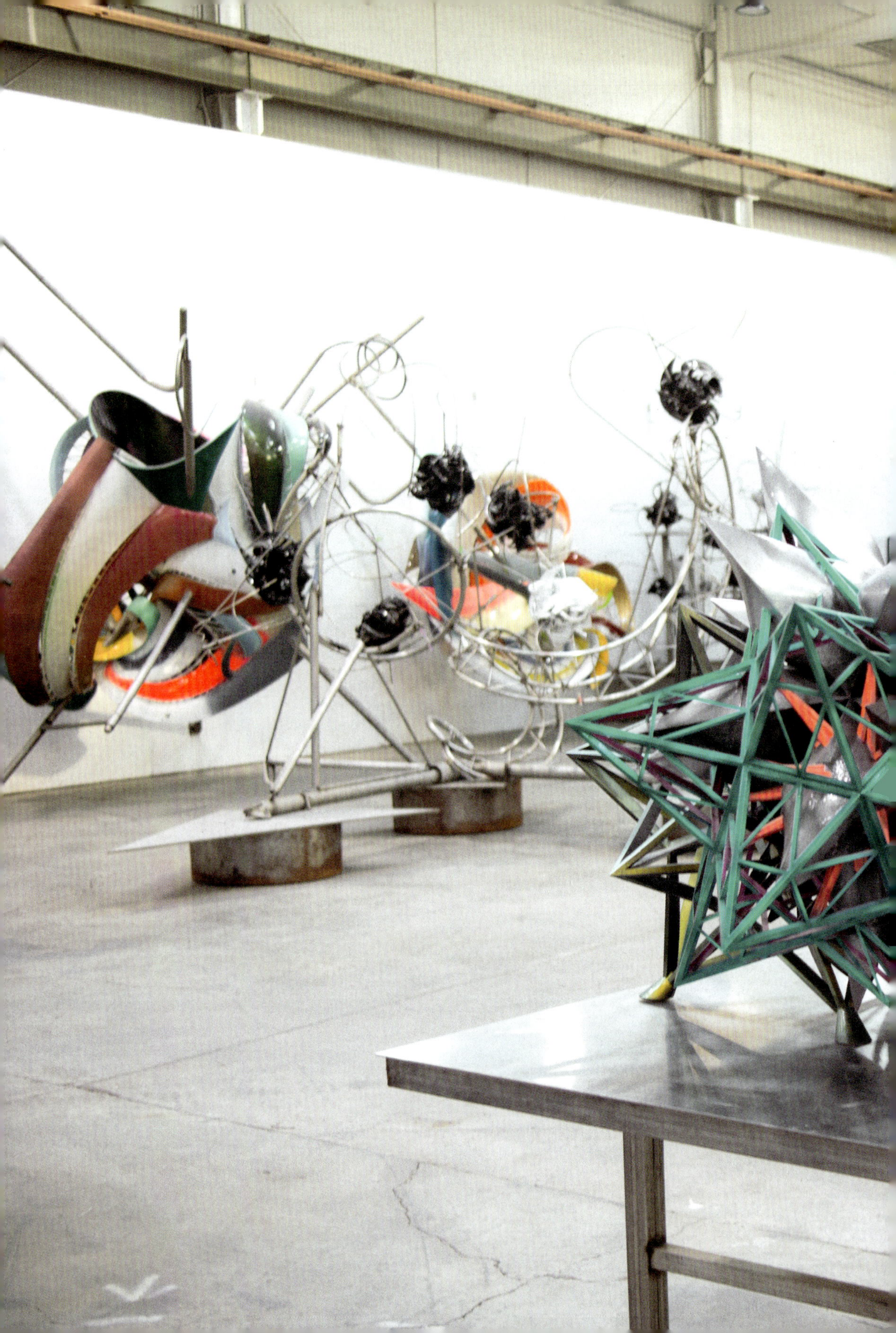

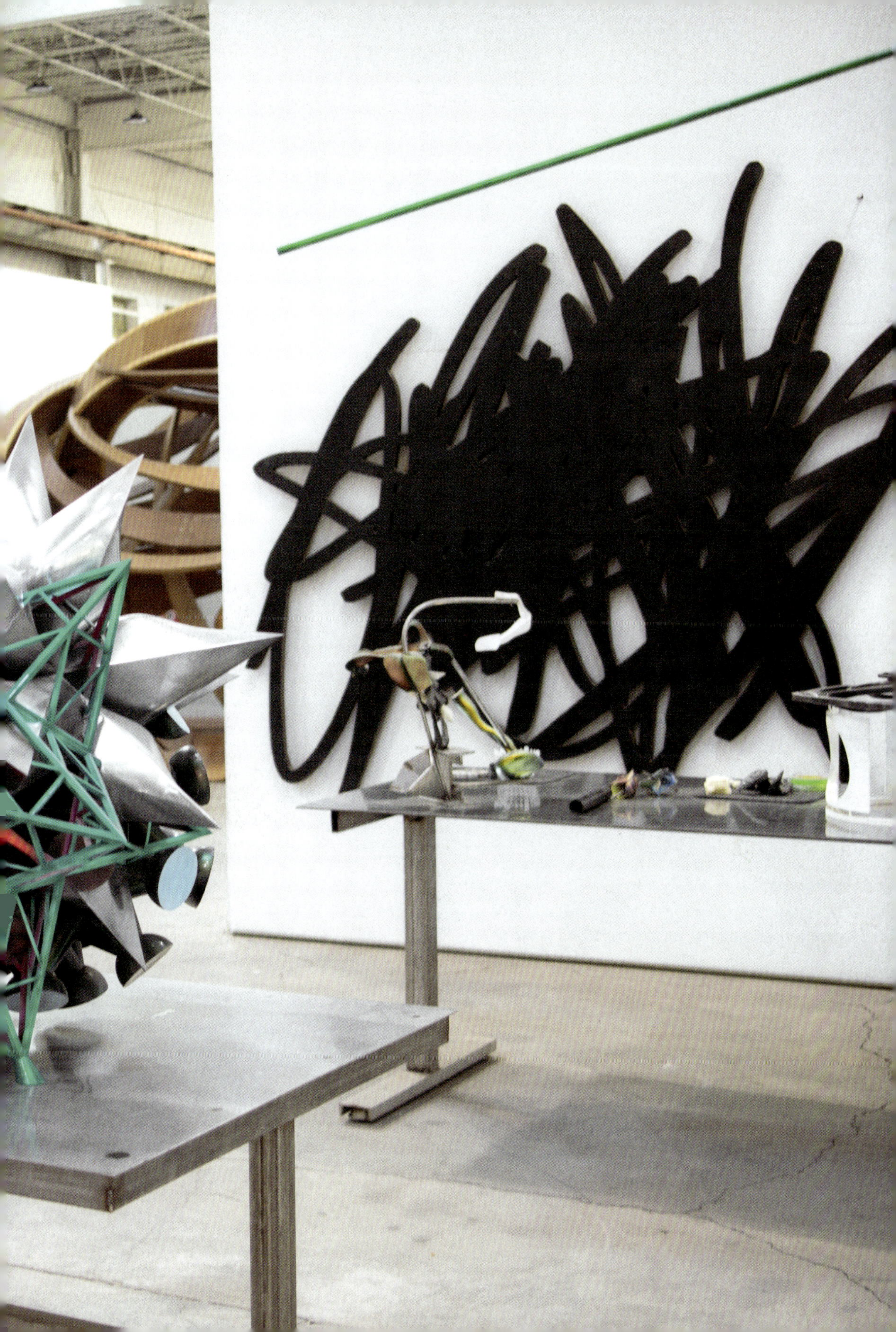

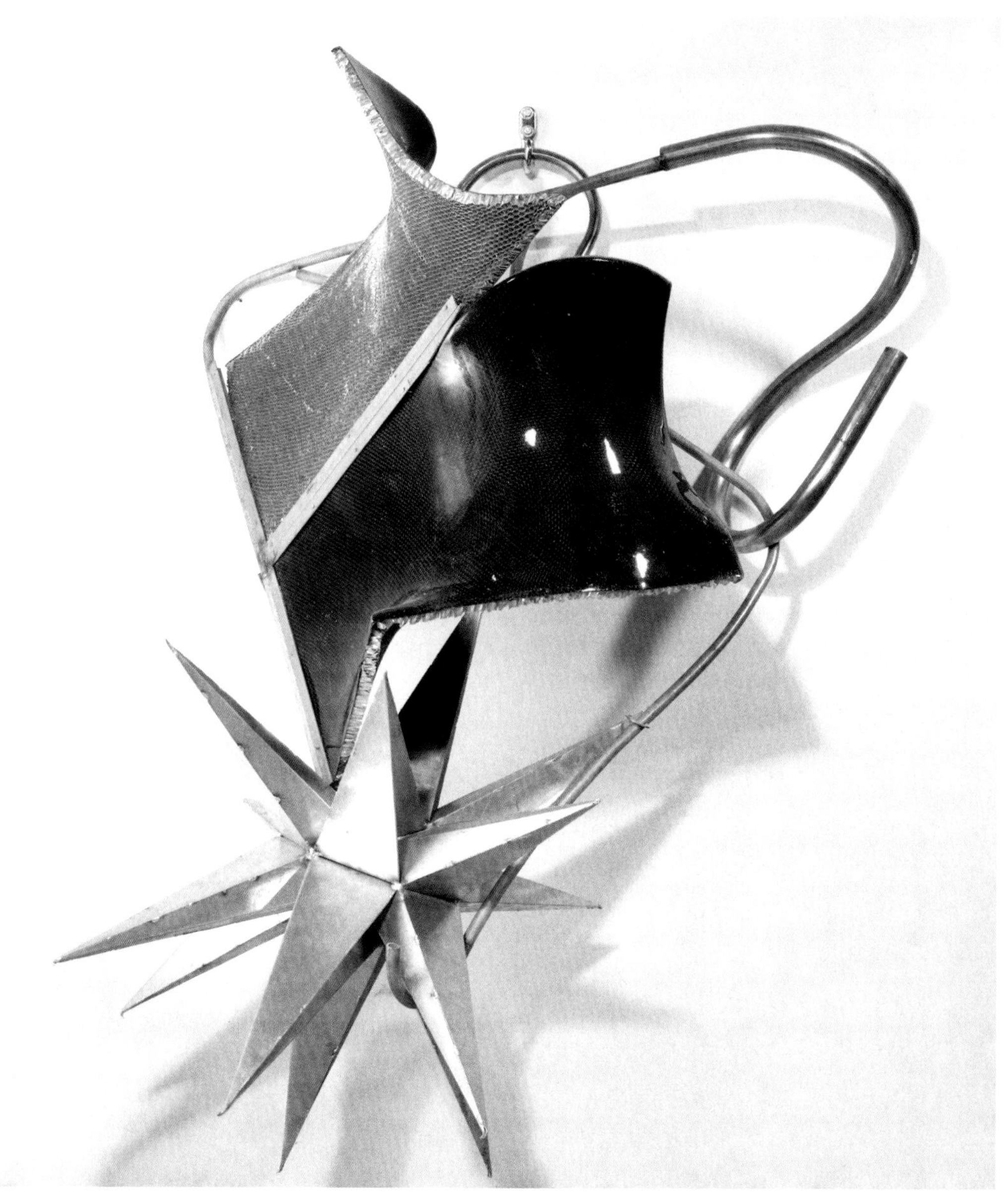

(FIG.13) *boeta*, 2004 (FS2004.009)

STELLA'S STAR SYSTEM

From the beginning of his career, Frank Stella's central concern has been exploring the various permutations available for the expression of visual space. At the onset it was pictorial space, which in the ensuing decades gradually expanded into a full-blown engagement with sculpture. The artist's thinking about space has been informed by an expansive knowledge of Western art, including, among other things, Baroque painting, Russian Constructivism, and Abstract Expressionism. In the early 1970s, when Stella began to make shallow relief works, he was adamant about their being seen frontally as "pictures," attended by all the historical baggage of painting since the Renaissance. But to look at Stella's work only as the product of a reaction to art history is extremely limiting. The artist's influences and interests are complex, spanning an array of disciplines, including science, literature, architecture, technology, music, and that most-commented-on obsession, automobile racing, an endeavor that revels in the experience of space through speed.

Although Stella is resolutely an abstract artist, identifiable forms have come and gone in the artist's practice over the years, including protractors, French curves, and smoke rings. But curiously, his career thus far has been bracketed by the appearance of a form that is simultaneously abstract and figurative: the *star*. The visual manifestation of a star, in all its variations, is the realization of a theoretical construct that is ultimately based in mathematics. And of course, we are speaking here of the geometrical form, not the stars that populate the heavens.

Stella's interest in the depiction of space has hinged on the revolution that transformed the Renaissance into the Baroque period, particularly the painting of Caravaggio.

In one of his Charles Eliot Norton lectures at Harvard University in 1983–84, Stella stated:

> It seems clear that Caravaggio's compelling realism extends to the space around his figures as well as to the figures themselves. In fact, in painting after painting we are forced to notice Caravaggio's real genius—a projective displacement of space.... We need some kind of image to help form an idea about the design and purpose of Caravaggio's pictorial space. The image that comes to mind is that of a gyroscope—a spinning sphere, capable of accommodating movement and tilt.[1]

But as this quote hints, the revolution regarding concepts of space that categorized the Baroque period wasn't limited to the visual arts. This revolution involved a sea change in thinking about space in general that laid the groundwork for the modern world.

Both Caravaggio and the astronomer and mathematician Johannes Kepler were born in 1571. Kepler was a key figure in the scientific revolution of the seventeenth century, with his life overlapping that of Galileo. Despite its attachment to the fading field of astrology, Kepler's first major astronomical work *Mysterium Cosmographicum* (1596) marks the beginning of modern astronomy due to its definitive rejection of an earth-centered universe. As an astronomer, Kepler was engaged with trying to make sense of the orbits of the planets and their distance from the sun and believed that an underlying geometrical harmony organized the universe. He postulated that the structure of the solar system was determined by the nesting of the five Platonic solids—octahedron, icosahedron, dodecahedron, tetrahedron, and cube—within spheres, with each sphere's relative size corresponding to the distance from the sun of the orbits of the planets then known: Mercury, Venus, Earth, Mars, Jupiter, and Saturn. Kepler's well-known drawing in *Mysterium*

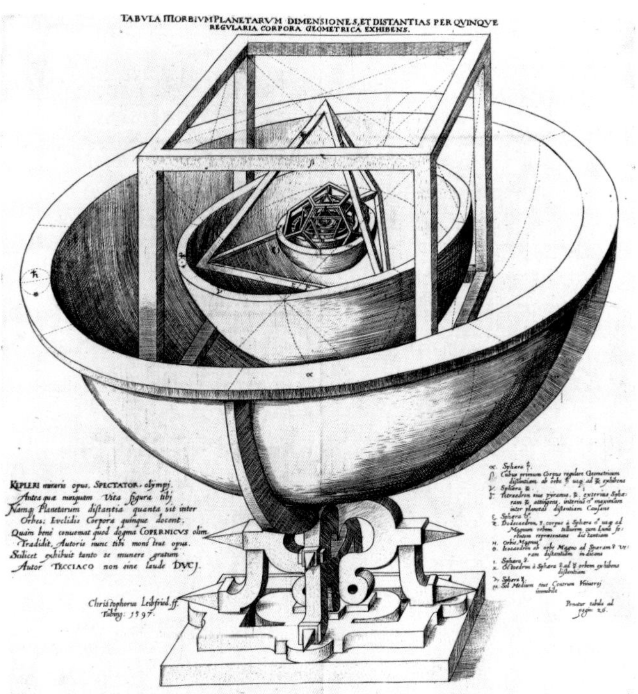

(FIG.14) Johannes Kepler, Model of the Solar System, from *Mysterium Cosmographicum*, 2nd ed., 1621

Cosmographicum (fig.14) that illustrated his Platonic-solid model of the solar system brings to mind Stella's description of the type of space depicted by Caravaggio: a free-floating, spherical gyroscope free of external influences. Beginning in the late 1990s, as Stella's work moved away from pictorialism to fully embrace three dimensions, its character increasingly resembled the vertiginous and cyclonic, with orbiting vectors caught in a seeming gravitational pull that often slingshots them back out into surrounding space.

Kepler was the first person to describe the result of extending the edges of polyhedrons until they met, defining what has come to be known in geometry as "stellated polyhedra." In 2004 Stella made *boeta* (fig.13), his first work to include a wholly three-dimensional star. The star in *boeta* is immediately recognizable as such, but is not as mathematically perfect as his later computer-designed stars; rather, it is a form spot-welded together

27

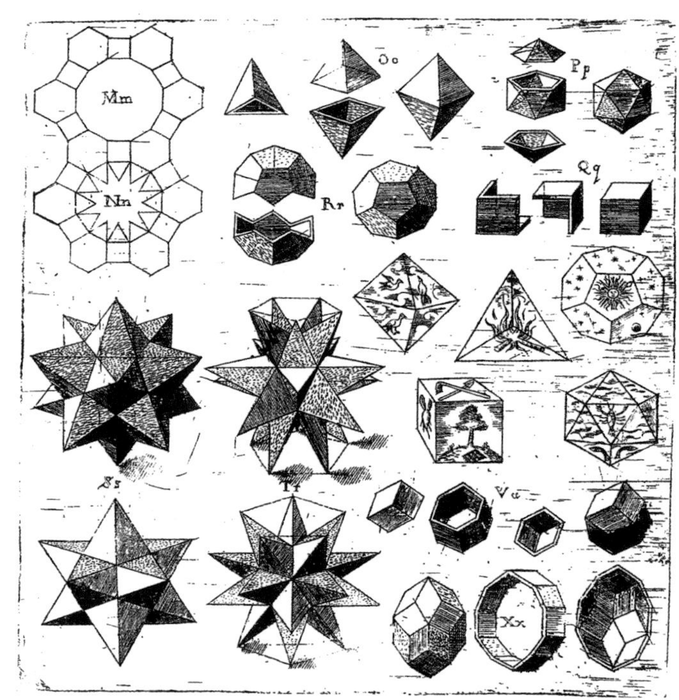

(FIG.15) Illustration of polyhedra and stellated polyhedra from Johannes Kepler's *Harmonices Mundi*, 1619

from a series of irregular stainless steel tetrahedrons. A form much like the star in *boeta*, but based on regular tetrahedra, appears at the center of an illustration in Kepler's 1619 book *Harmonices Mundi* (fig.15), in a section that relates two-dimensional geometry to that of three.

In looking at Stella's star paintings, prints, and drawings from the 1960s, the connection to his recent star sculptures, other than their shared radiational character, might not be obvious. A resolutely flat work like the painting *Port Tampa City*, 1963, is composed of eight tiled parallelograms, each with two corners of 135° and 45°. By fitting similar parallelograms into the negative space formed by the edges of the painting, one can extend the work into an infinite field of tiled parallelograms. The upper left corner of the page from Kepler's *Harmonices Mundi*, while not illustrating the eight-pointed star of *Port Tampa City*, does show a twelve-pointed star and its relationship to the surrounding

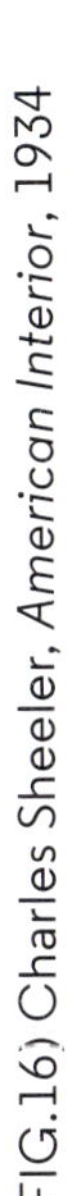

(FIG.16) Charles Sheeler, *American Interior*, 1934

tiled, geometric space. Kepler's illustration reveals the relationship between the tiling of two-dimensional space and the folding of tiling into three. Two of Stella's painting series from the 1960s, *Protractors*, 1967–70, which includes titles such as *Basra Gate I*, 1968, and *Damascus Gate (Stretch Variation I)*, 1970,[2] along with *Moroccan*, 1965, hint at another deep connection with abstract, flat, geometrical space: the complex tessellation found in Islamic art. Much like Stella's rejection of illusionistic space in the first decade of his career, traditional Islamic art is resolutely nonrepresentational, using geometry to animate space in abstract, universal terms. The dramatic silhouette and scale of *Port Tampa City*, however, deflects attention from the painting's more familiar connection with tessellated space, the Star of Bethlehem, one of the most traditional star motifs in quilting and textiles. In the painting *American Interior* by Charles Sheeler (fig.16), another artist whose work often exhibits pronounced geometry, the Star of Bethlehem appears in the carpet design on the floor of the artist's former South Salem, New York, living room.

Stella has repeatedly mentioned throughout his career a desire for his works of art not to be contained by their physical borders but rather to have the ability to activate the surrounding space. The potency of a work like the print *Star of Persia I*, 1967, can be explained by its geometry: six tessellated equilateral triangles, with the exterior face of each missing a triangular notch delineated by the concentric lines that echo each triangle's form. Without these notches the overall form would be a simple hexagon. These small triangles implicate other geometrical forms outside the periphery of the print's silhouette. In fact, if one were to tessellate space with *Star of Persia I* by replicating its form and by touching together the points of the resulting stars, the negative space created would form perfect six-pointed stars composed of two overlapping equilateral triangles, a shape commonly known as the Star of David (fig.17).

Stella has maintained an interest in both symmetry and the extravagantly intricate. This spectrum extends at one end from his early concentric *Black Paintings*, the two-dimensional star works from the early 60s, and the recent individual sculptural stars to his ongoing interest with physically replicating the amorphous nature of smoke rings and his spiraling works that approach Art Nouveau in their sinuous complexity. It is interesting to note that the periods of pronounced symmetry are *symmetrically* located almost sixty years apart, forming brackets on his career thus far. But none of the recent star sculptures exhibit perfect, crystalline symmetry; all have been altered in various ways through piercings, distortion of faces, fabrication techniques, or even biomorphism. It seems that Stella's interest is always to take the known form and manipulate it, often by adding additional layers of spatial information. The artist's geometry has increasingly become non-Euclidean, describing a space where straight and parallel lines don't exist, and Platonic form is consistently undermined.

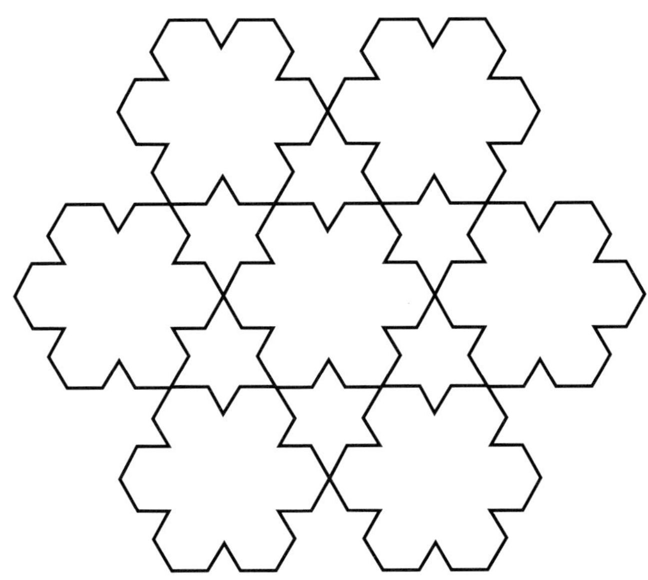

Lurking on a shelf in the artist's studio (and included in the exhibition that accompanies this publication) is a singular, organic object that seems out of place. It is a seedpod of the Travelers Palm (*Phenakospermum guyannense*), a tropical plant native to Suriname, French Guiana, and the eastern Amazon basin (fig.10). Composed of a cluster of eleven smaller, individual pods that radiate from a stem, this object, like many of Stella's star sculptures, is poised between symmetry and chance organization. His interest in this "star pod" is complex, and as with many other aspects of his work, Stella is reticent to expound on its specific meaning. But his interest in including it in the exhibition (with the urging of the curators) points to the fact that the artist's influences are varied, and the appearance of the pod in the context of the exhibition is a nonverbal way of opening up the experience of Stella's work to more expansive interpretation. Accompanying the pod are several works that clearly reference its form, including *Maquette for Star*, 2017, and *Botanical Star on Stainless Background*, 2018.

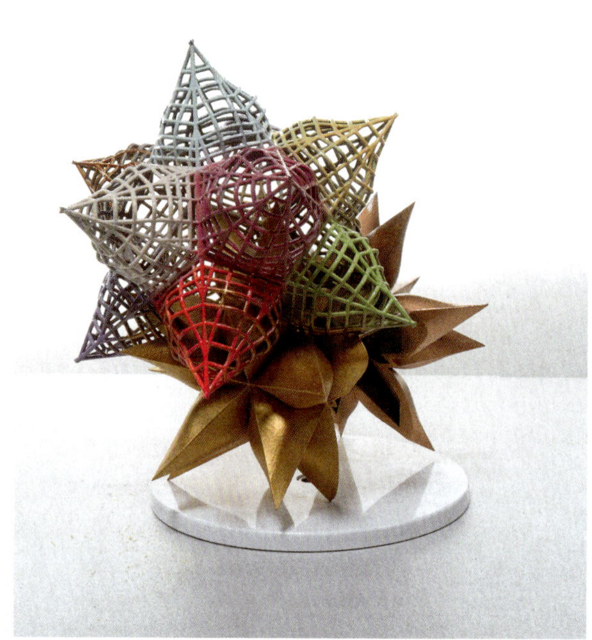

Stella has quipped "An artist's bibles are D'Arcy Thompson's *On Growth and Form*, which can be considered the Old Testament, and the McMaster-Carr Catalogue, which can be looked at as the New Testament."[3] The fundamental importance to Stella of *On Growth and Form* and the catalogue of the leading US supplier of hardware, tools, raw materials, and equipment are in need of an explanation. McMaster-Carr is a source of practical solutions to the "how" of construction and fabrication, and is germane to Stella's complex studio practice, while Thompson's book, first published in 1917, is the seminal text on how the physical laws of nature influence biology.[4] Stella has two copies of *On Growth and Form* in his library, and its presence points to the artist's interest in the physical and natural sciences. At its core, the book explores how mathematics is the determining factor of most forms found in nature, relating such things as the spiral growth of plants and shells to the Fibonacci sequence, skeletal structure to engineering truss design, and the effects of surface tension on the form of cells and cellular structures. More descriptive than experimental, it is a

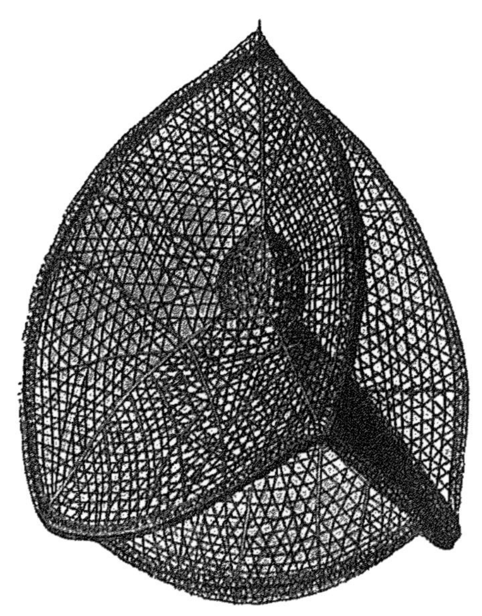

text that has had broad appeal to artists, designers, and architects since its publication.

One consistent "corruption" of the star form in Stella's work is the frequent rendering of the points of the star sculptures as open, lattice-like grids, such as in *Nessus and Dejanira*, 2017, and *Model for the Phoenix Suns I*, 2019 (fig.18). Not only are these surfaces anything but solid, but they also balloon out into space as if puffed up from within. Compare these surfaces with the illustration of the skeleton of a microscopic radiolarian in Thompson's book (fig.19). Both achieve rigidity with a minimization of materials through enclosing space within a curved grid. In biology as well as engineering, curved surfaces are more rigid than those that are flat, and Stella's use of this technique is not so much for structural reasons as for aesthetic. These types of surfaces are more descriptive of space, and it is no coincidence that the deformed grid is not only a biological construct, but also the way that computers map space to form surfaces and objects. In computer design this type of surface is referred to as a "space frame," and it lurks in everything from the fuselages of aircraft to the forms of characters

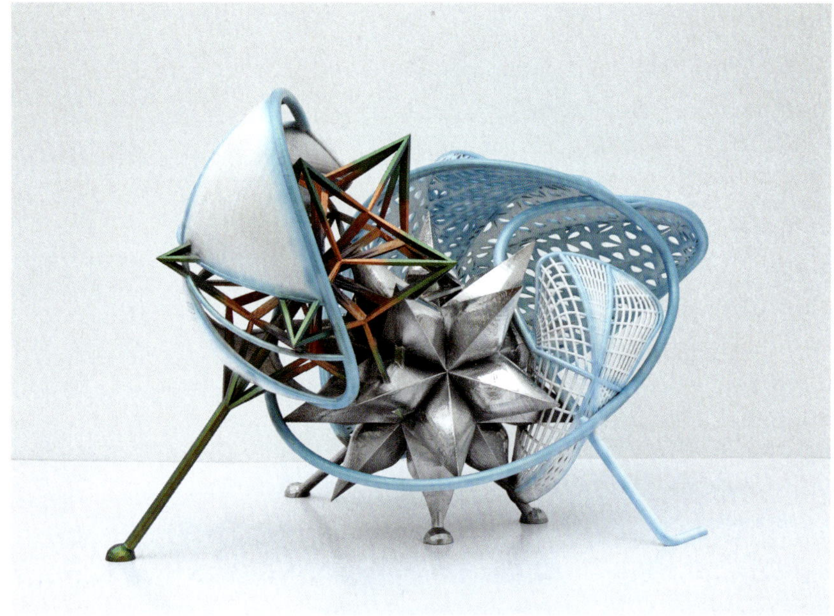

in Pixar animation. Stella was one of the first artists to use computers in making three-dimensional works, most notably in his depictions in the late 1980s of cigar smoke rings that were captured digitally and transferred into CAD programs. The complex geometry of recent sculpture such as *Frank's Wooden Star*, 2014, and *Fat 12 Point Carbon Fiber Star*, 2016 (fig.5), could not have been realized without sophisticated digital technology—for both design and fabrication. In computer space, deformation can be an expressive tool, and the ballooning out of the pentagonal points on *Fat 12 Point Carbon Fiber Star*, together with its reflective epoxy-resin surface embedded with carbon fiber, situate the object at the intersection of art, geometry, biology, aerospace design, and science fiction. As previously noted, Stella has a passion for car racing, and the design and material sensibility of much of his recent sculpture resembles the way rigidly geometric frames and suspension systems on performance cars are overlaid by sleek skins of composite materials. In the core of *Fat 12 Point Carbon Fiber Star* is a regular dodecahedron made of steel, to which twelve five-sided carbon-fiber points are attached. The sculpture is not a vehicle or an aircraft, but a creature of the twenty-first century that reminds us that materiality and construction are coequal with outward form.

In many of the artist's star works, such as *boeta*, the star appears not as a singular form, but rather as part of a composition jostling with other elements—or even multiple stars. In numerous works, such as *Stainless split star with truss segments*, 2016, the star is presented as fragmented, with sections either completely missing or detached. Stella has embedded multiple stars on curvilinear armatures, flung them on sections of twisting truss, and included them in compositions that feature found objects or rapid prototyped versions of found objects. The spatial complexity of these works is sometimes bewildering, going beyond the baroque to reflect the evolution of spatial paradigms since Caravaggio and Kepler's time. Renaissance perspective and the flatness of modernism have been left in the dust by knowledge of the gravitational warping surrounding black holes and our creation of the infinite labyrinth of cyberspace. Looked at in this light, works such as *K.159*, 2013, or *K.359*, 2014 (fig.20), might be thought of as cosmic collisions or music-like mash-ups created by digital sampling. But no matter how Stella splits his stars or how he buries them in surrounding turmoil, the star's commanding geometry always makes them readily apparent. Every star, both terrestrial and cosmic, has a center point that respectively radiates geometry outward or is compressed by gravitation. In a career that has been defined by a tenacious pursuit of innovation and diversity, it seems that the star is a center where Stella can express both rest and restlessness.

Richard Klein, Exhibitions Director

---

1. Frank Stella, *Working Space* (Cambridge, MA: Harvard University Press, 1986), 11.
2. Stella recently reinterpreted *Damascus Gate (Stretch Variation I)* as a huge mural that was installed in 2019 in Boston's Seaport district.
3. From a conversation between the author and the artist at his studio in Rock Tavern, New York, September 11, 2019.
4. D'Arcy Wentworth Thompson, *On Growth and Form*, abr. ed., ed. J. T. Bonner (1917; Cambridge: Cambridge University Press, 1971).

Plant City, 1963
Zinc chromate and oil on canvas
102½ x 102½
(Rubin 211)

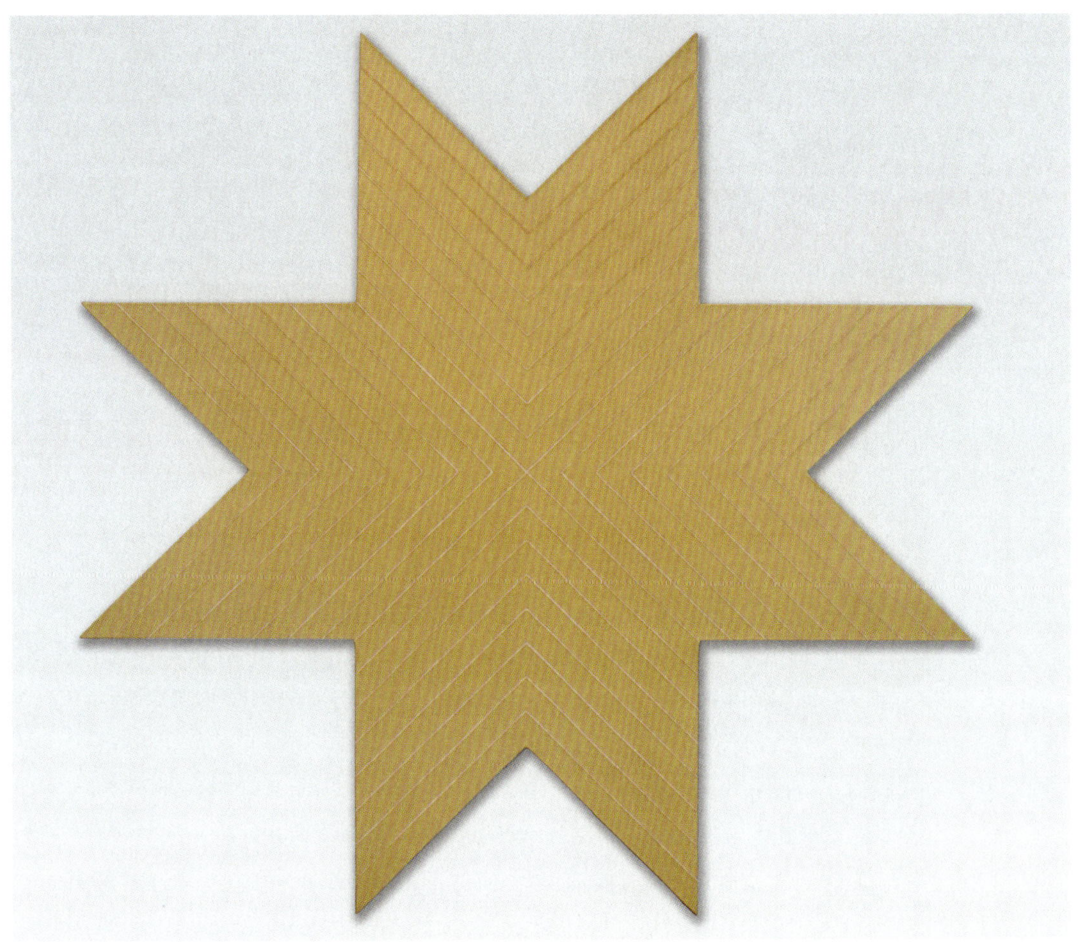

Port Tampa City, 1963
Red lead on canvas
102 x 102
(Rubin 215)

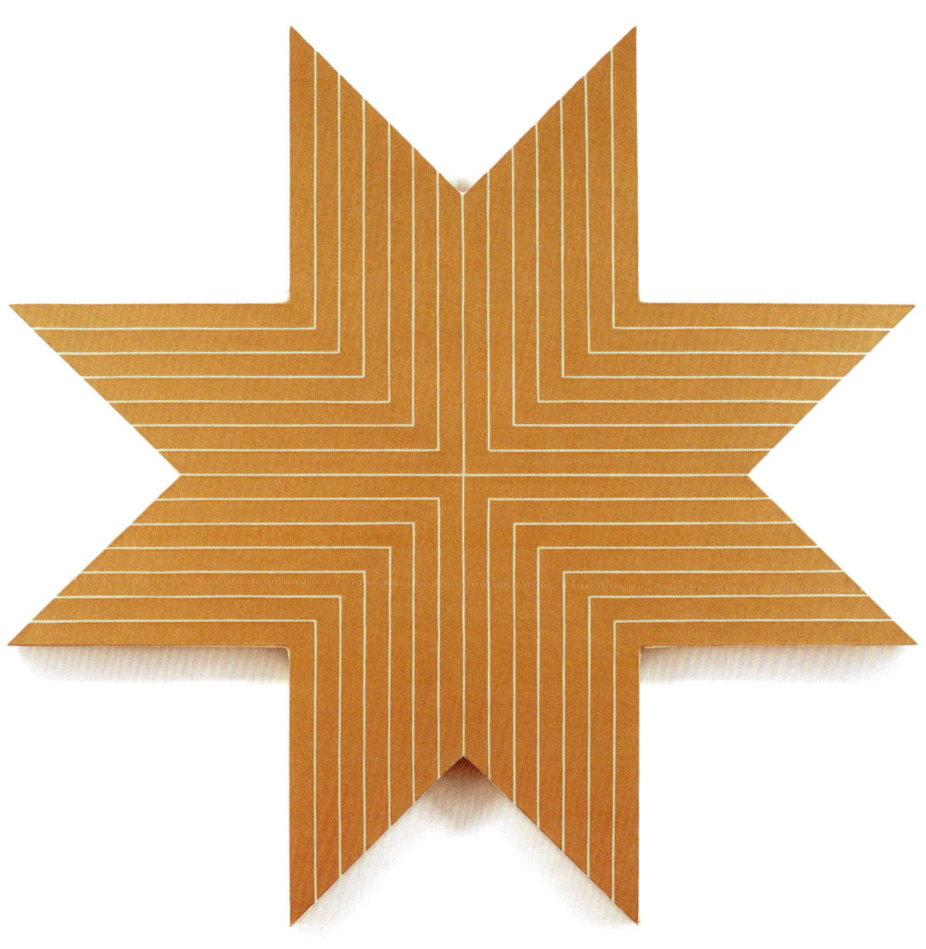

Untitled, 1964
Pencil and crayon on graph paper
17 x 21⅞

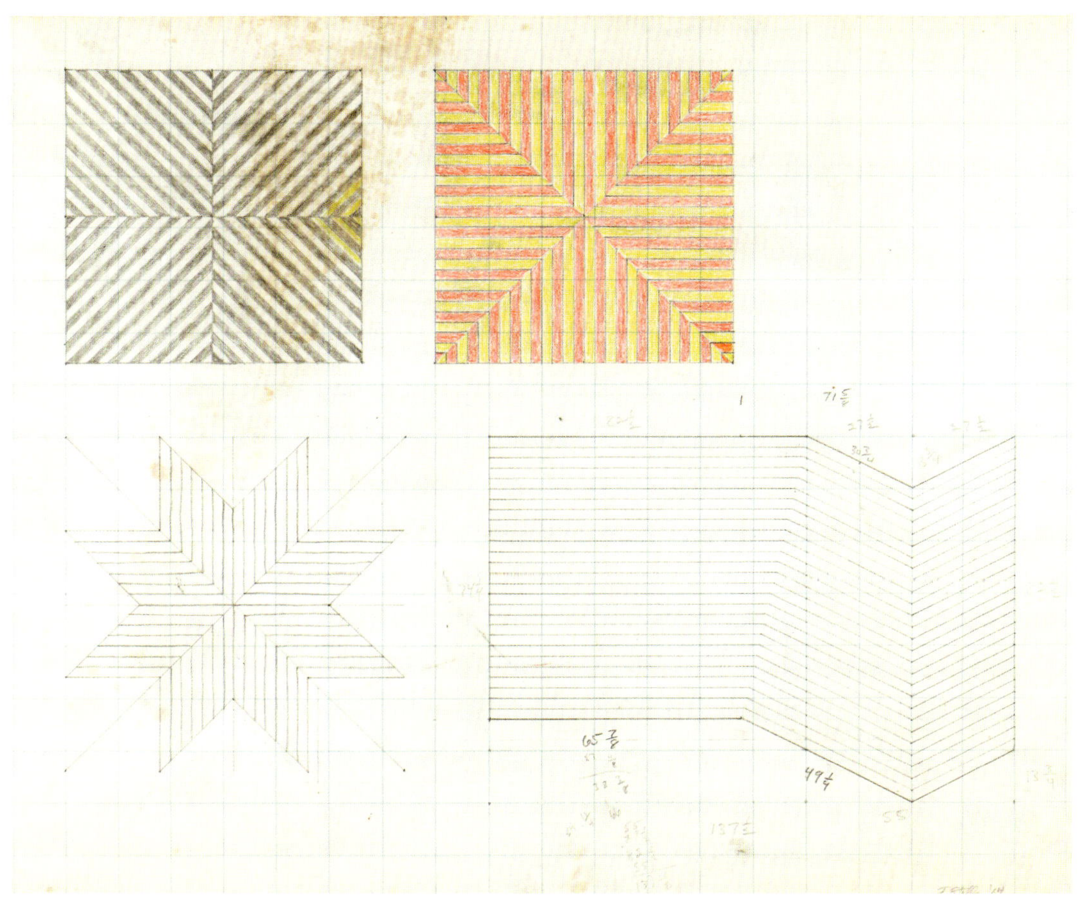

Star of Persia, 1967
Graphite on graph paper
24½ x 27
(FS67.178)

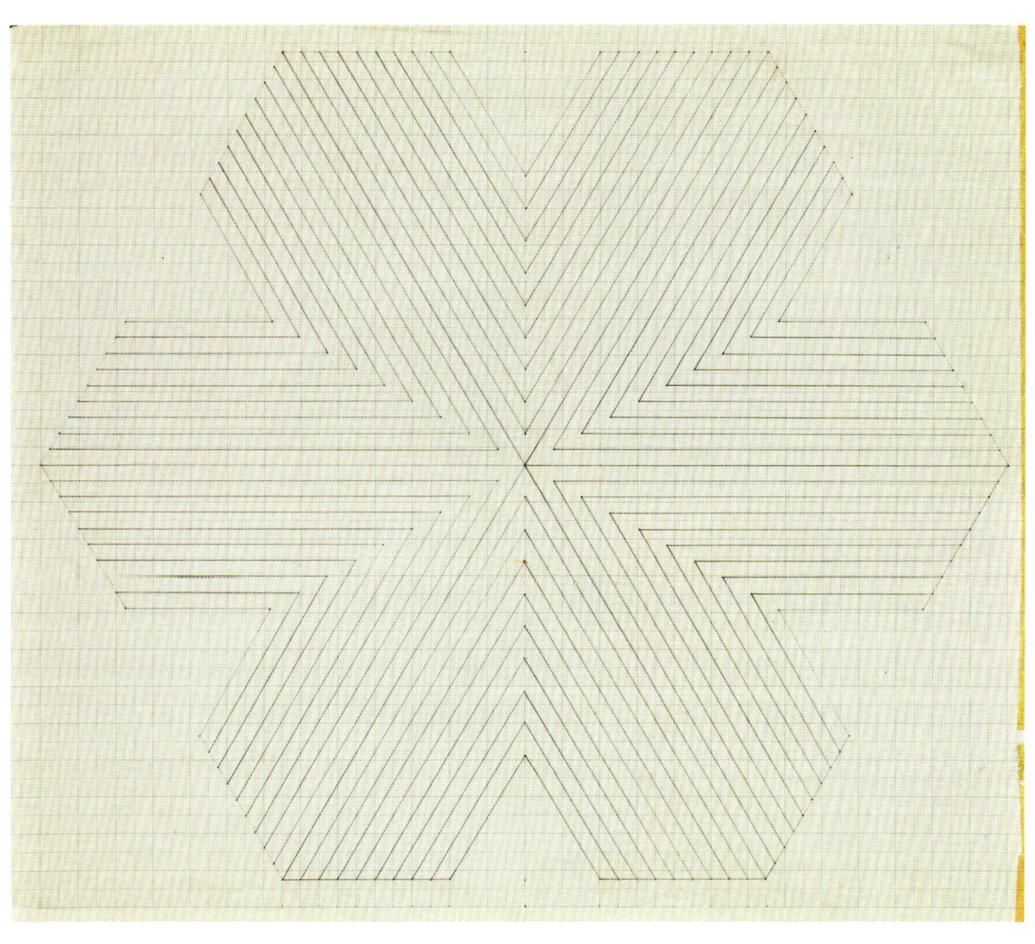

Star of Persia I, 1967
Lithograph on English Vellum Graph paper
Edition #14 of 92
26 x 31
FS67.110
(Axsom/Kolb 1)

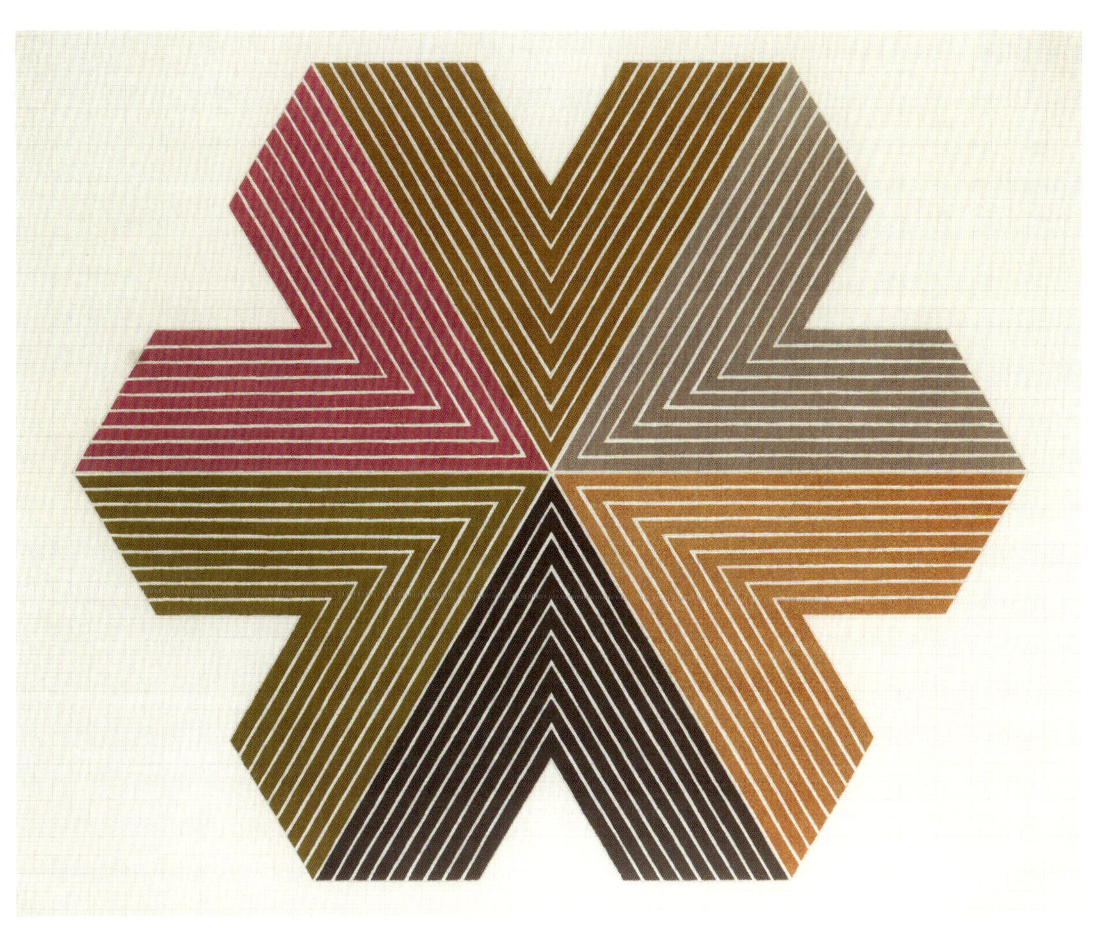

Star of Persia II, 1967
Lithograph on English Vellum Graph paper
Edition #8 of 92
26 x 31
FS67.111
(Axsom/Kolb 2)

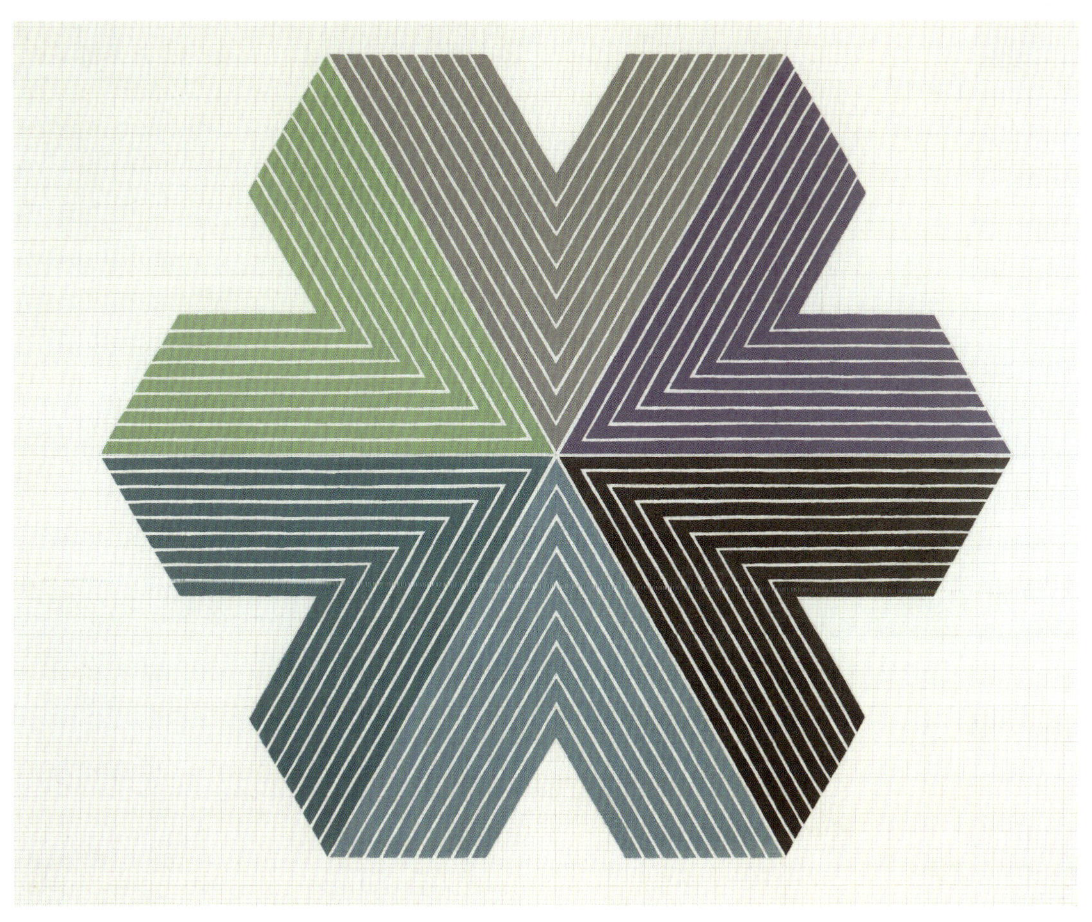

Irving Blum Memorial Edition, 1967
Lithograph on English Vellum Graph paper
26 x 32
FS67.159
(Axsom/Kolb 3)

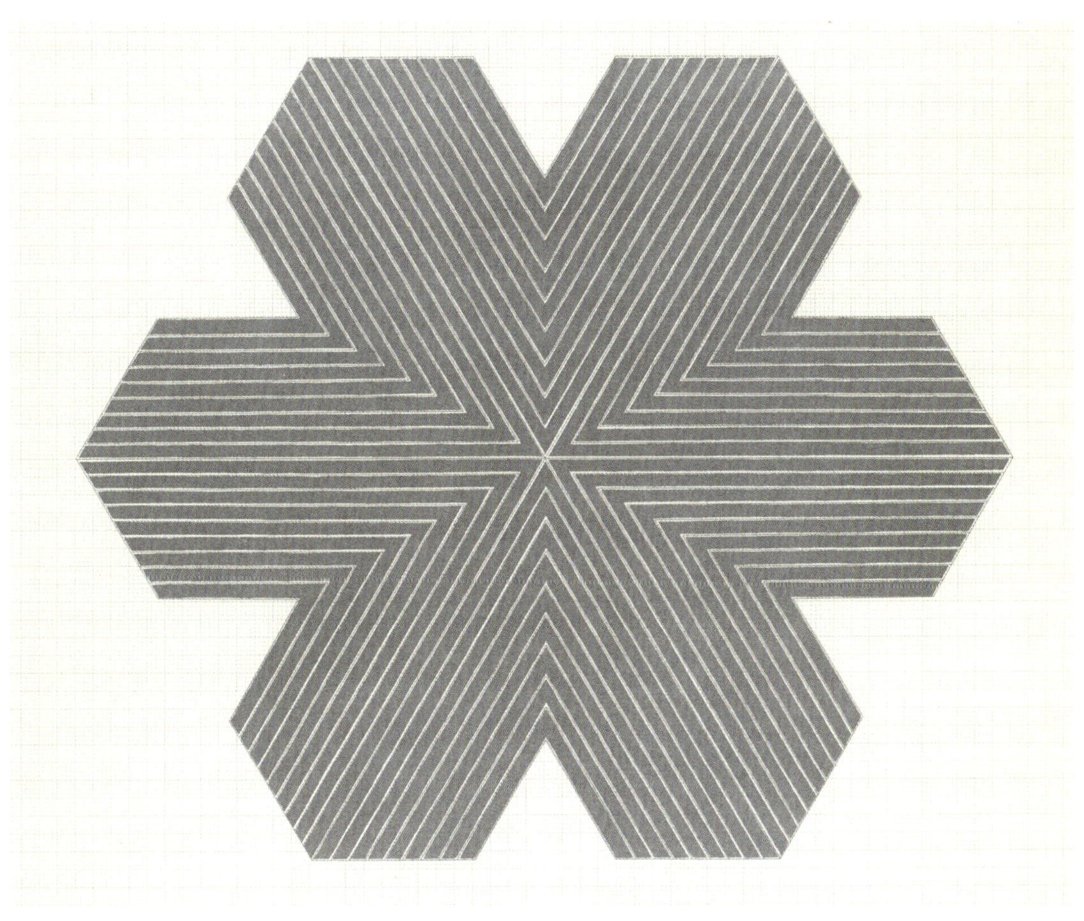

K.109, 2006
Stainless steel tubing, nylon RPT, spray paint
19 x 17 x 10
(FS2006.043)

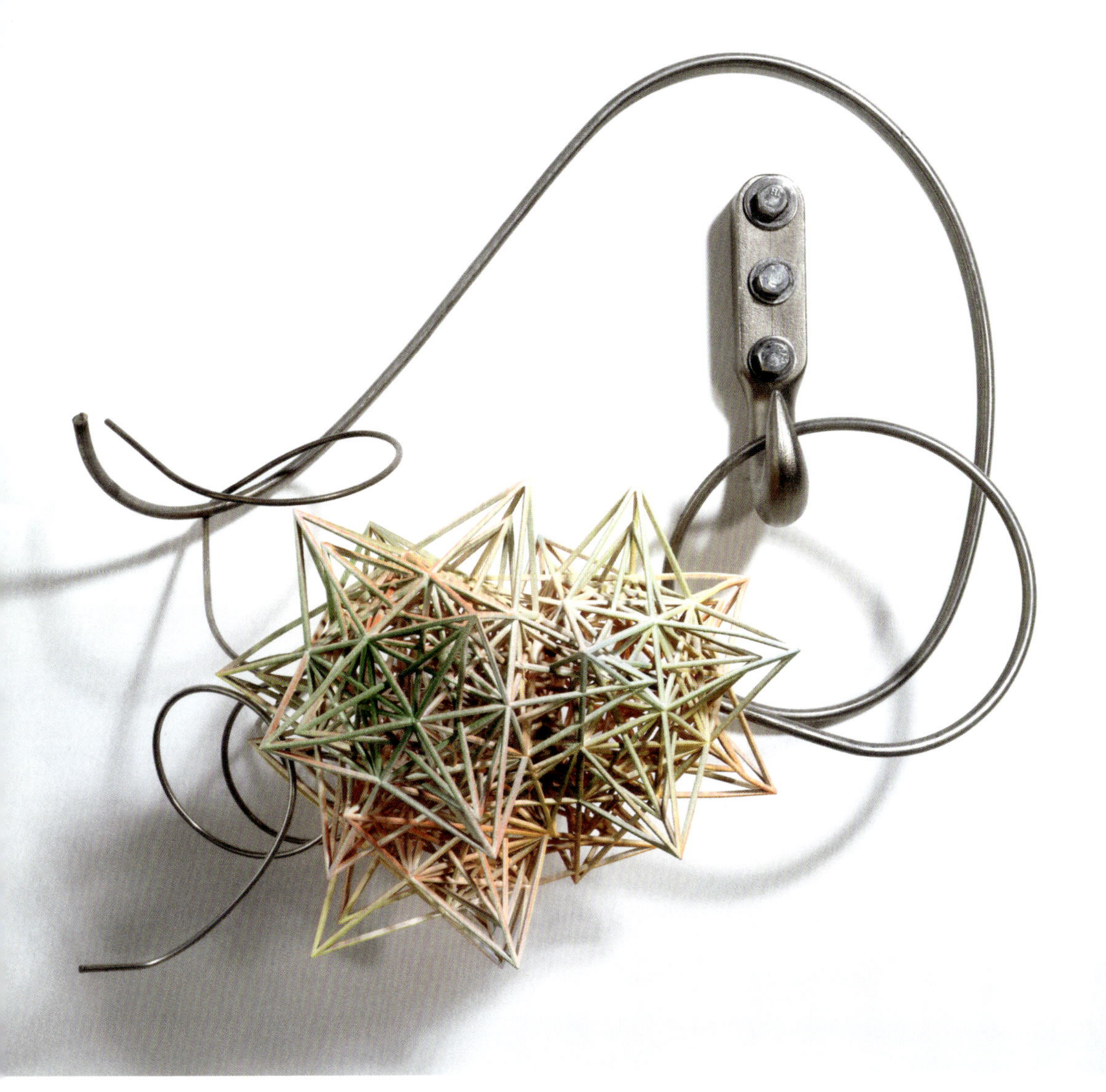

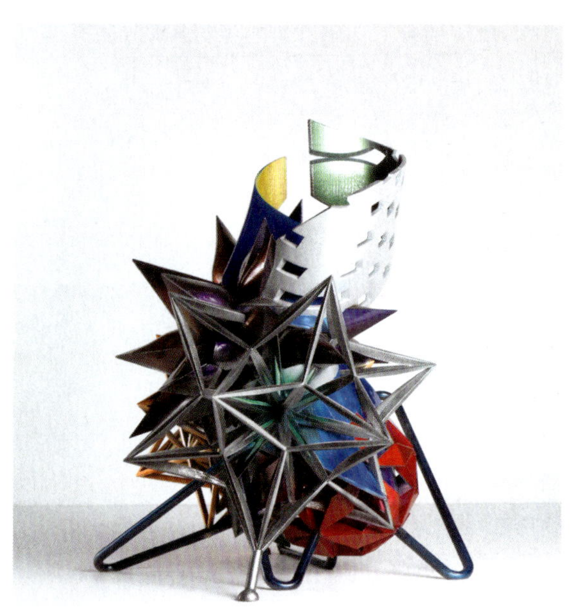

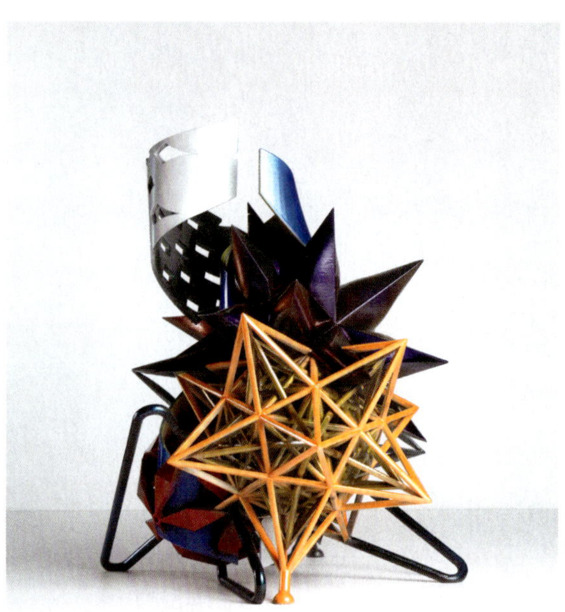

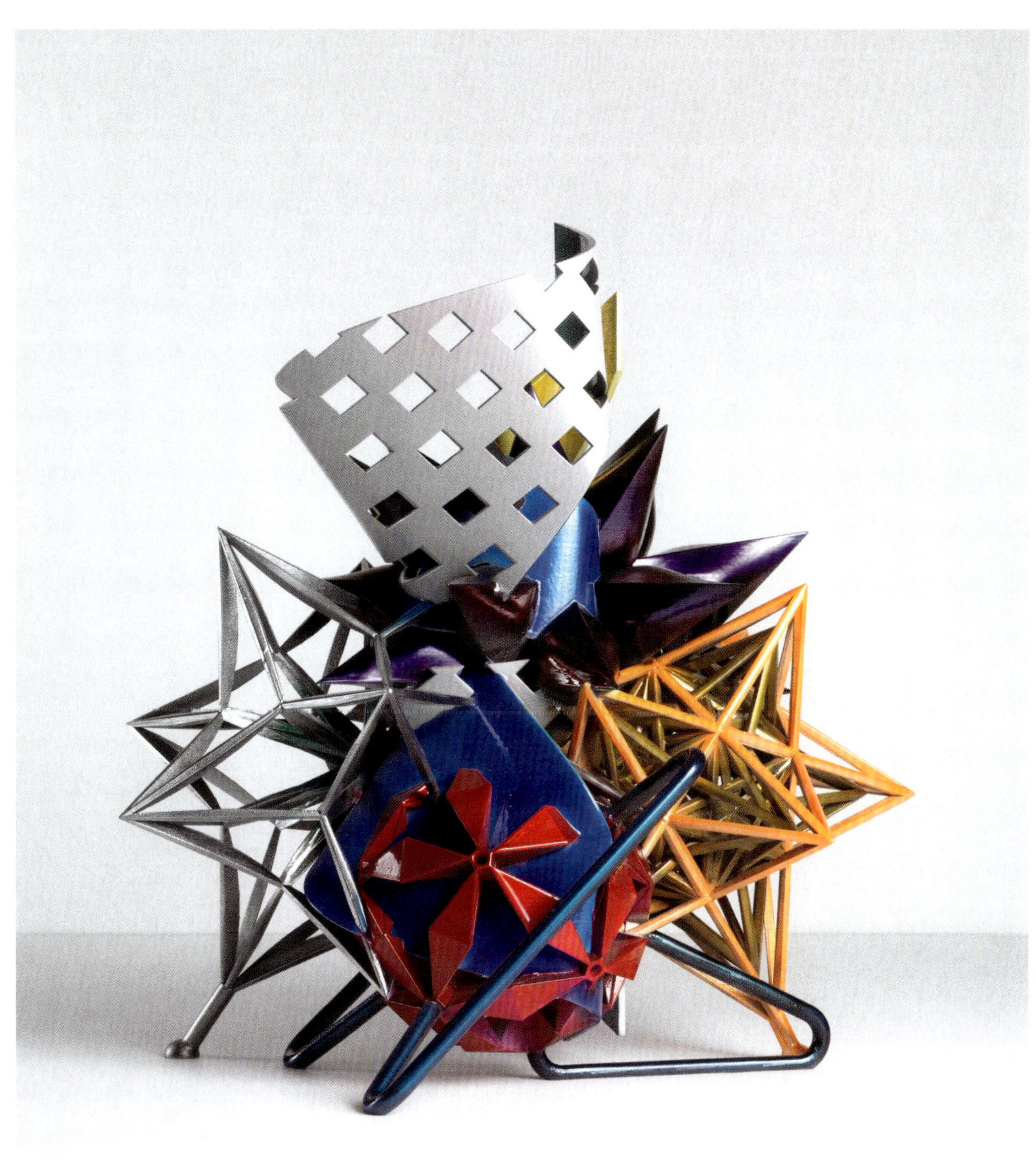

K.161a, 2011
Nylon and lacquer paint
20 x 20 x 20
(FS2011.017)

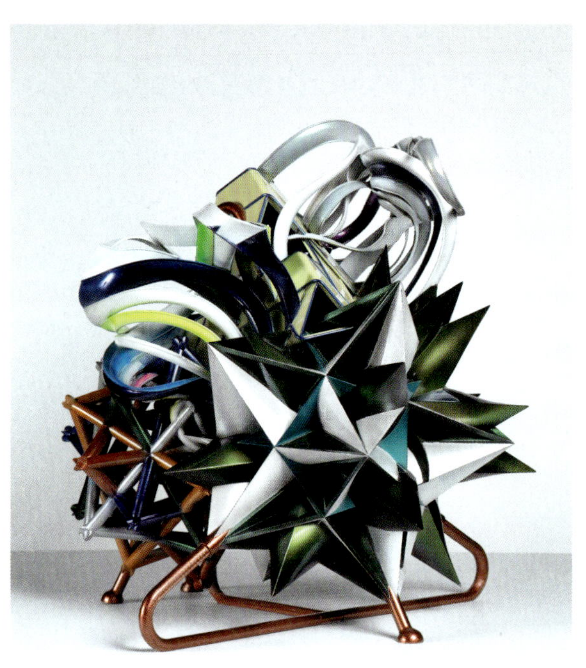

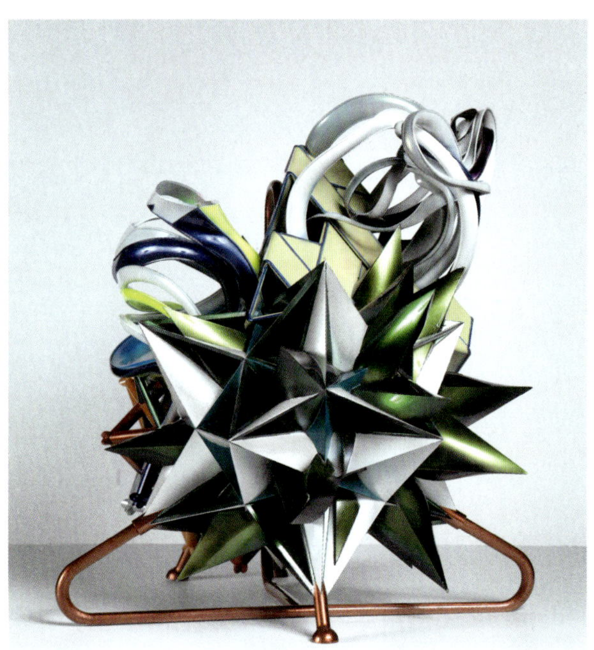

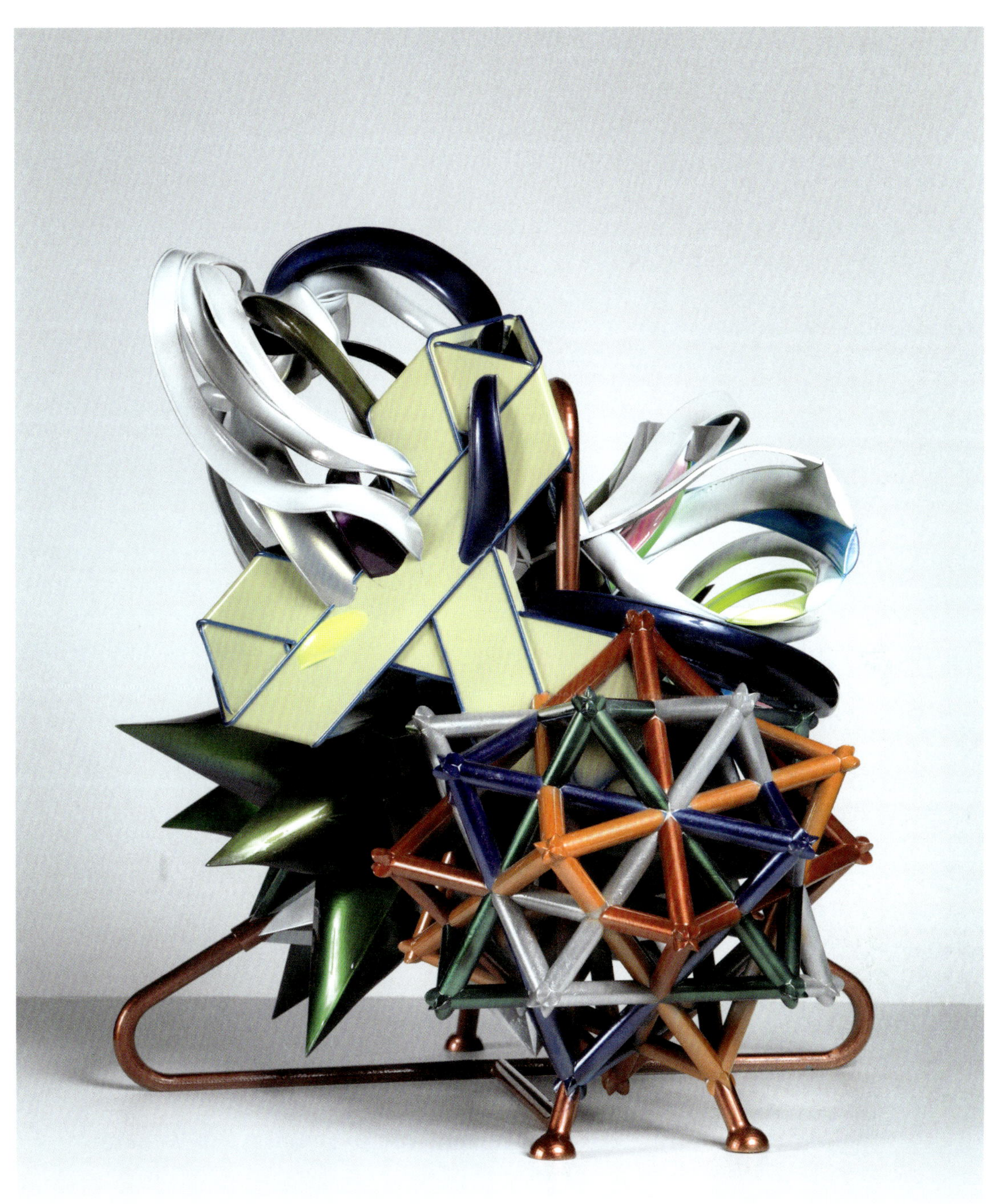

K.162, 2011
Nylon and lacquer paint
22 x 22 x 24
(FS2011.002)

K.432, 2013
ABS RTP and stainless steel
59 x 56 x 52
(FS2013.011)

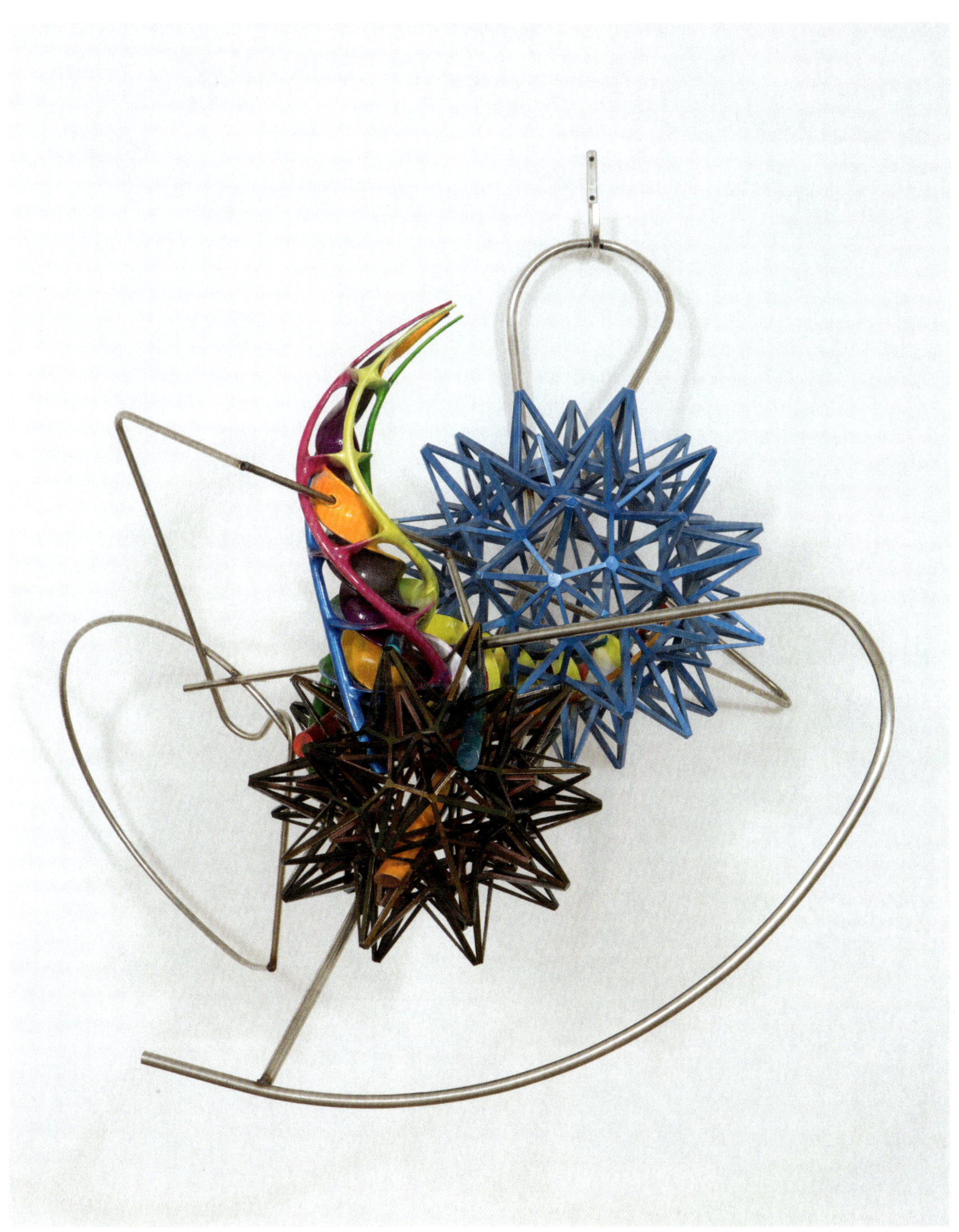

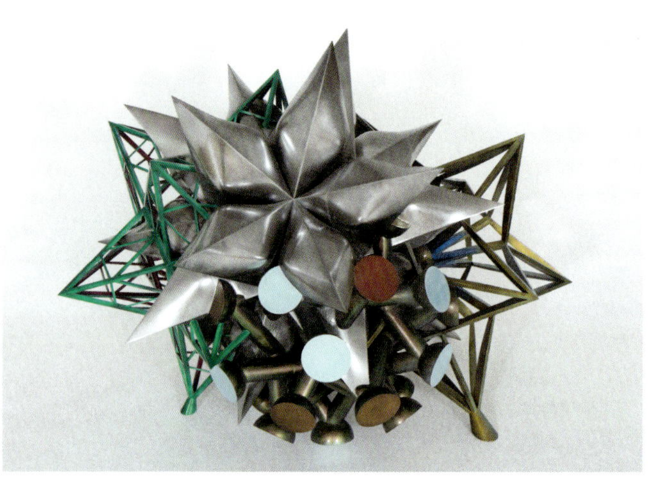

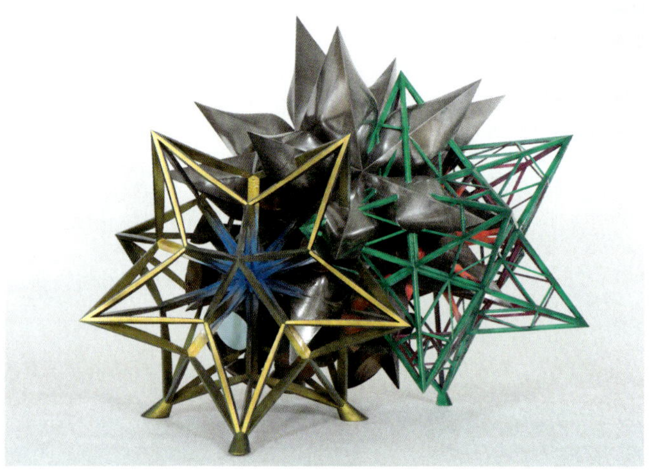

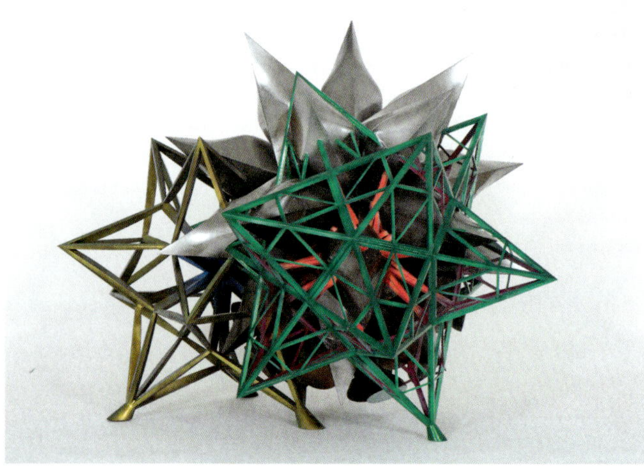

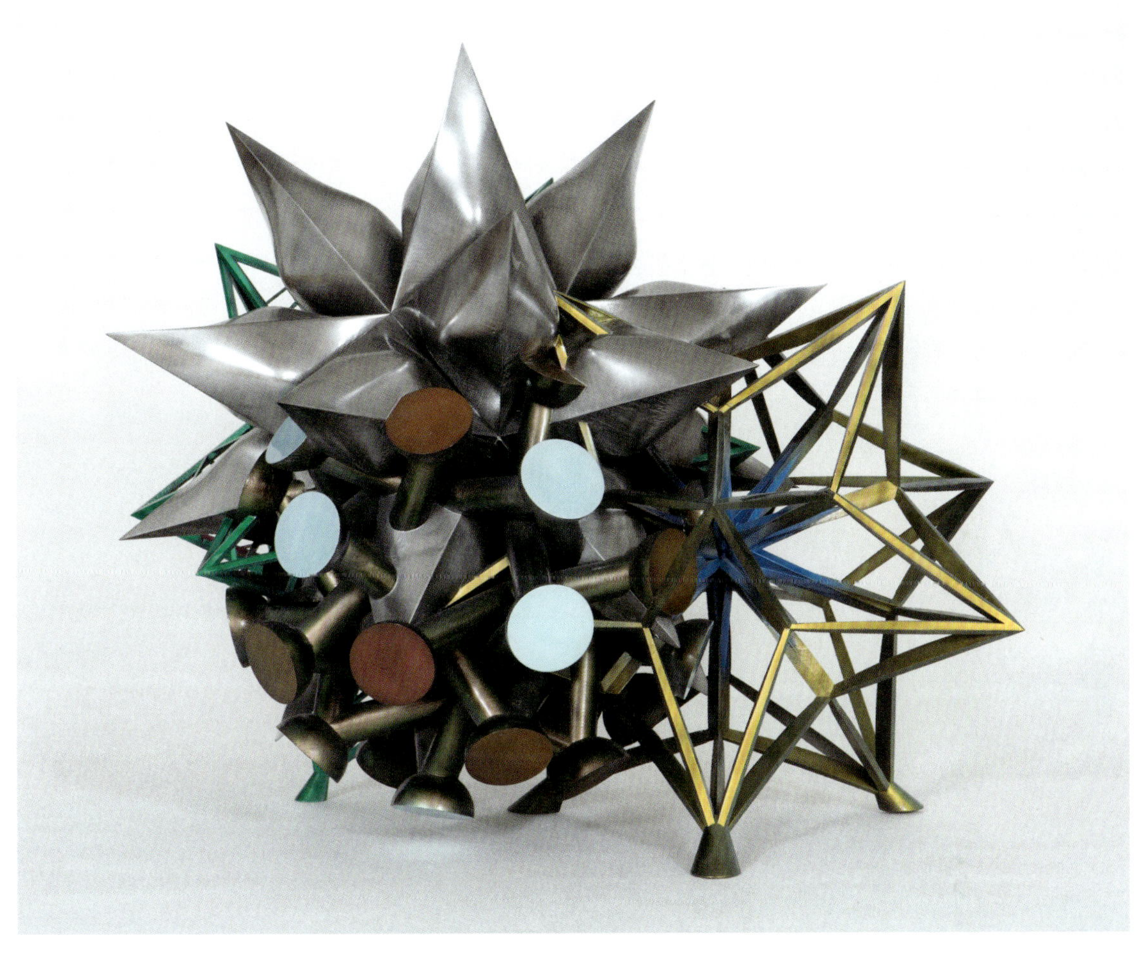

K.159, 2013
Polyamide (laser-sintered prototype part)
41 x 49 x 45
(FS2013.015)

October Maquette No. 3, 2014
Elasto plastic, honeycomb aluminum, Kevlar
13 x 11½ x 11¼
(FS2014.060)

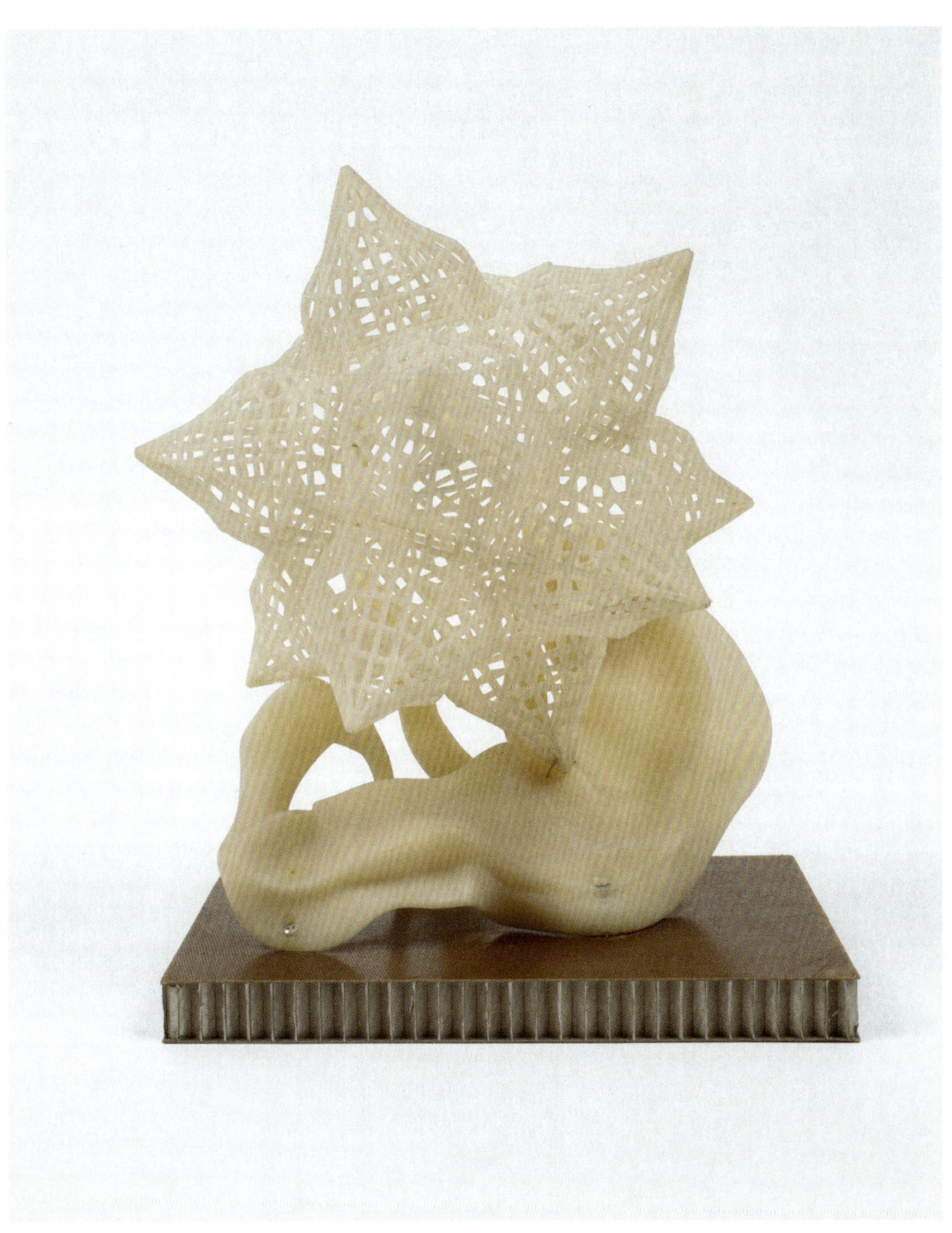

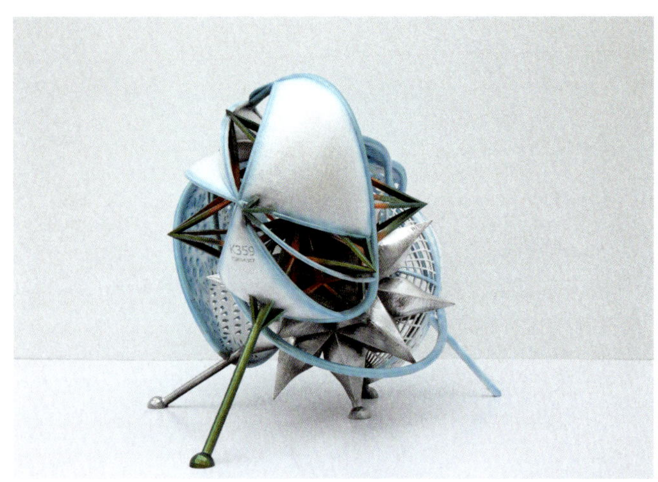

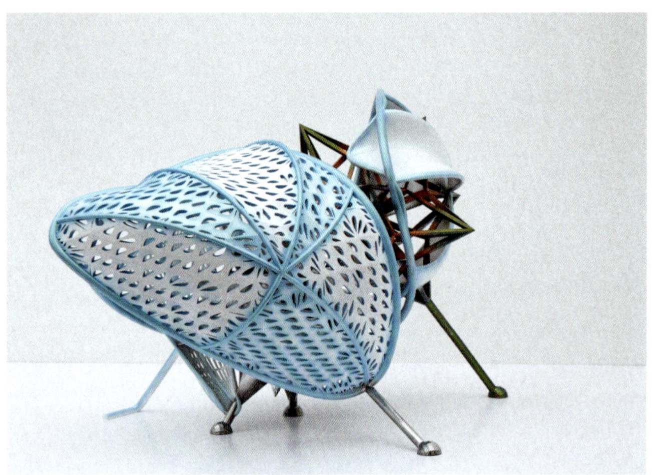

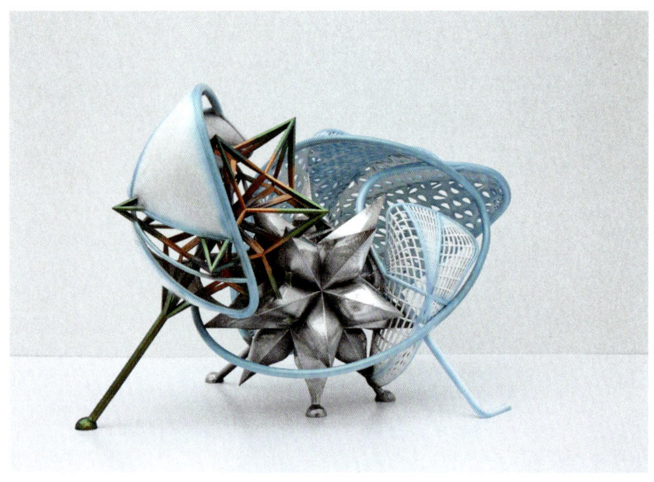

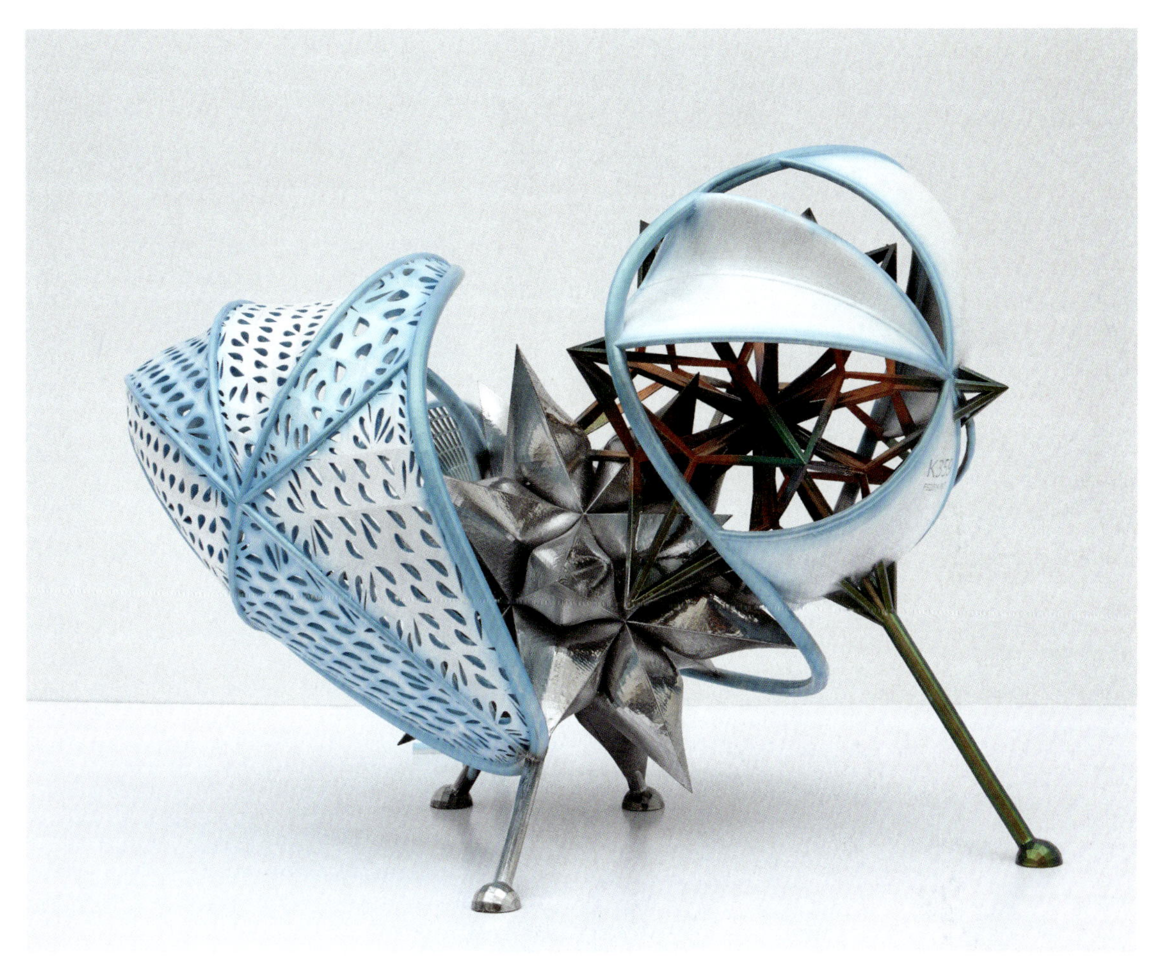

K.359, 2014
ABS RPT
27½ x 40 x 24
(FS2014.017)

K.140, 2008, 2014
Tusk RPT with stainless steel tubing
45 x 62 x 36
(FS2008.002)

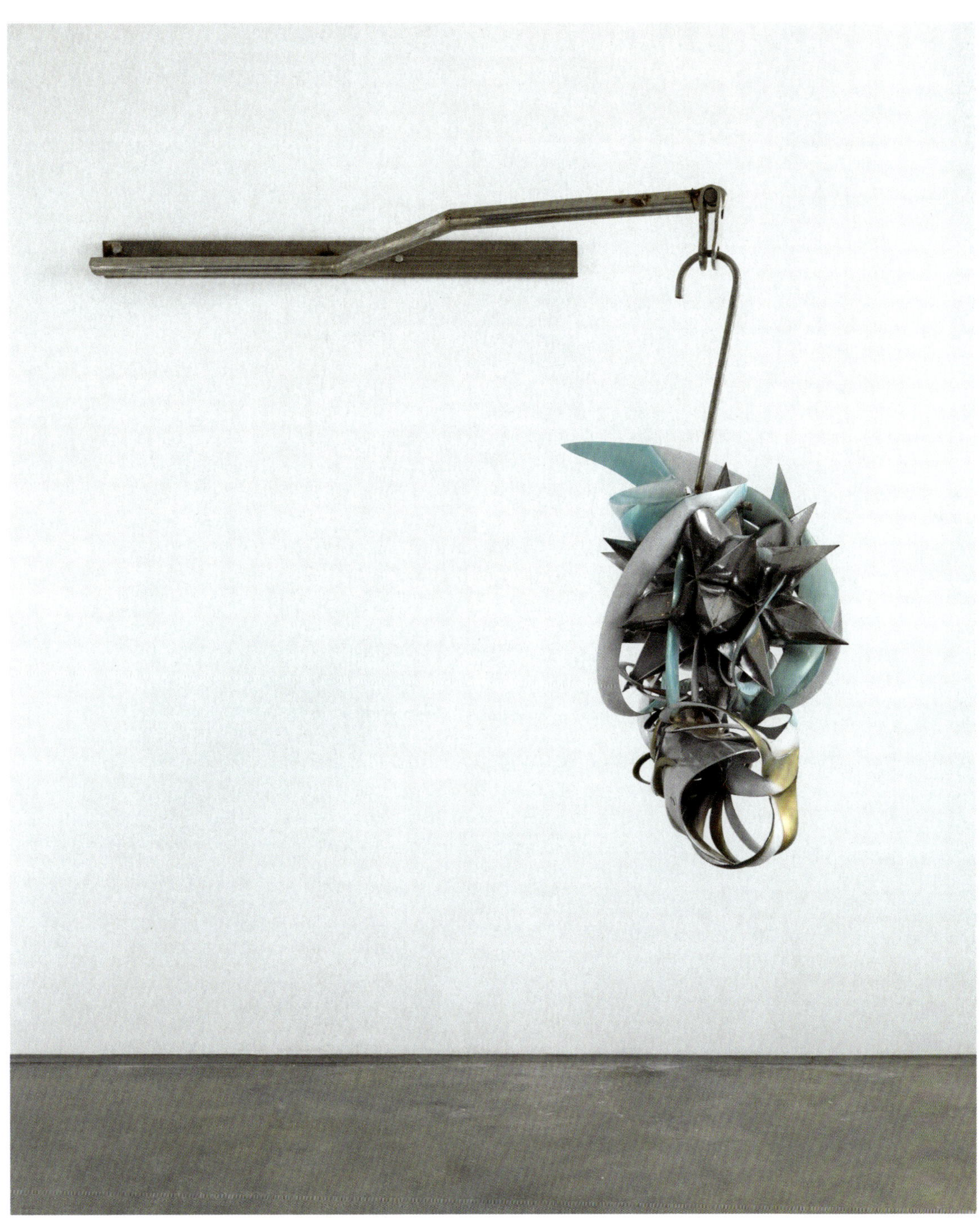

Puffed Net Star (Smoke 1), 2014
Painted RPT with metal
21 x 12 x 11
(FS2014.070)

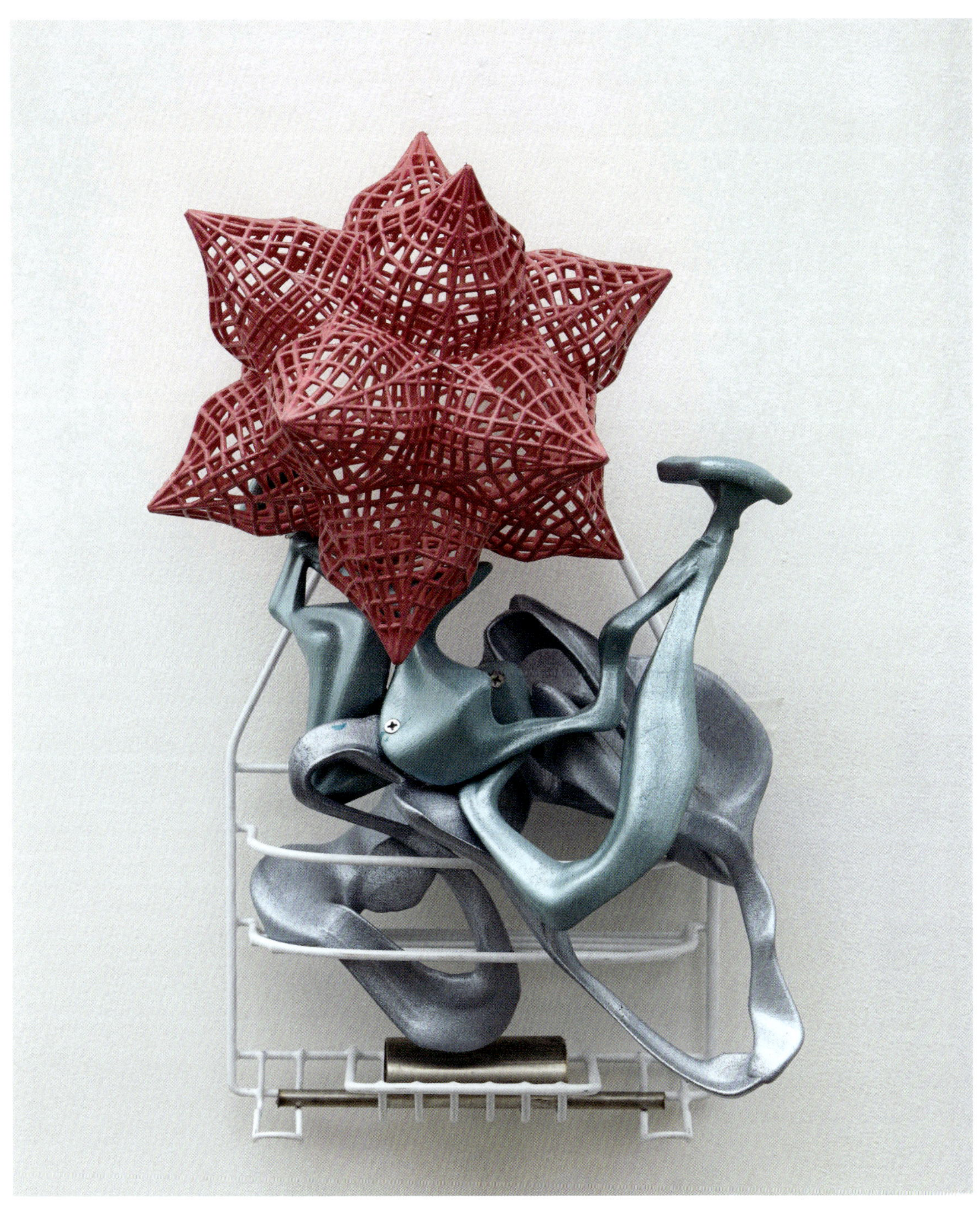

Puffed Star II, 2014
Polished aluminum
224½ x 224½ x 224½
(FS2014.043)

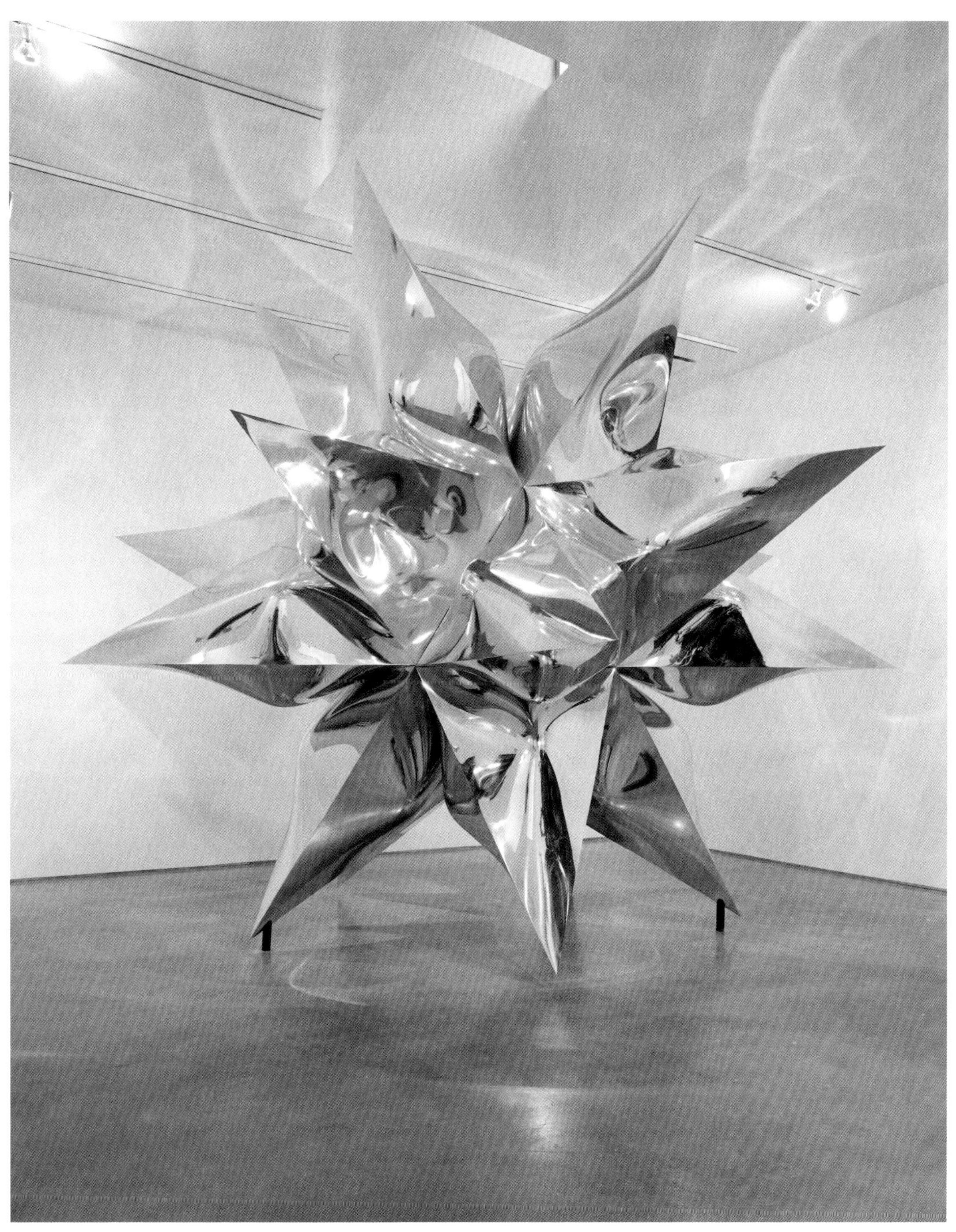

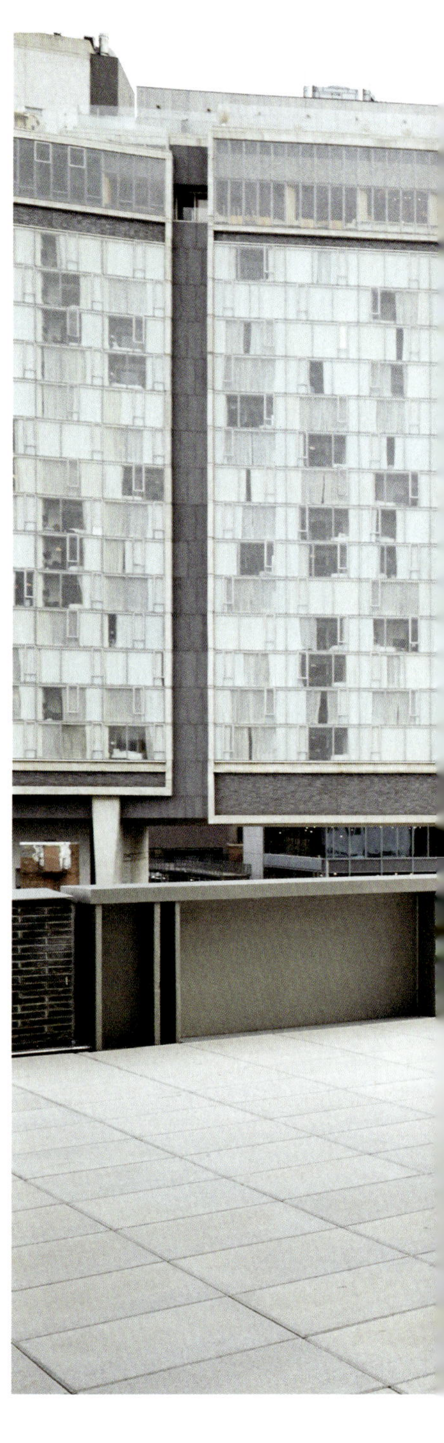

Black Star, 2014
Carbon fiber
224½ x 224½ x 224½
(FS2014.041)

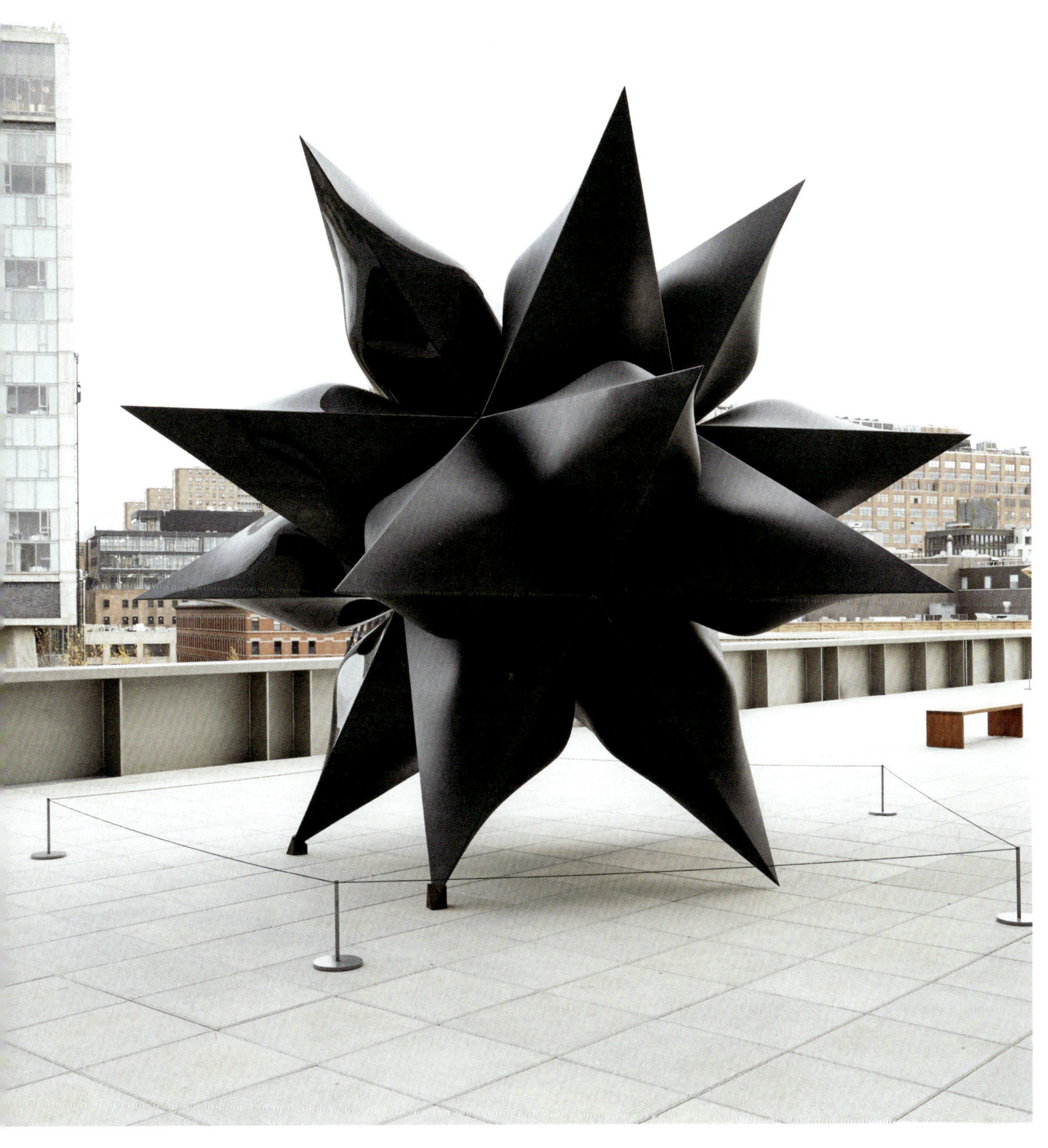

Frank's Wooden Star, 2014
Teak wood
157¼ x 157¼ x 157¼
(FS2014.047)

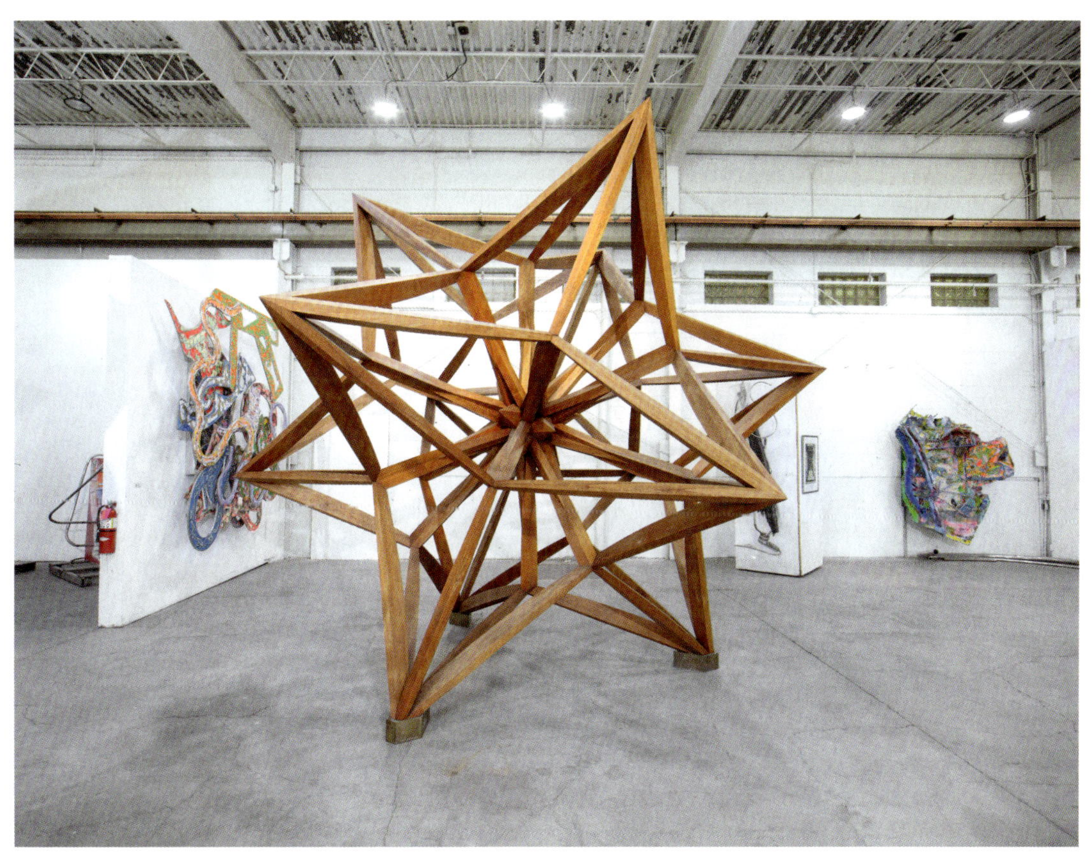

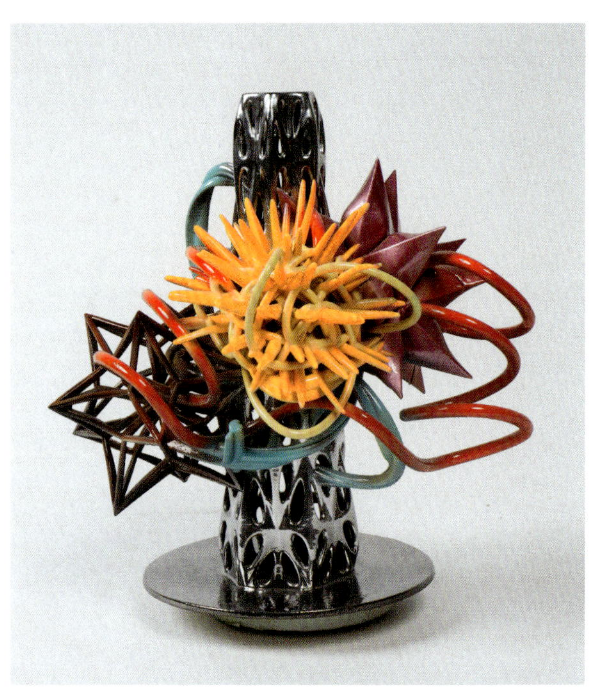

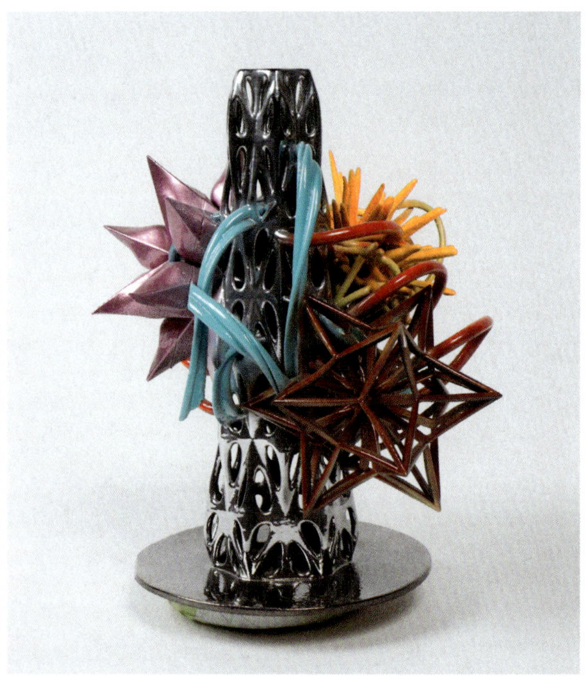

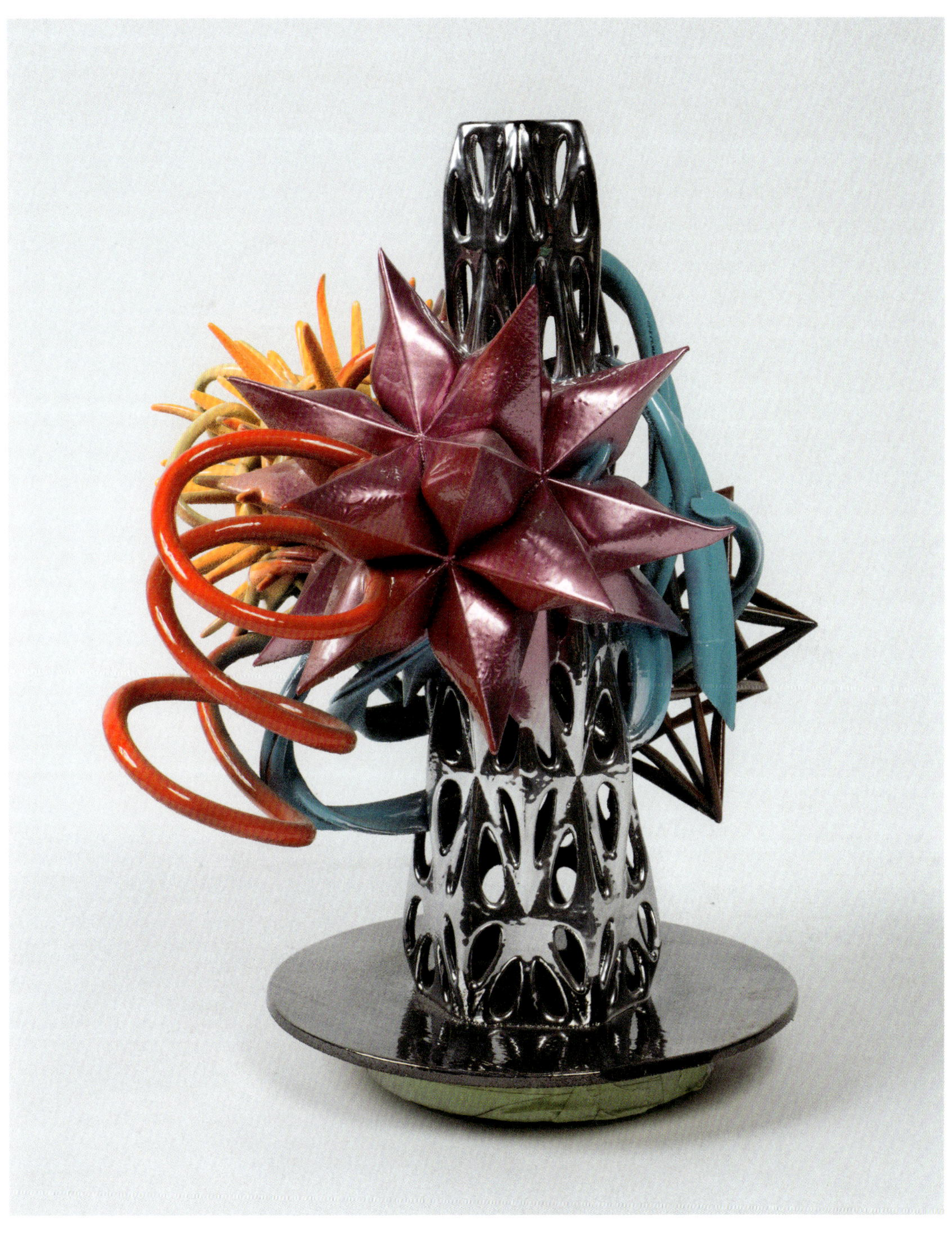

K.374 (Tower with Porcupine), 2015
Elasto plastic
13 x 12 x 8½
(FS2015.021)

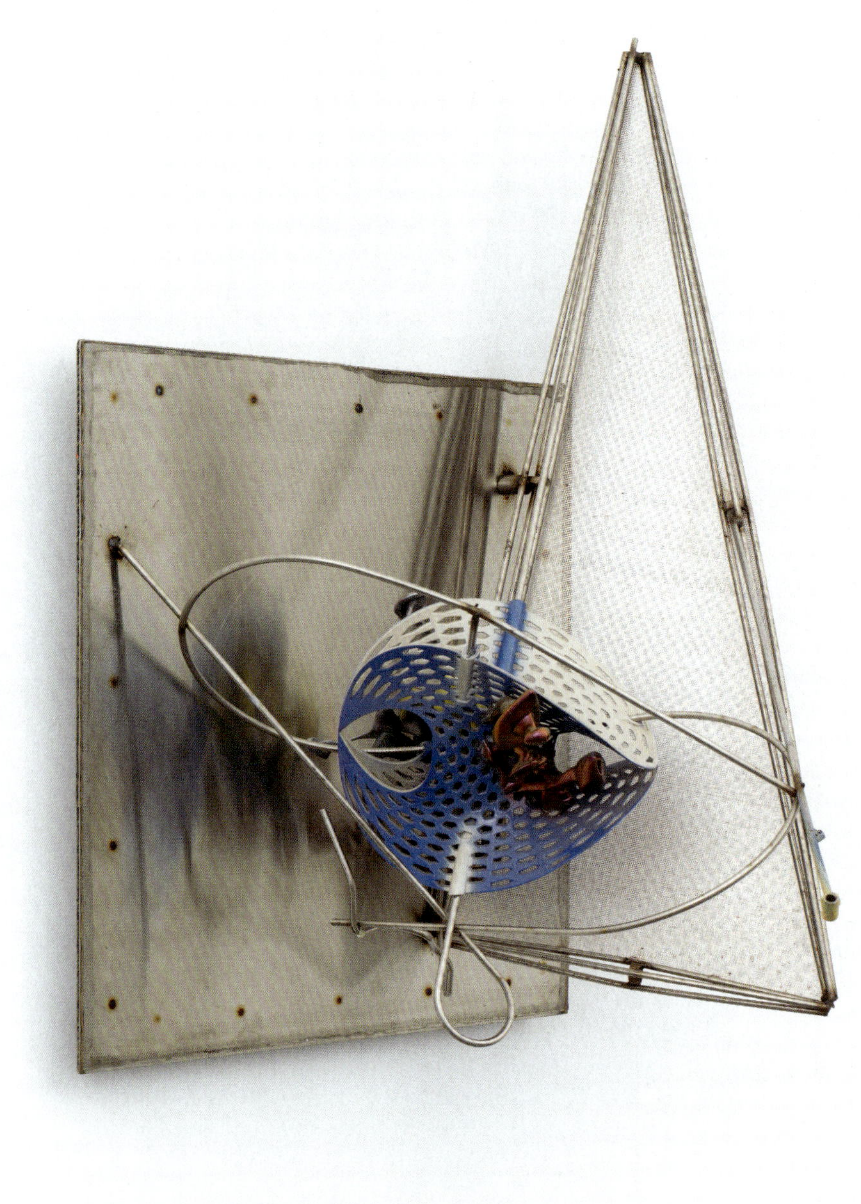

K.505 on Stainless Background, 2015
Elasto plastic, stainless steel
37 x 24 x 24
(FS2015.009)

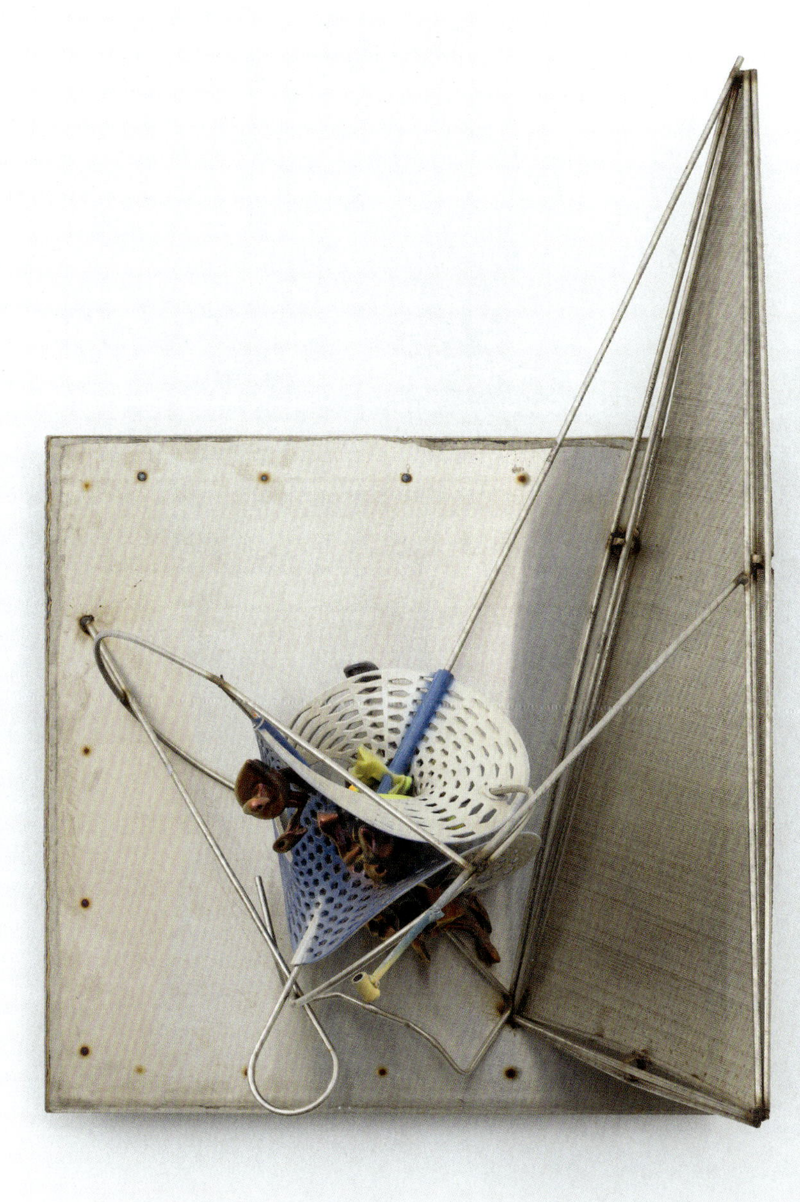

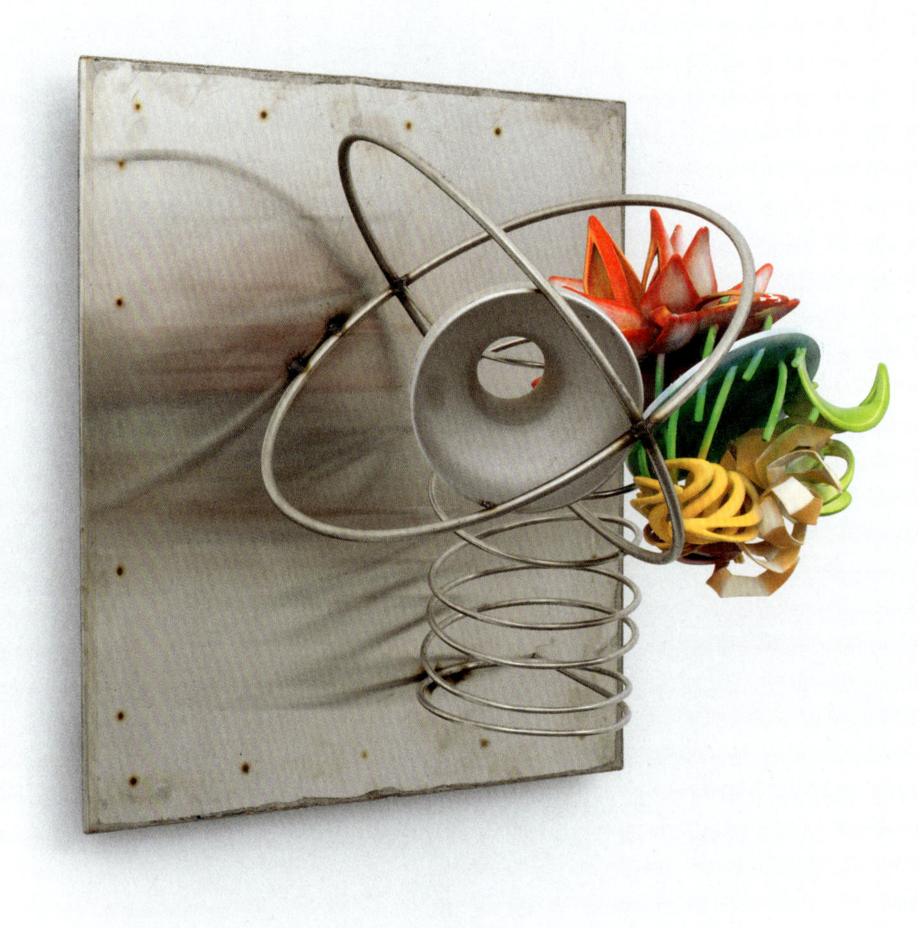

Bell Piece on Stainless Background, 2016
Elasto plastic RPT, stainless steel
24 x 24 x 18
(FS2016.066)

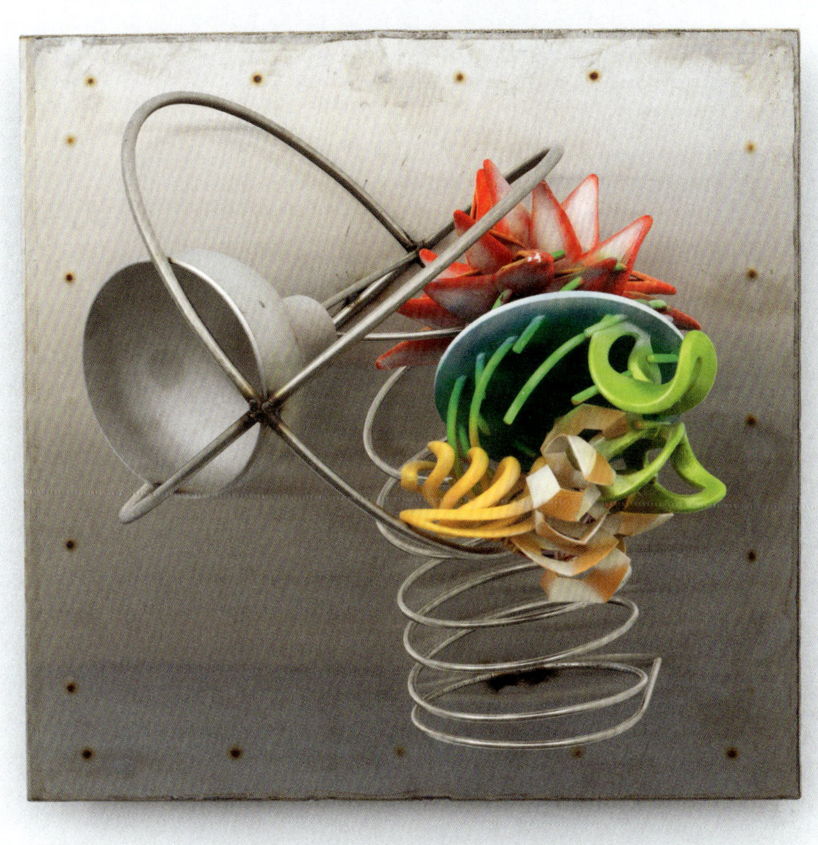

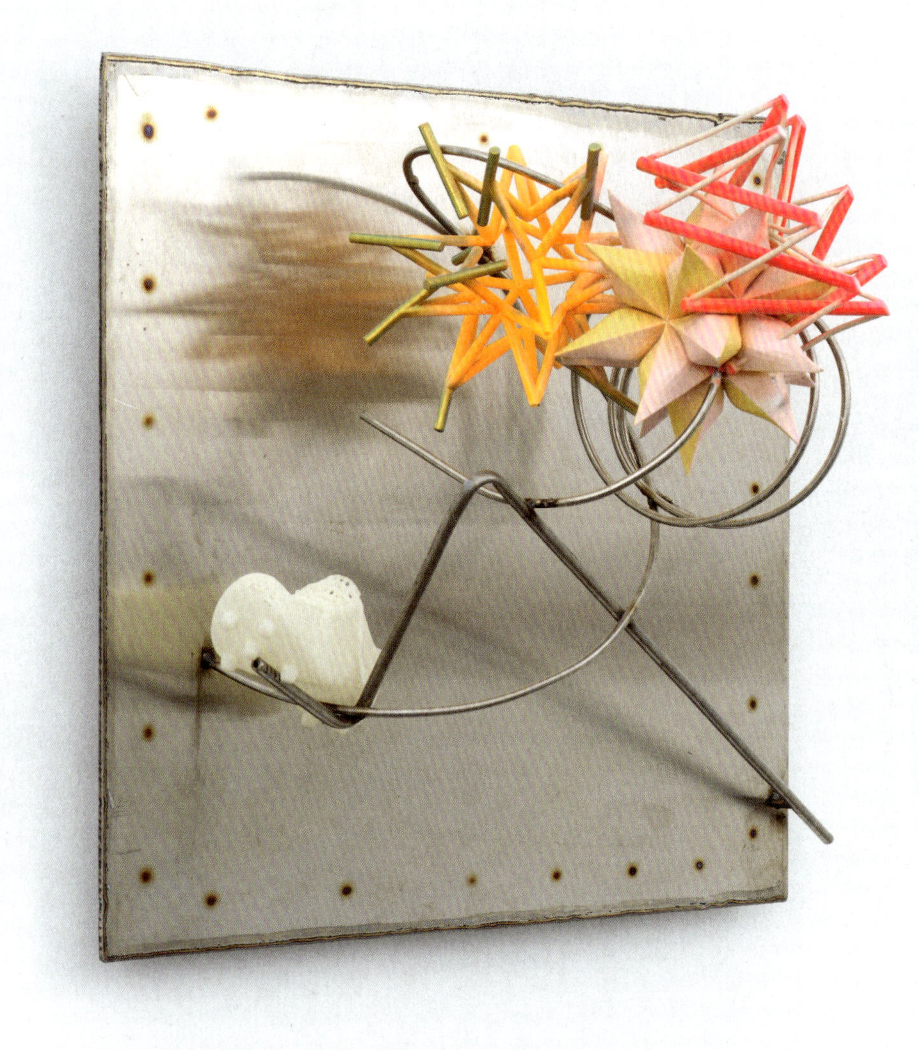

Shoe Piece on Stainless Background, 2016
Elasto plastic RPT, stainless steel
24 x 25½ x 17½
(FS2016.064)

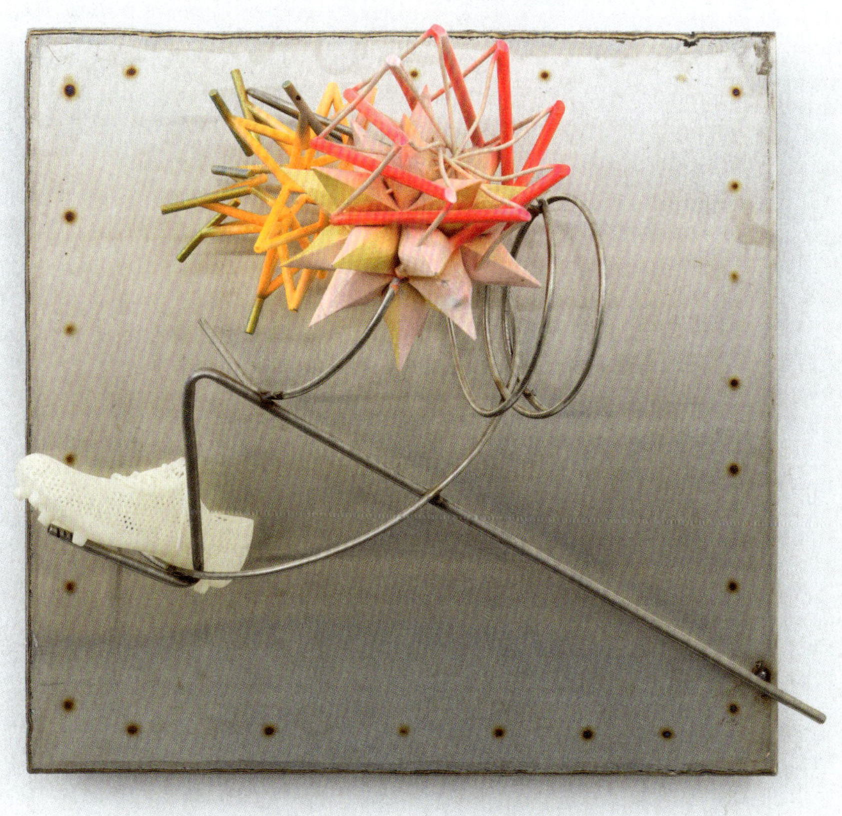

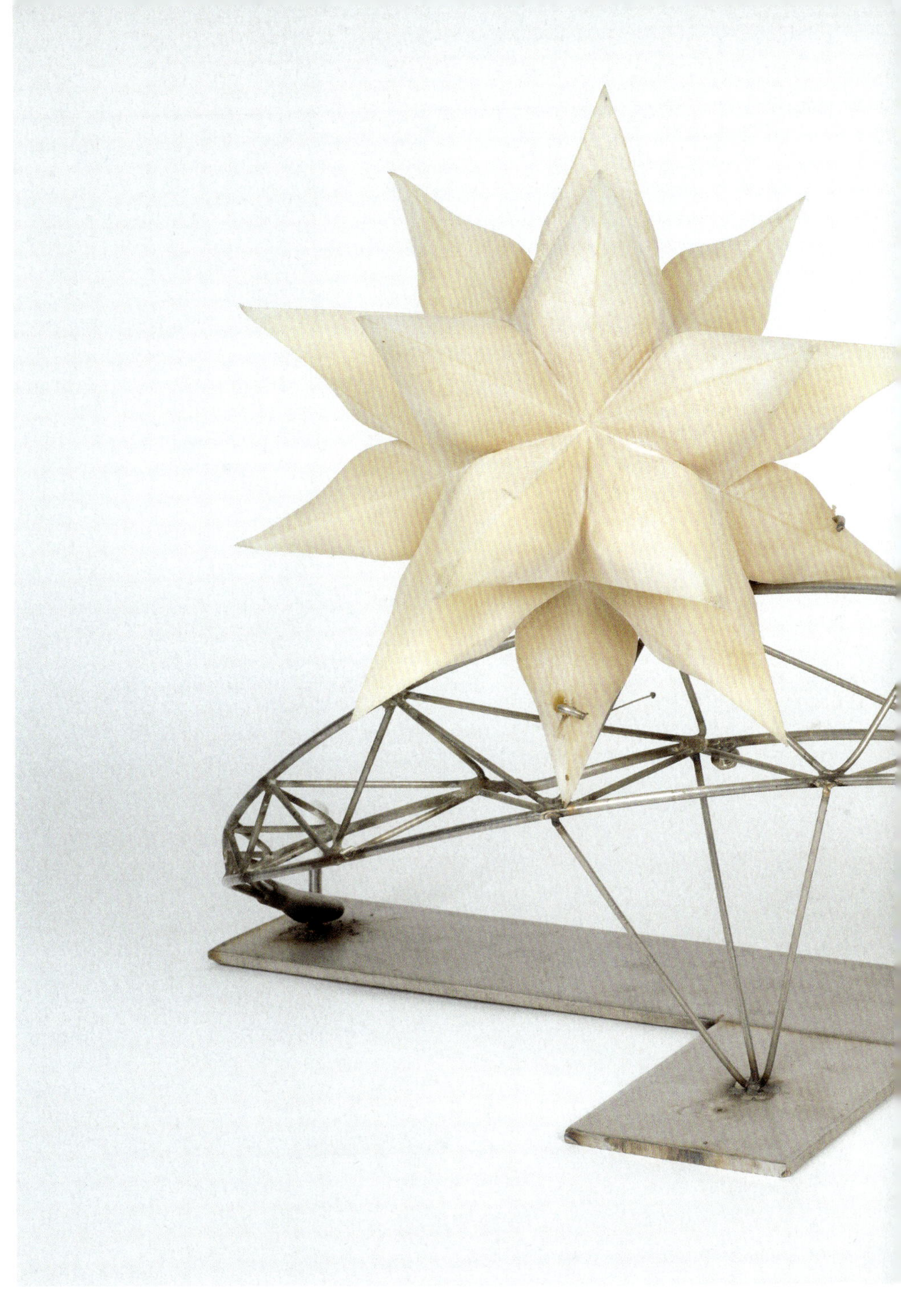

Truss with Stars I, 2016
Nylon RPT with stainless steel
17¾ x 31½ x 13½
(FS2016.052)

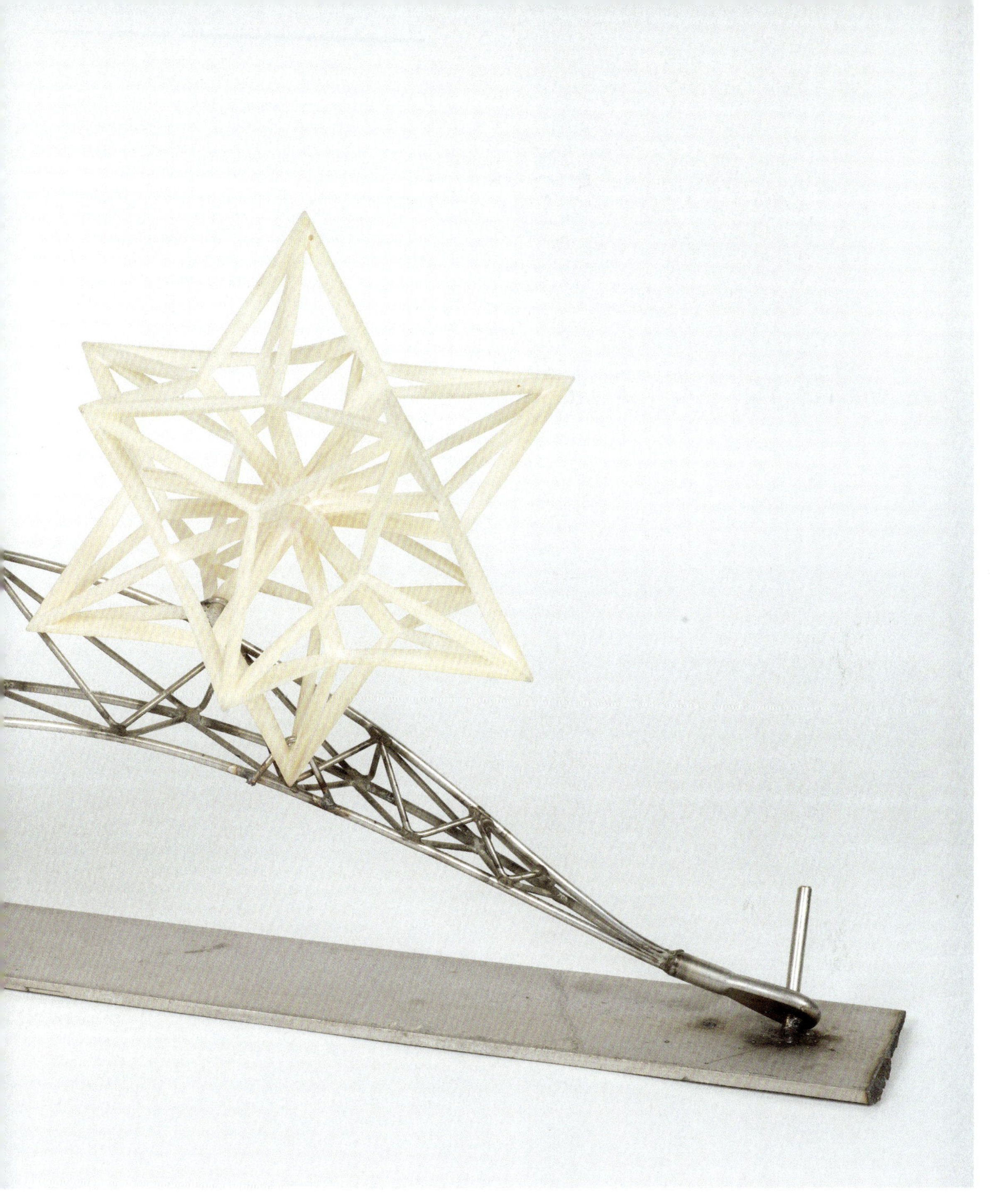

Fat Puffed Star Model, 2016
Nylon RPT
11 x 14 x 13
(FS2016.043)

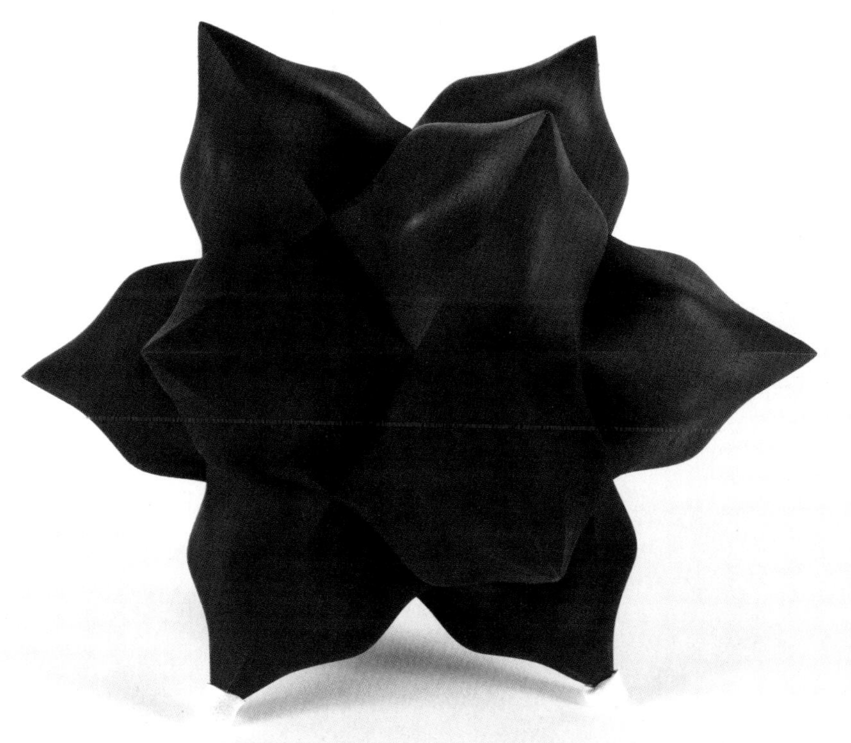

Fat 12 Point Carbon Fiber Star, 2016
Carbon fiber
252 x 252 x 204
(FS2016.033)

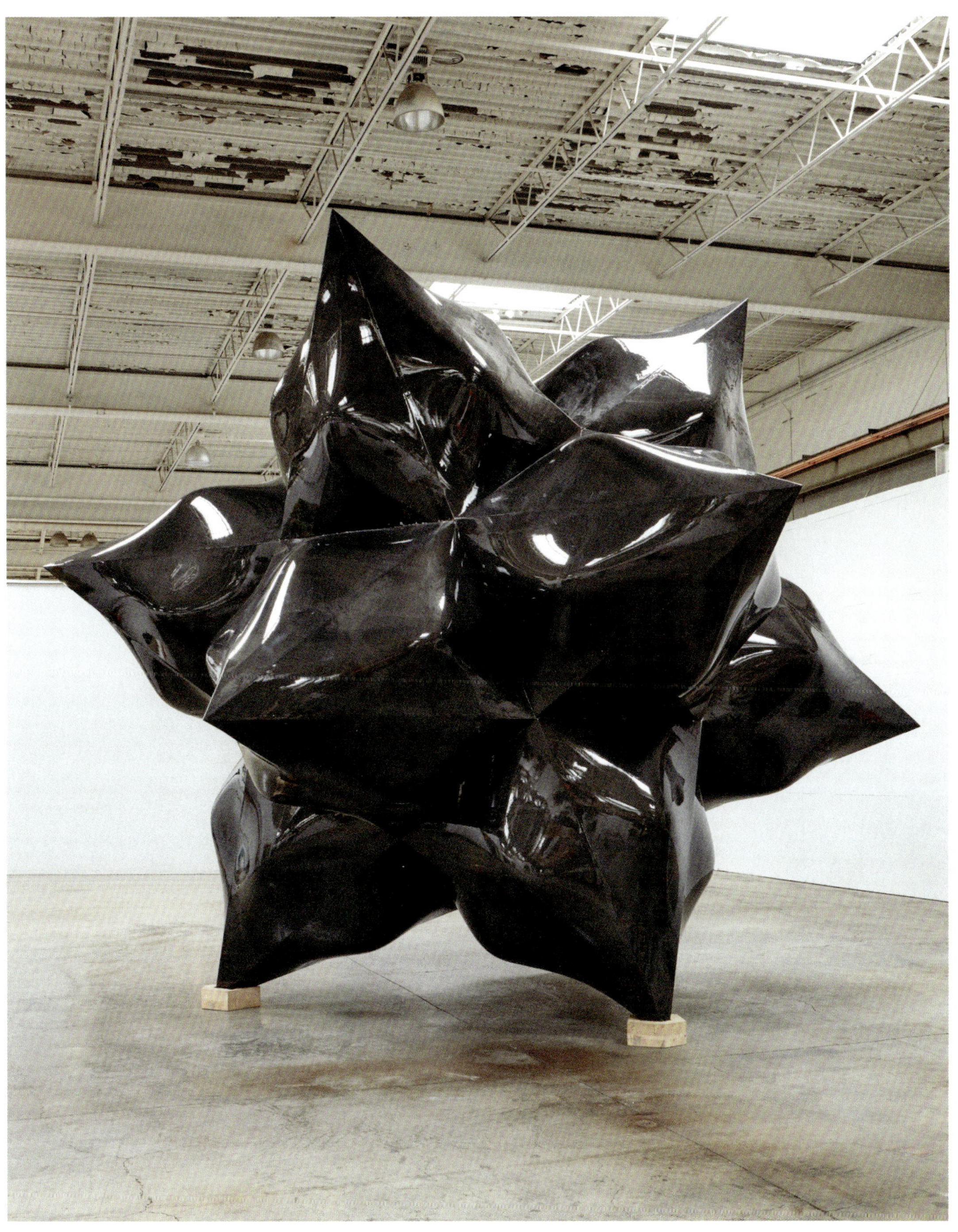

Alu Truss Star, 2016
Milled aluminum
168 x 168 x 168
(FS2016.056)

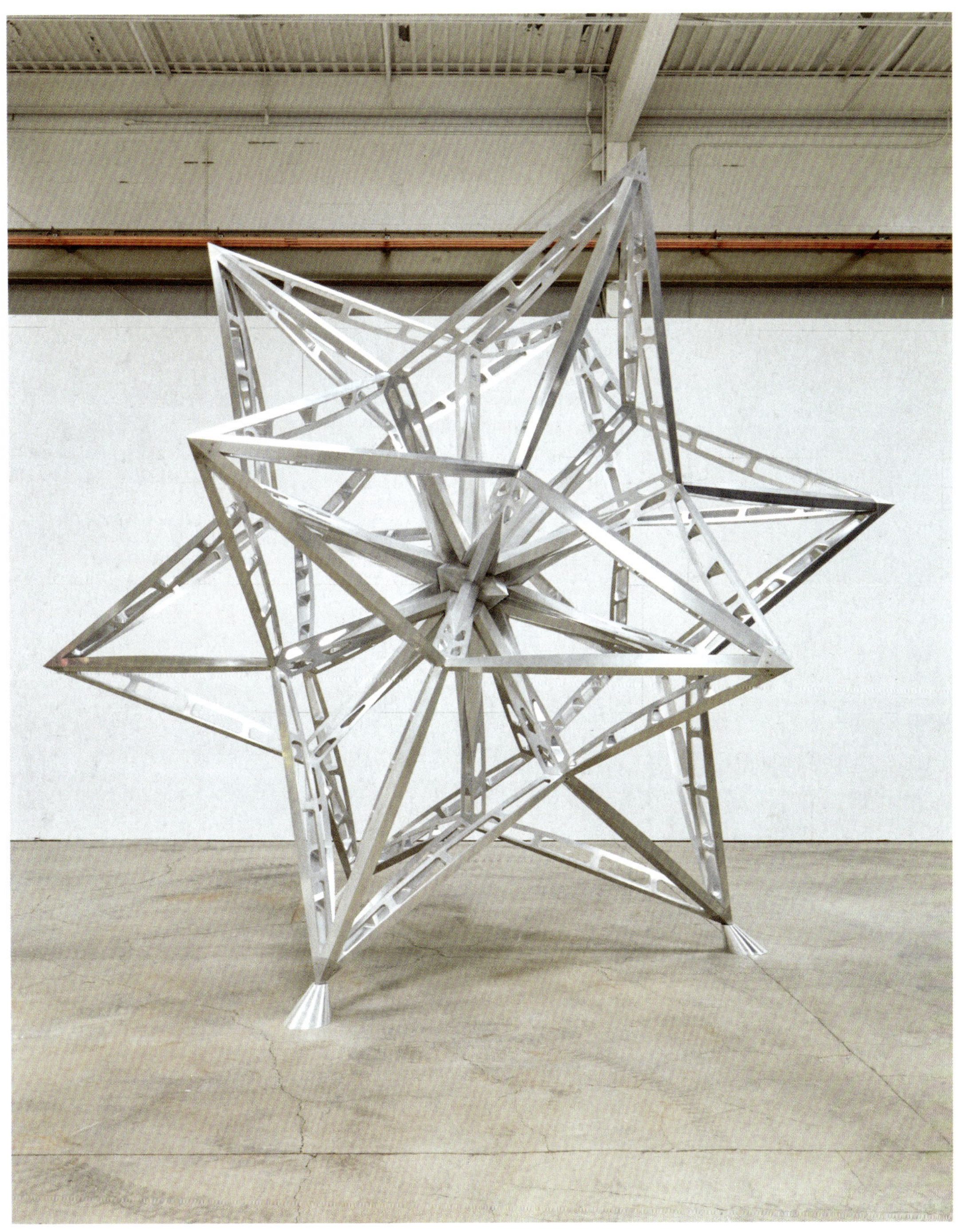

Jay's Carbon Fiber Star, 2016
Carbon fiber and RPT joints
111 x 94 x 94
(FS2016.071)

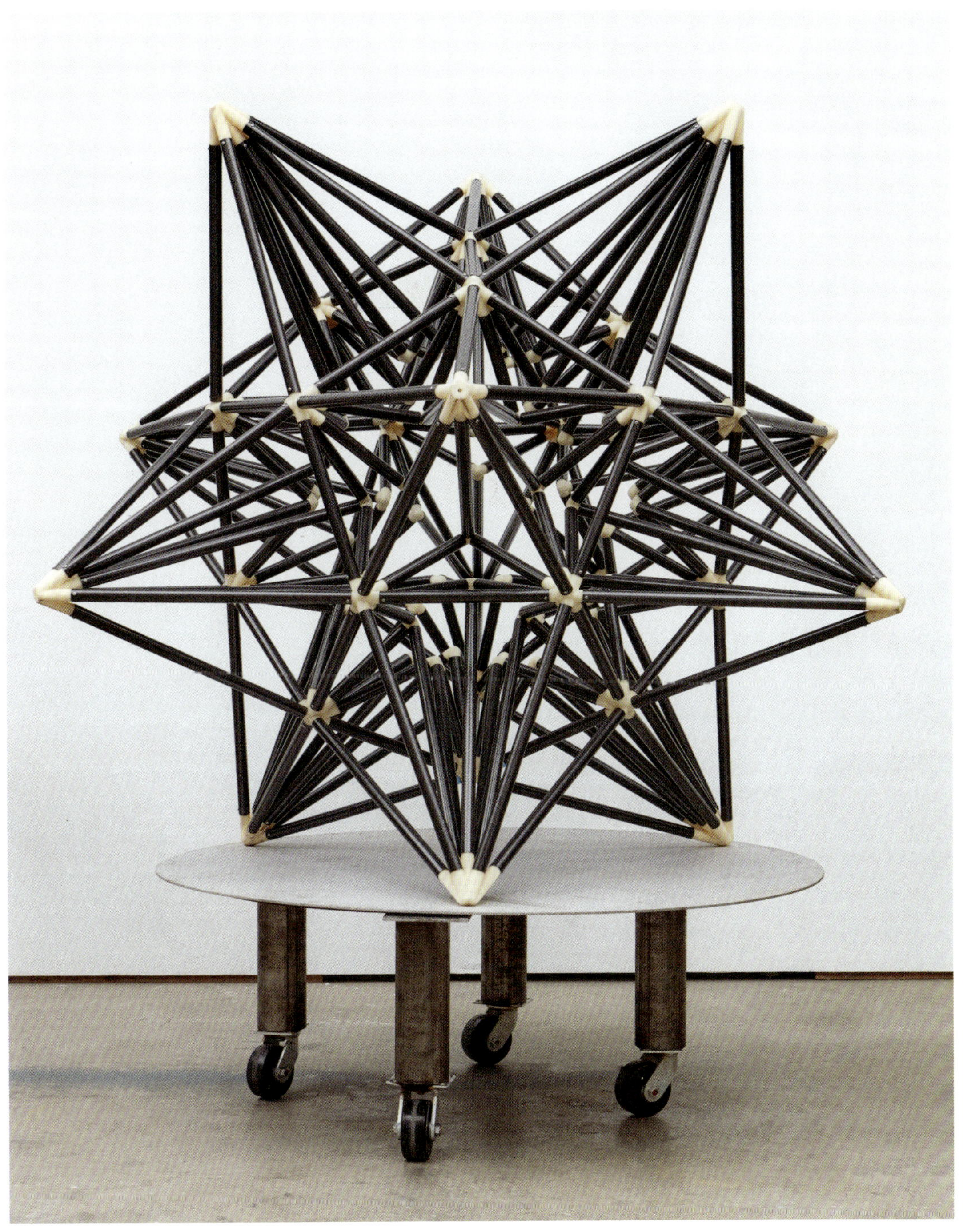

Stainless split star with truss segments, 2016
Stainless steel
88 x 67 x 84
(FS2016.081)

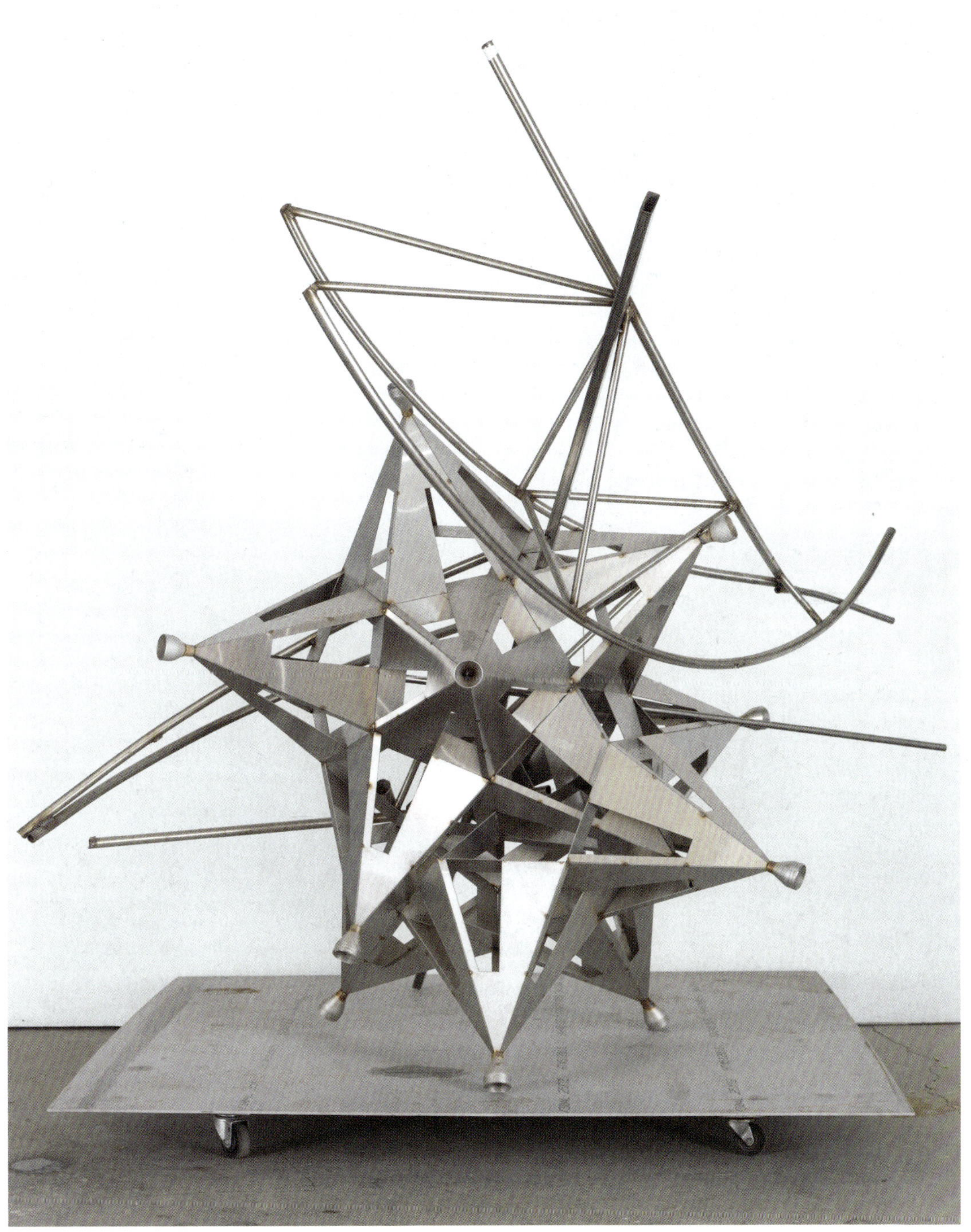

Star with Square Tubing, 2016
Stainless Steel
46 x 46 x 46
(FS2016.001)

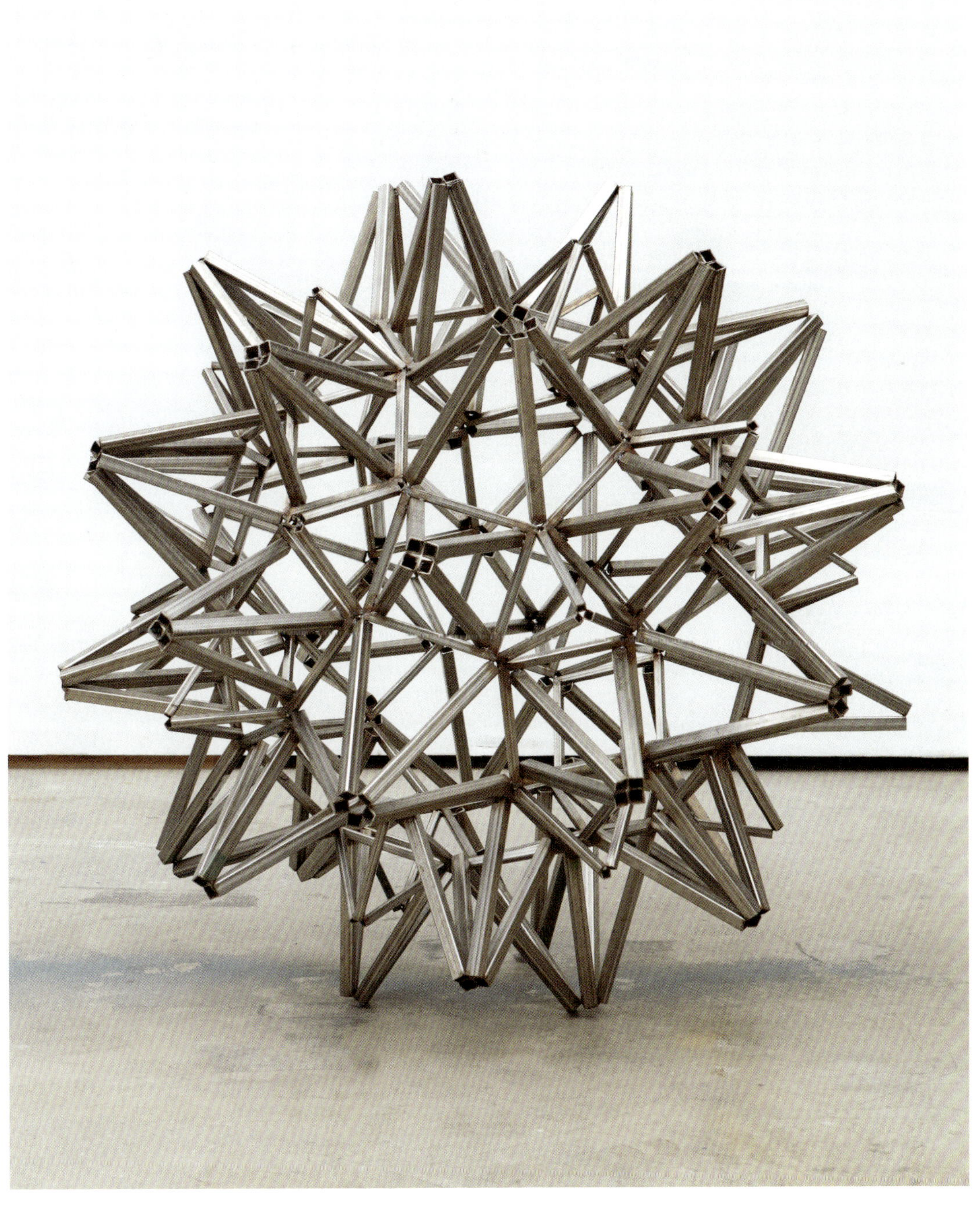

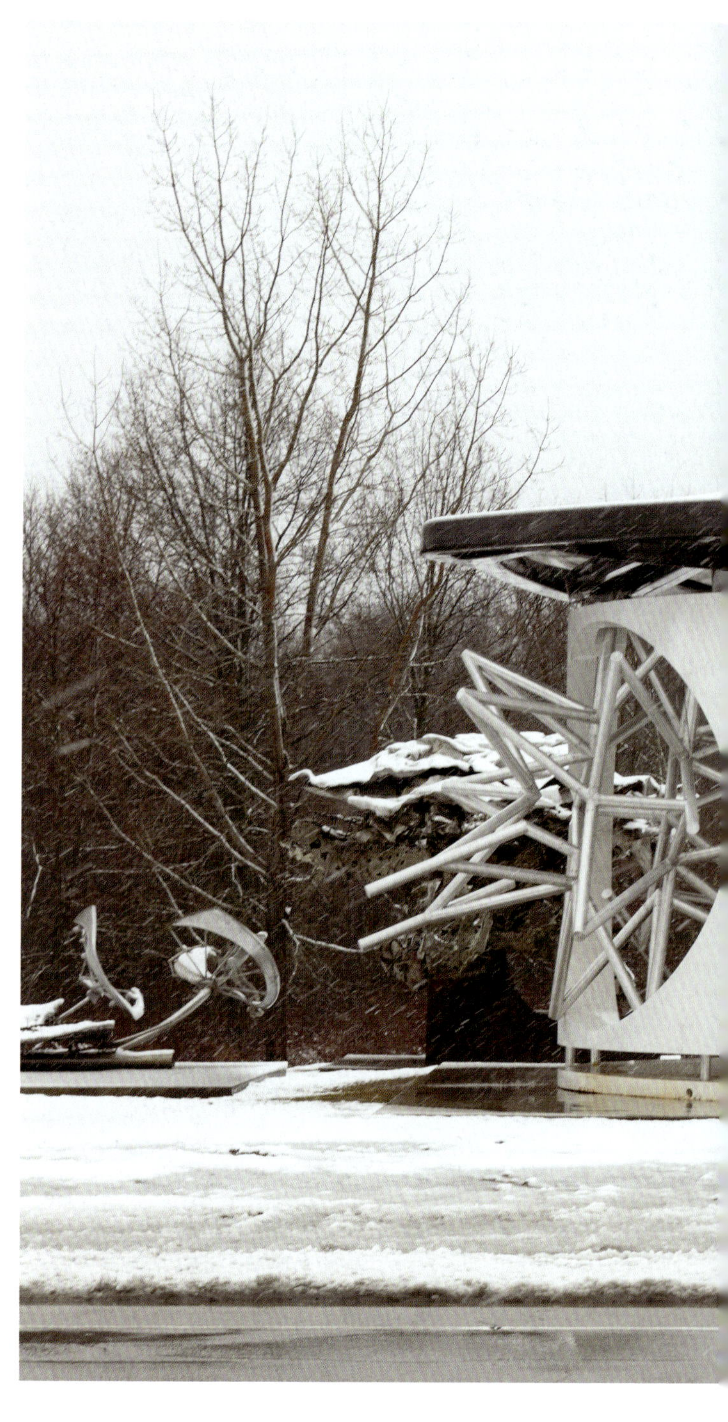

Pavillion, 2016
Carbon fiber roof, painted steel
base with three aluminum stars
300 x 552 x 552
(FS2016.058)

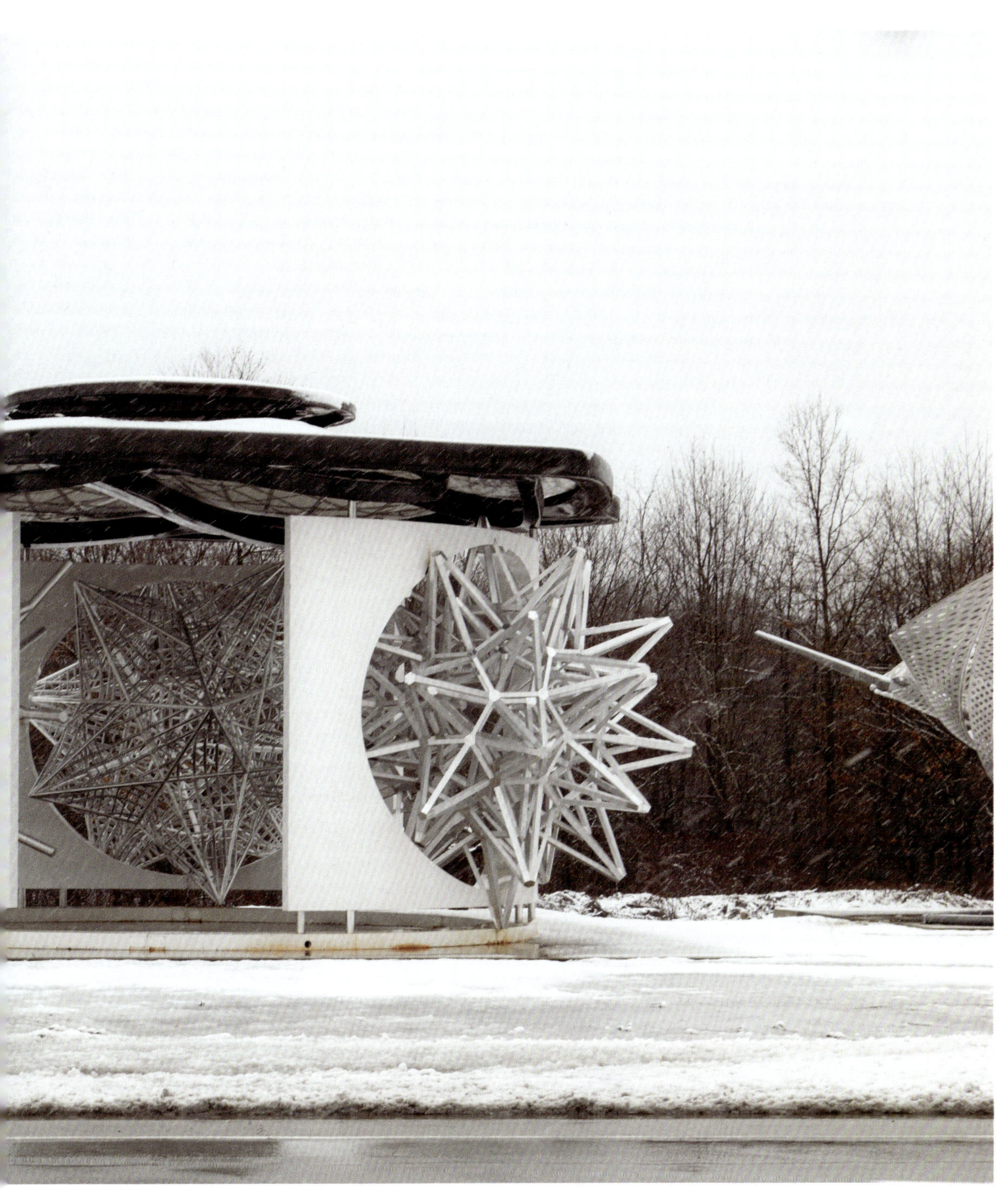

Flat Pack Star, 2016
Coated Baltic birch plywood
48 x 48 x 48
(FS2016.061)

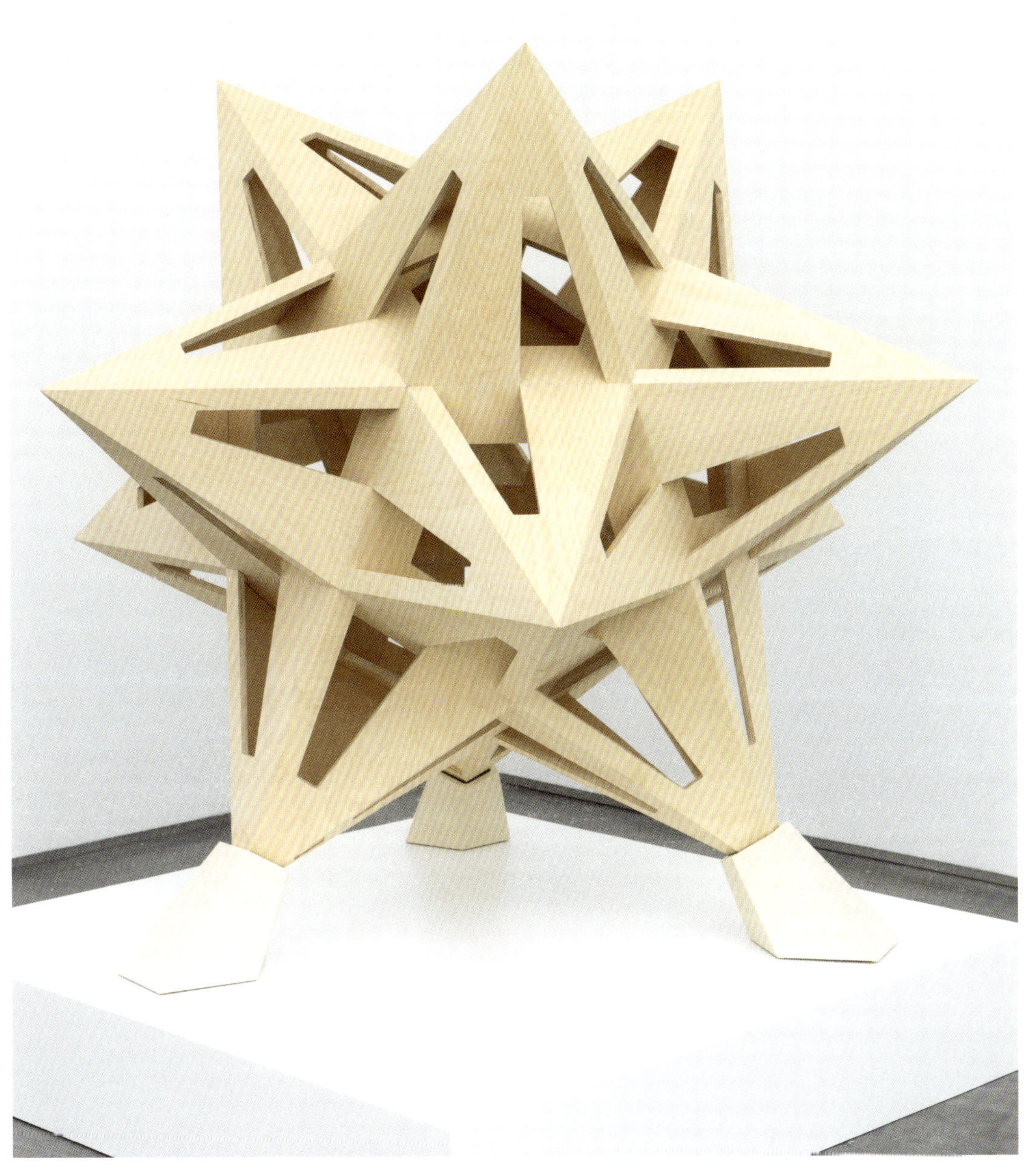

Corian Star, 2017
Corian
47 x 47 x 47
(FS2017.012)

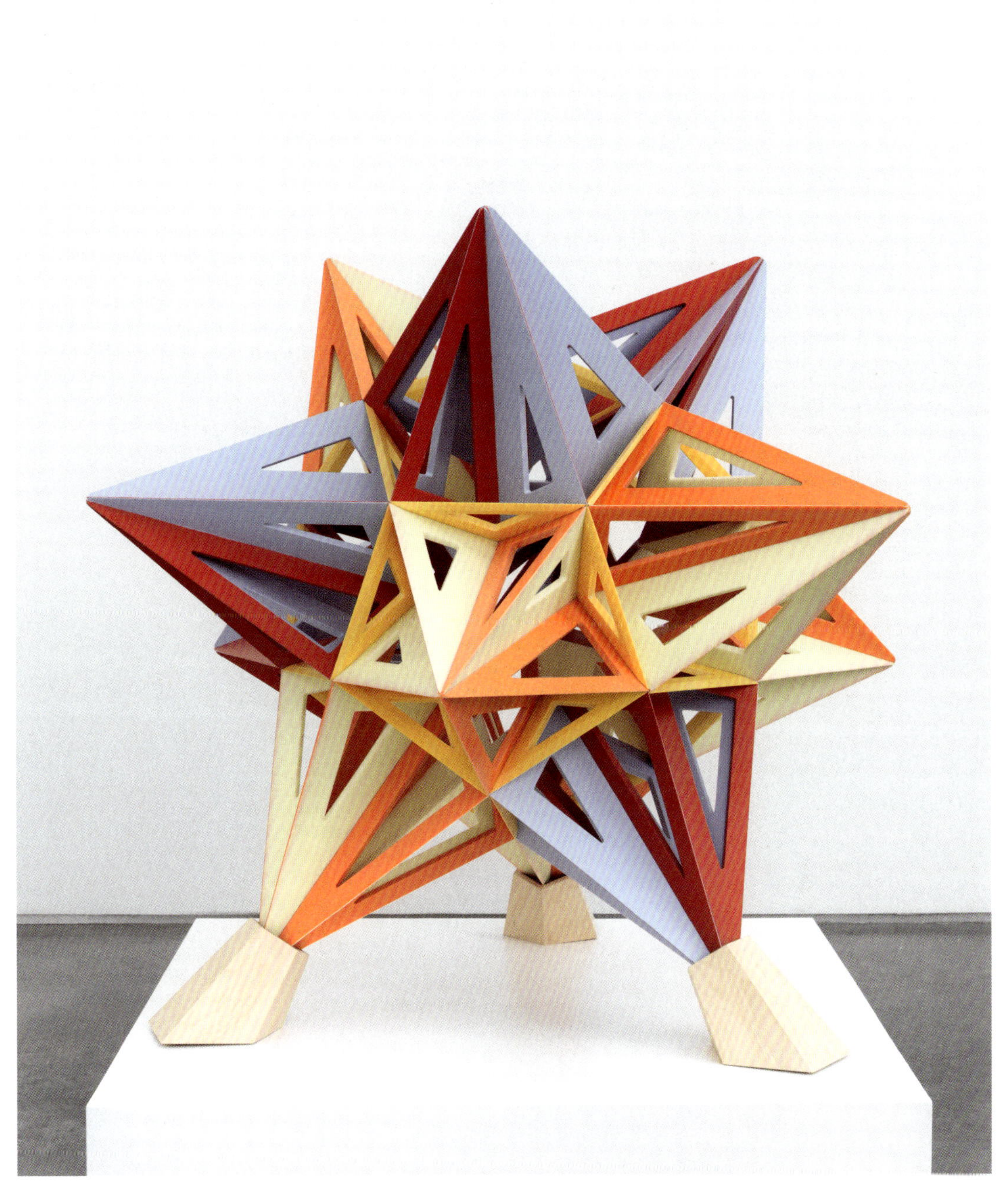

Jay's Star, 2017
Stainless steel
75 x 85 x 85
(FS2017.023)

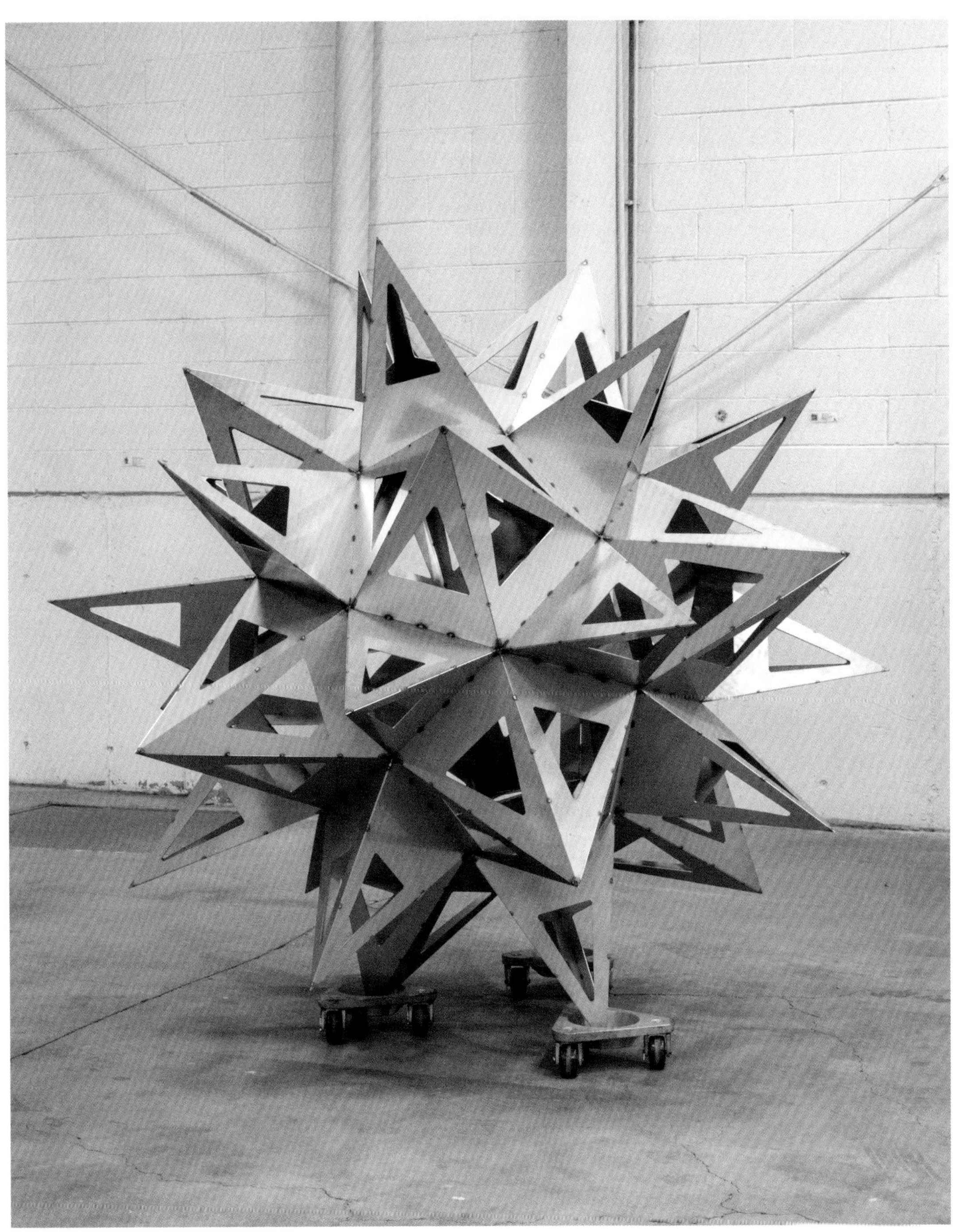

Stick Star, 2017
Stainless steel
106 x 96 x 96
(FS2017.013)

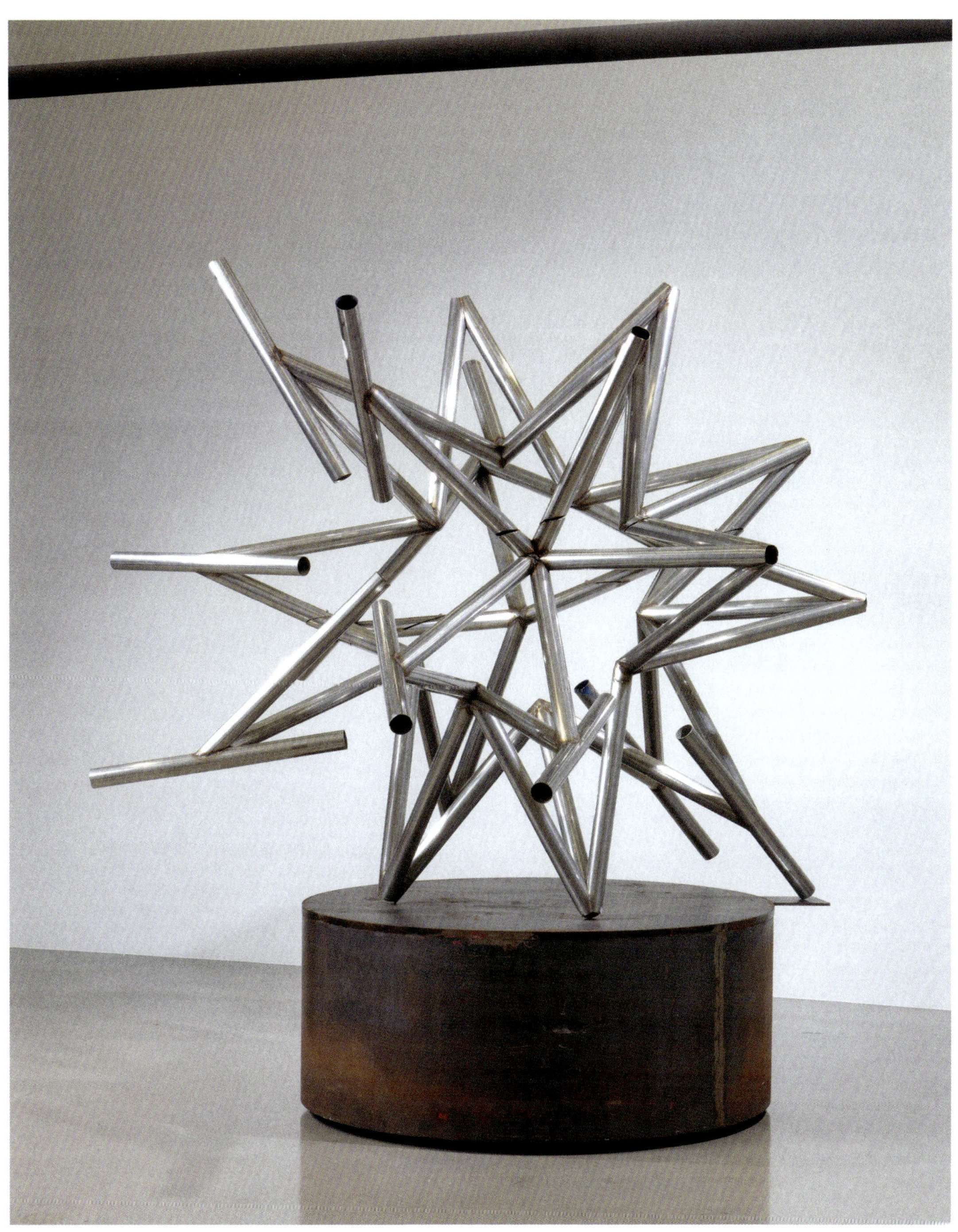

Jasper's Split Star, 2017
Aluminum
202 x 257 x 249
(FS2017.007)

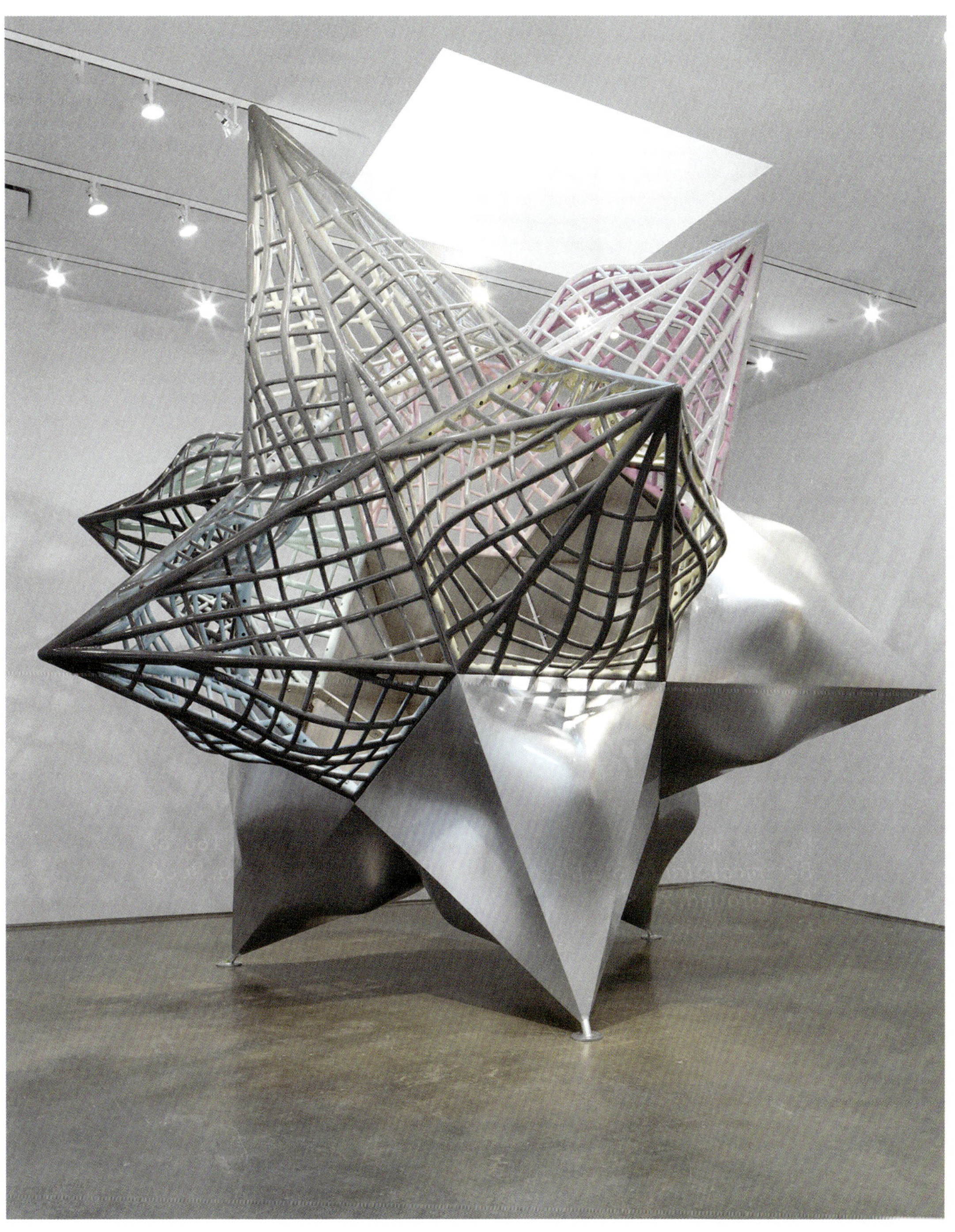

Maquette for Star, 2017
Strong flexible RPT
10 x 12 x 12
(FS2017.035)

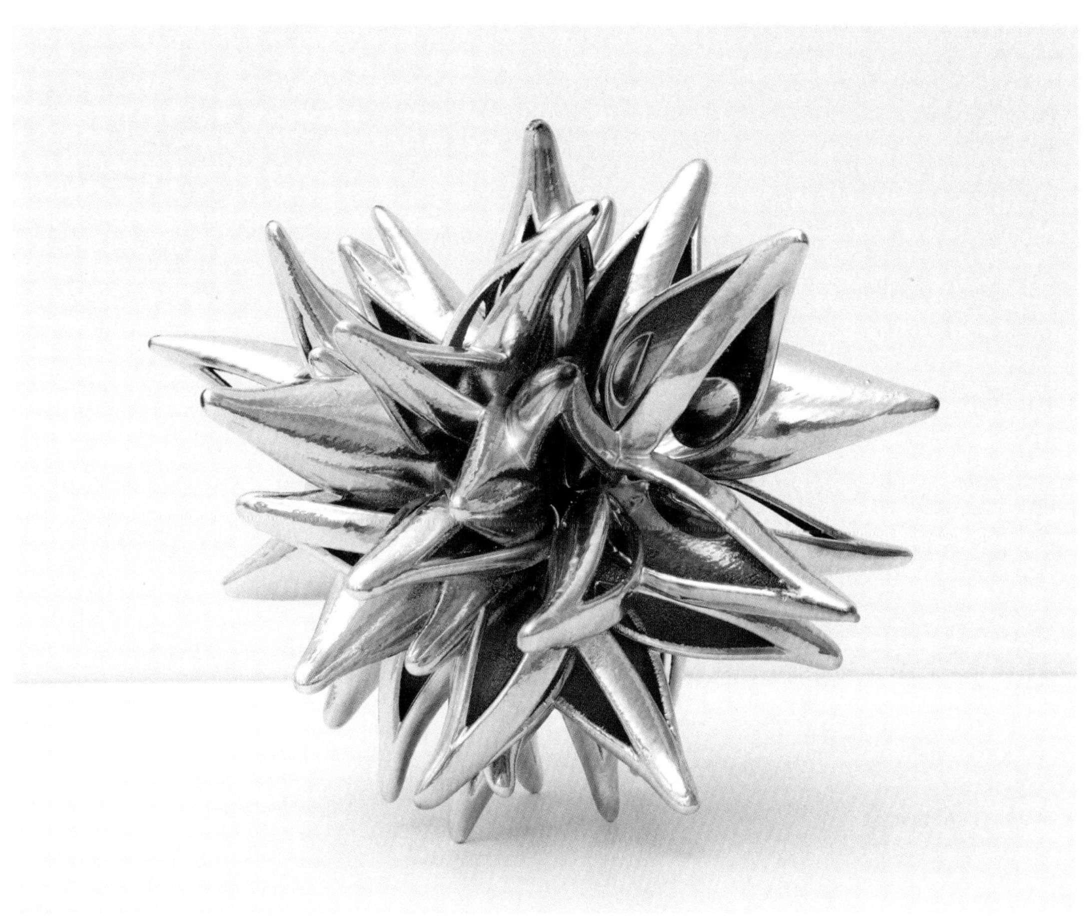

Nessus and Dejanira, 2017
Aluminum and fiberglass
143 x 139 x 118
(FS2017.011)

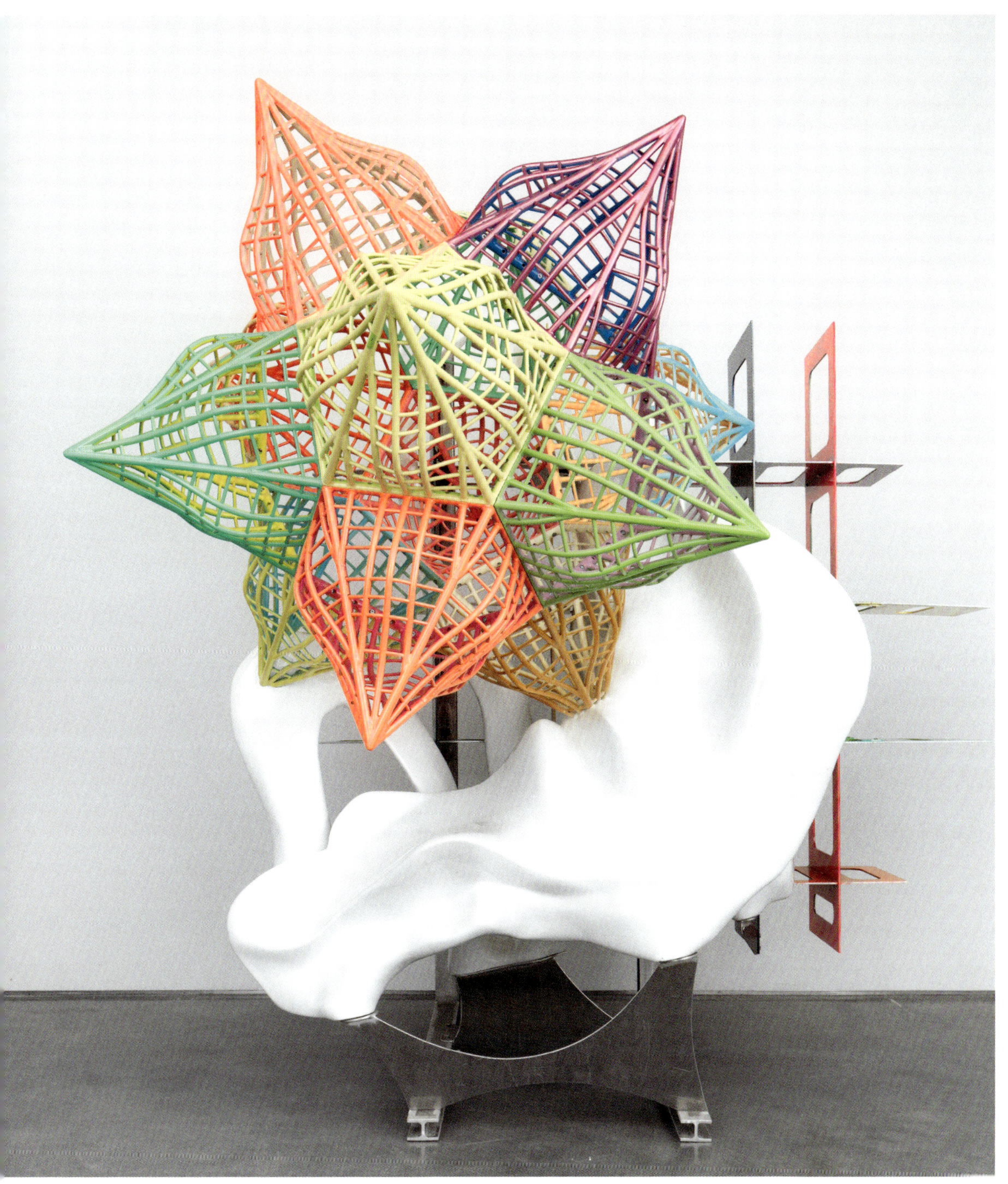

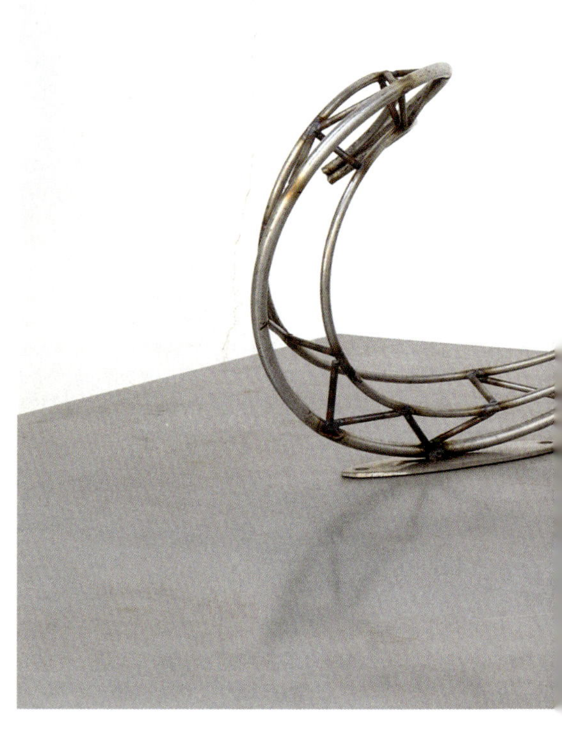

Truss with Stars II, 2018
Elasto plastic, paint, steel
21½ x 38 x 16½
(FS2018.025)

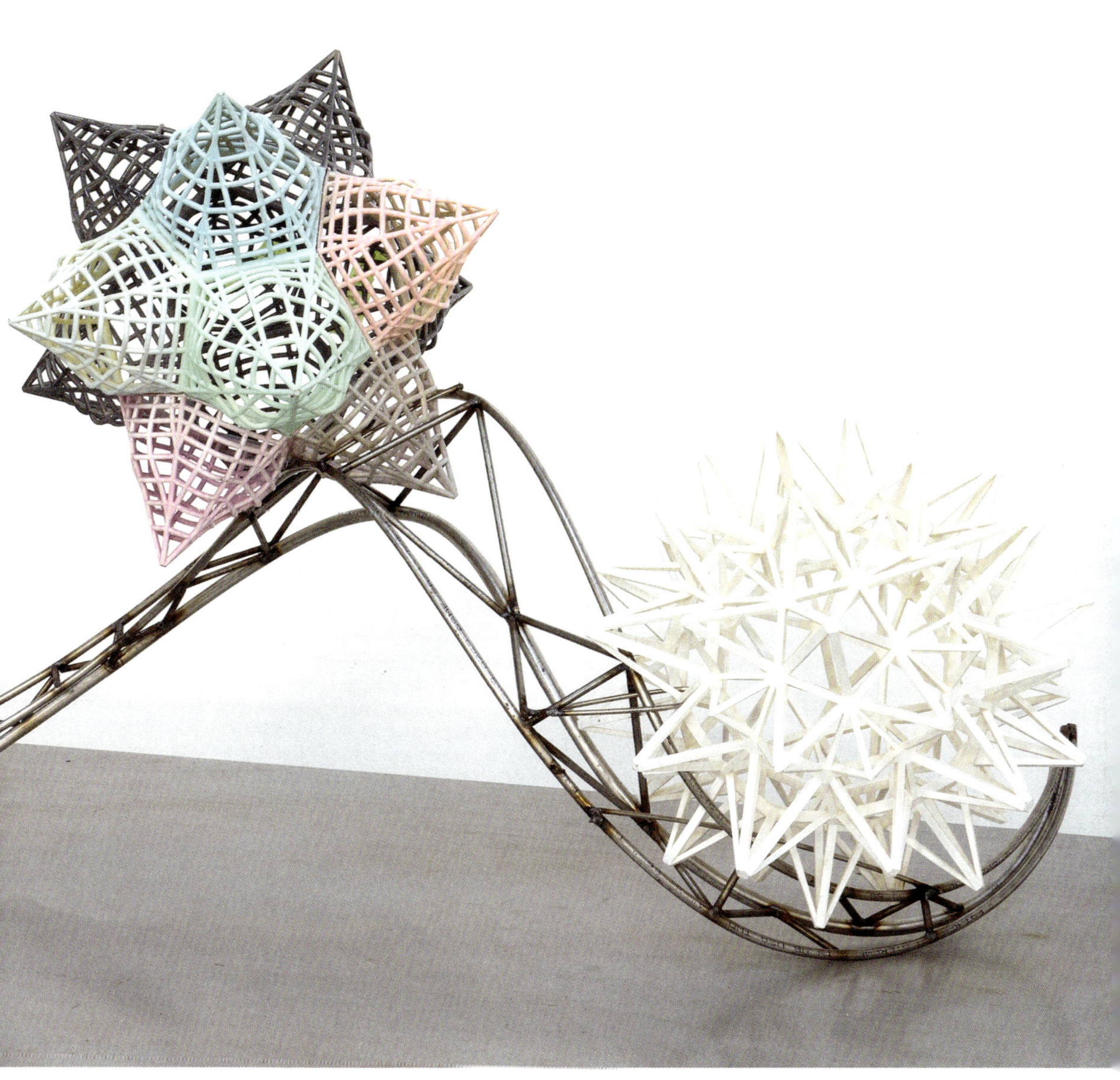

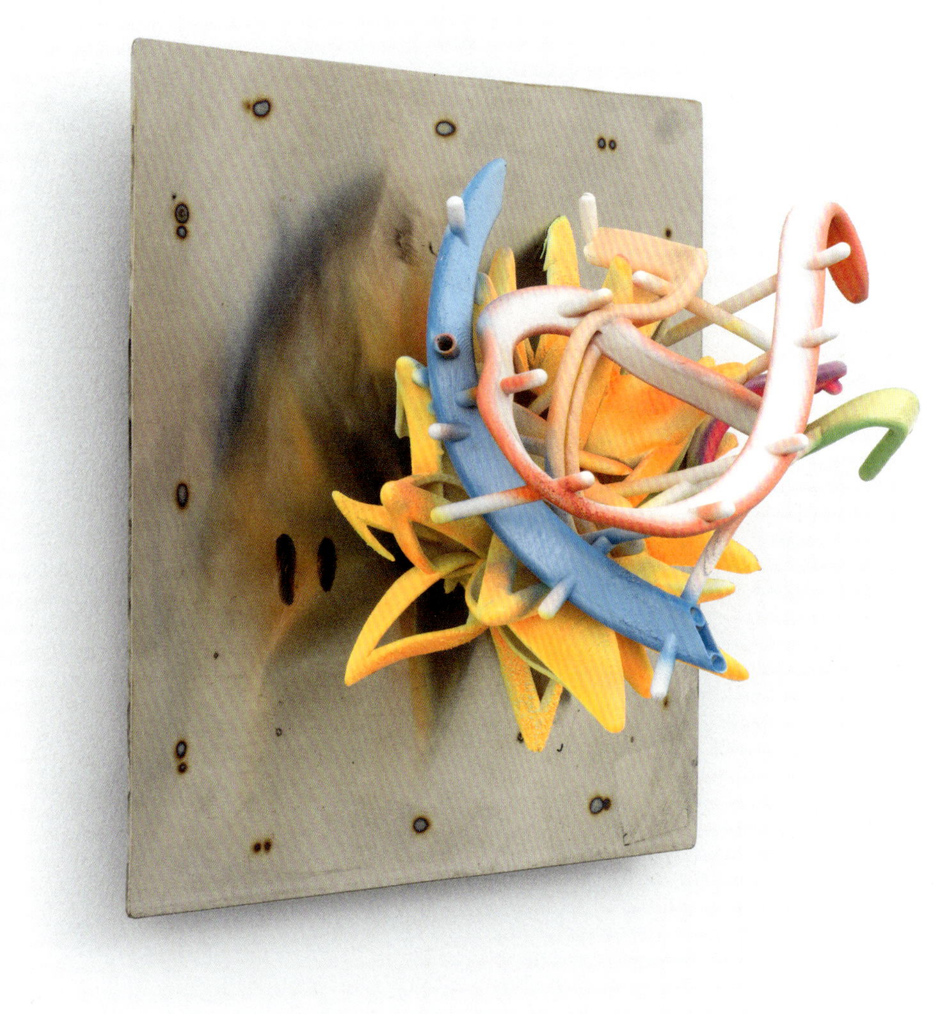

Botanical Star on Stainless Background, 2018
Elasto plastic, paint, stainless steel
16½ x 16½ x 10½
(FS2018.033)

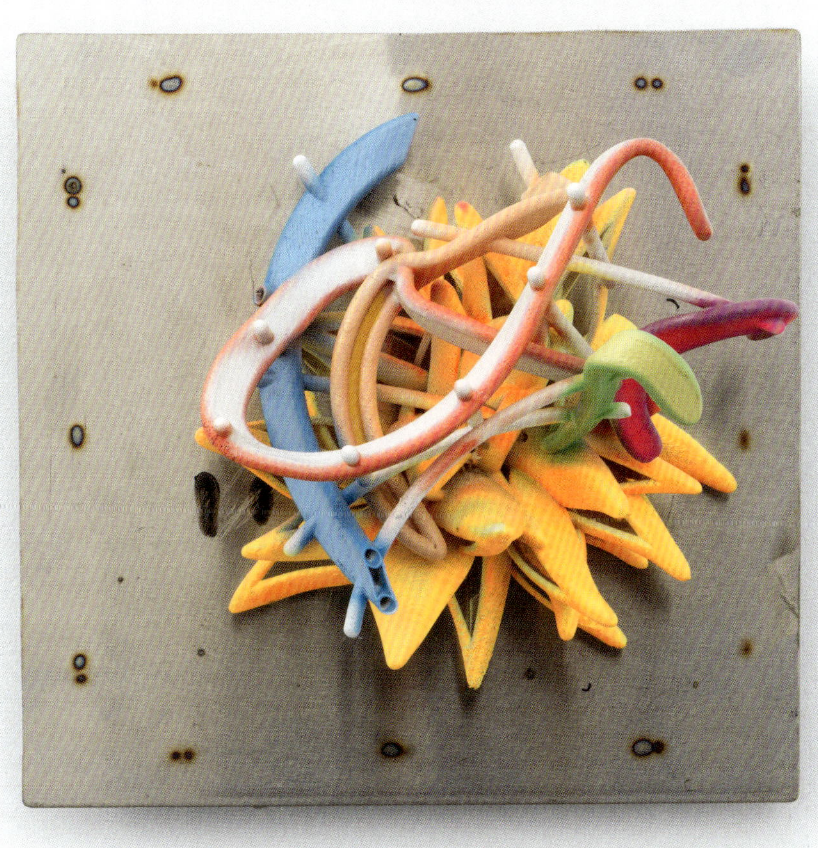

Model for the Phoenix Suns I, 2019
Elasto plastic and paint
13 x 13 x 12
(FS2019.031)

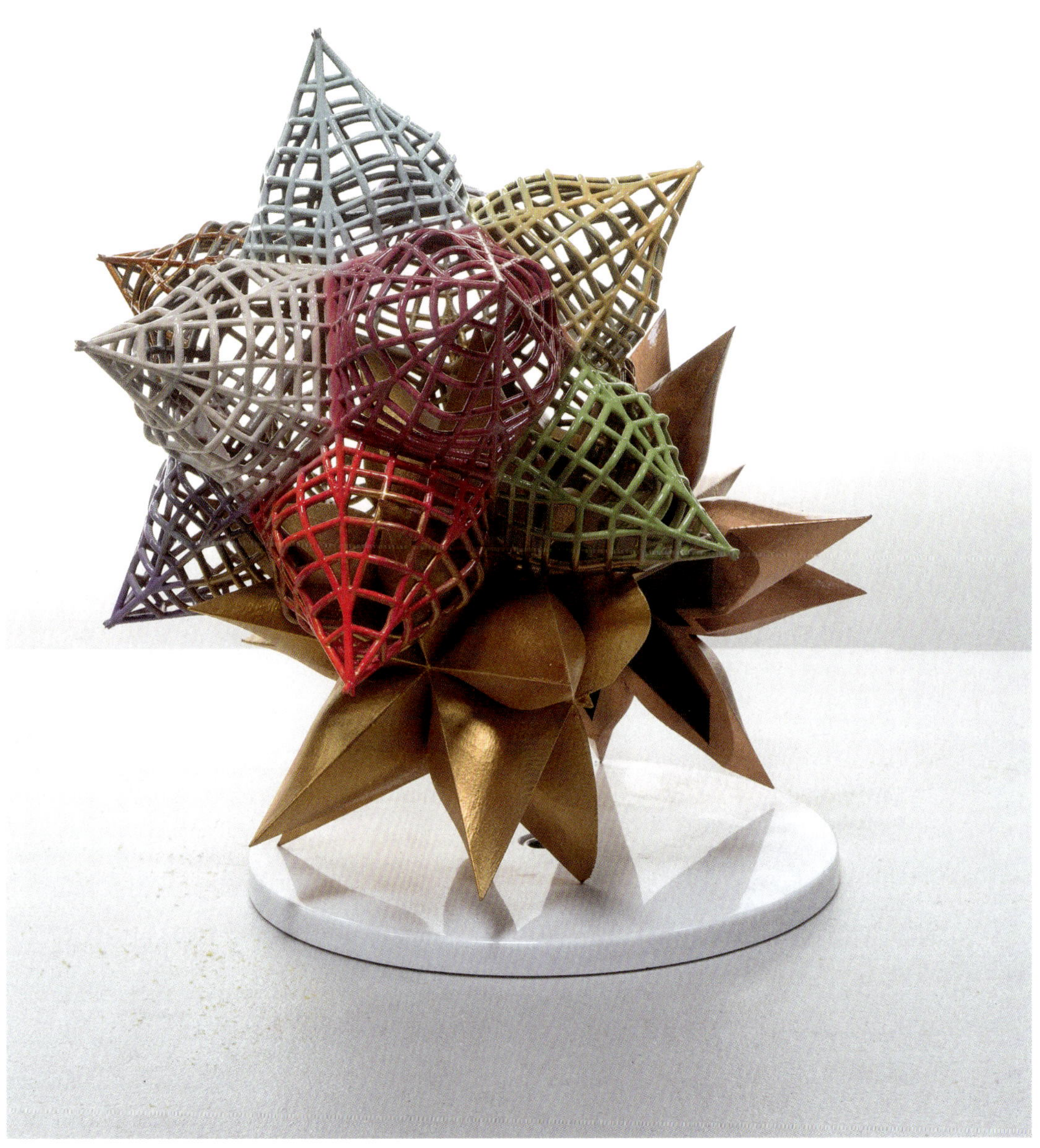

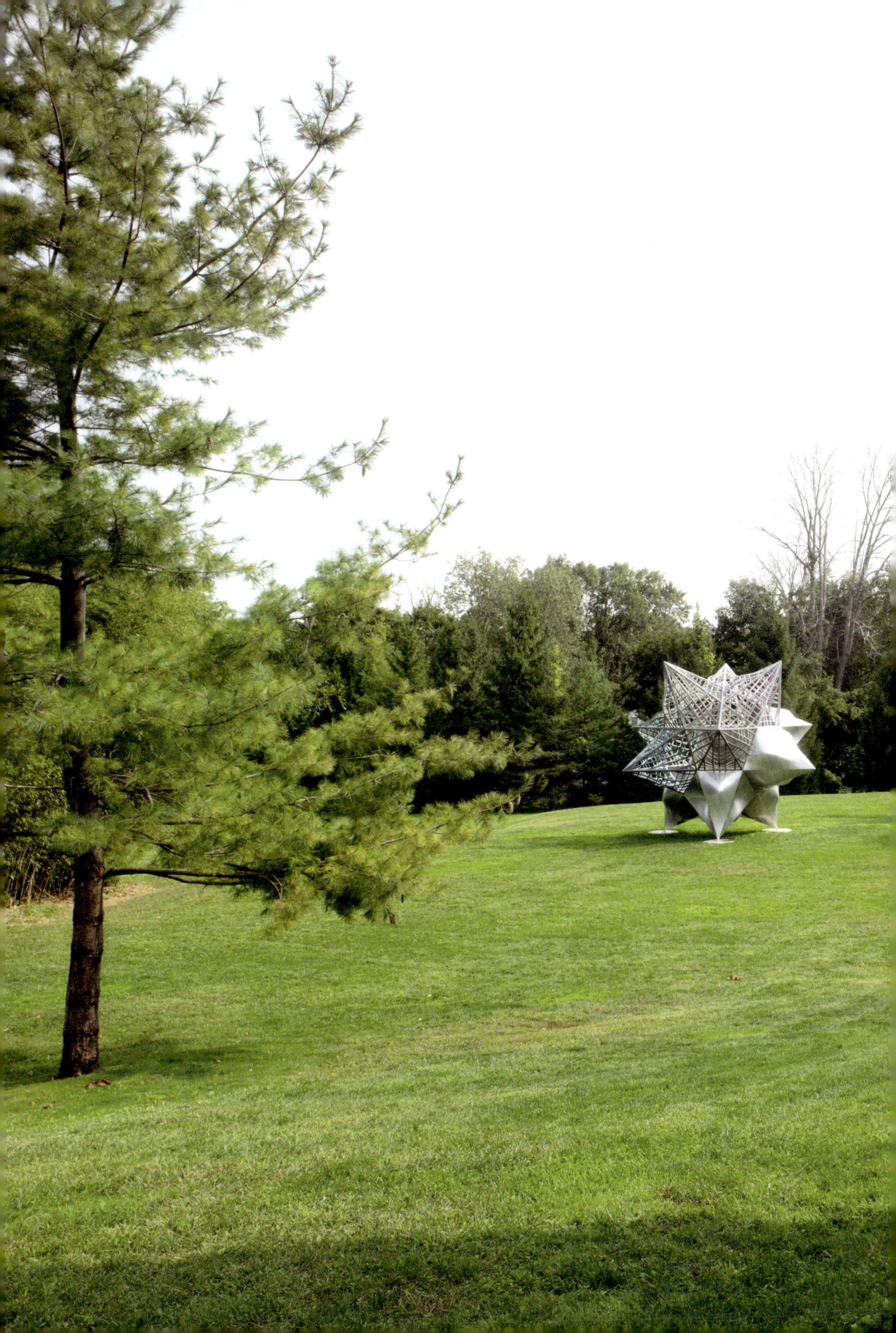

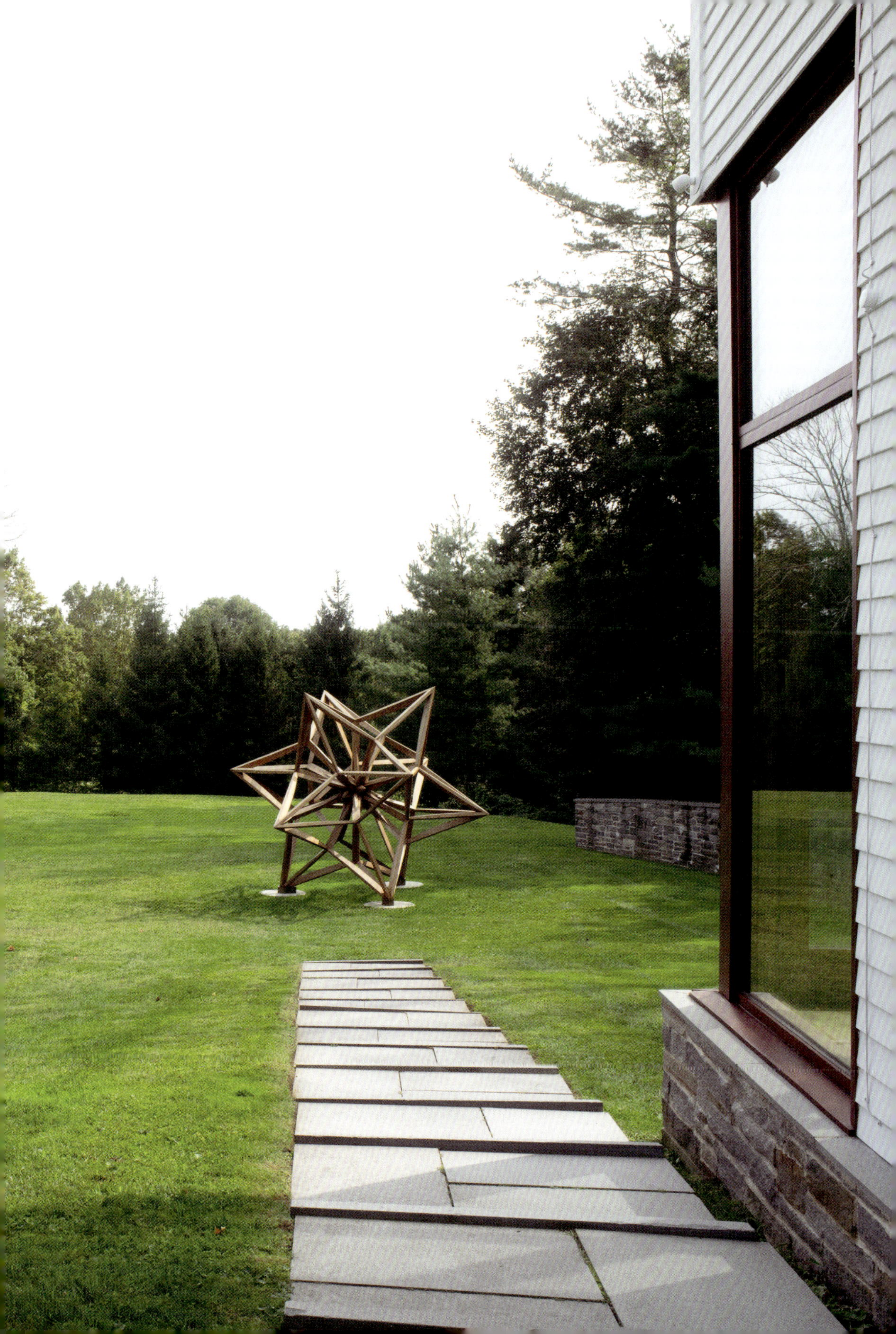

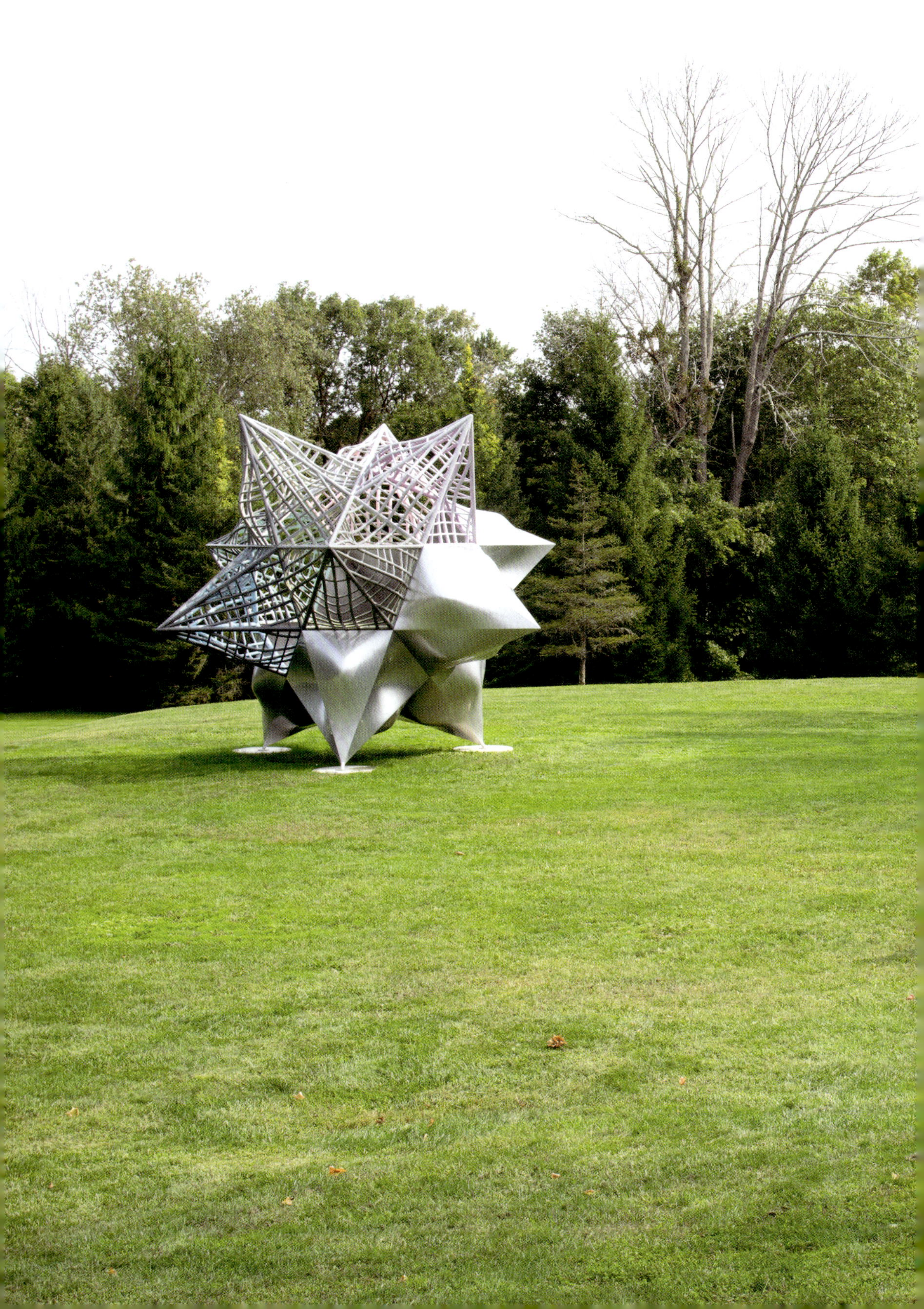

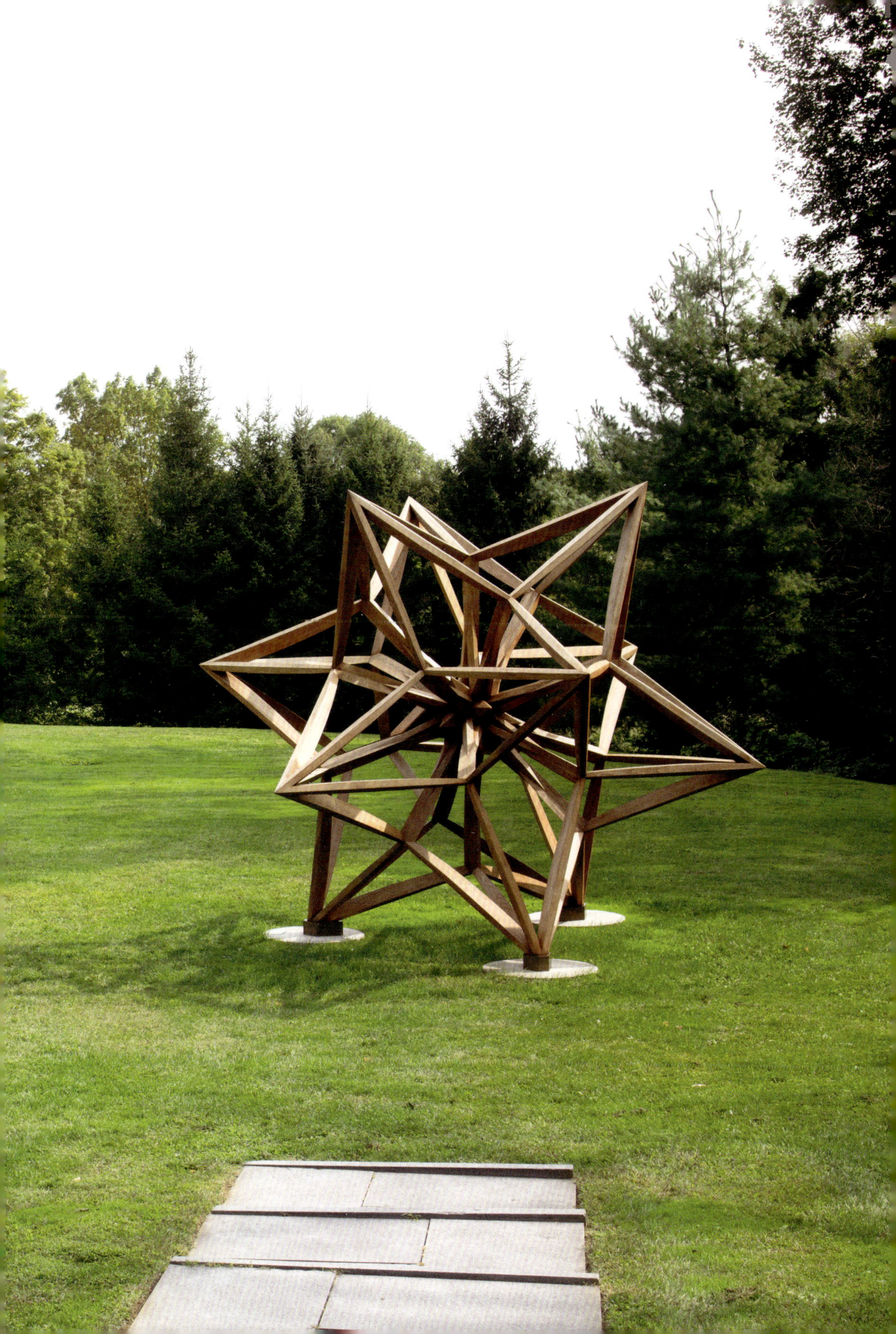

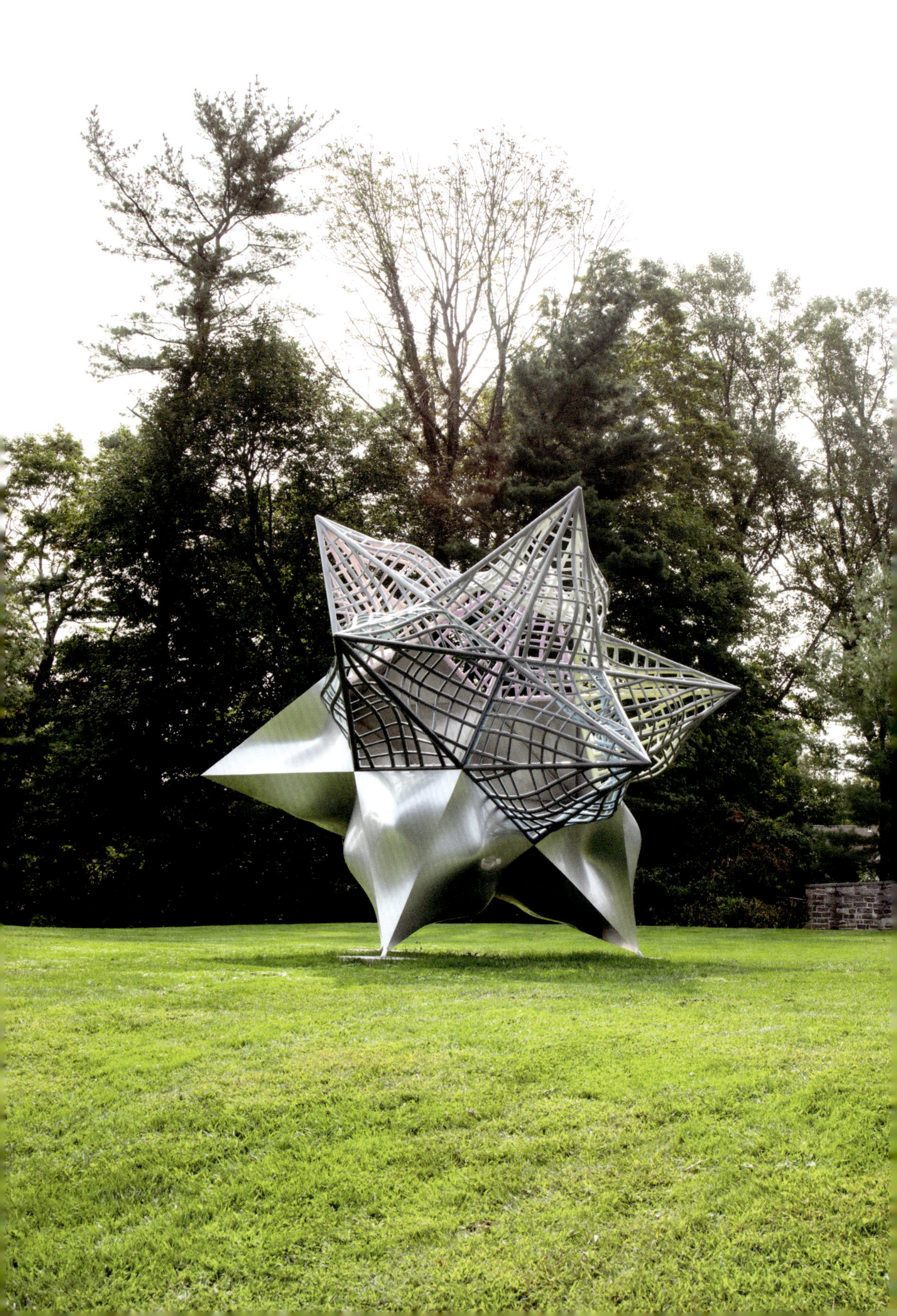

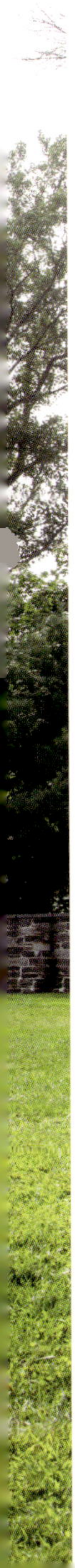

Jasper's Split Star, 2017
Aluminum
202 x 257 x 249
(FS2017.007)

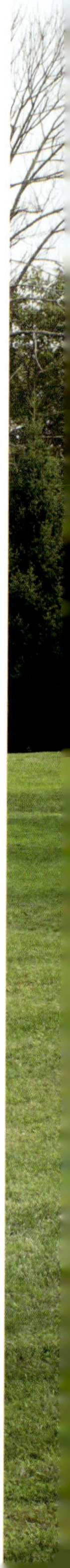

Frank's Wooden Star, 2014
Teak wood
157¼ x 157¼ x 157¼
(FS2014.047)

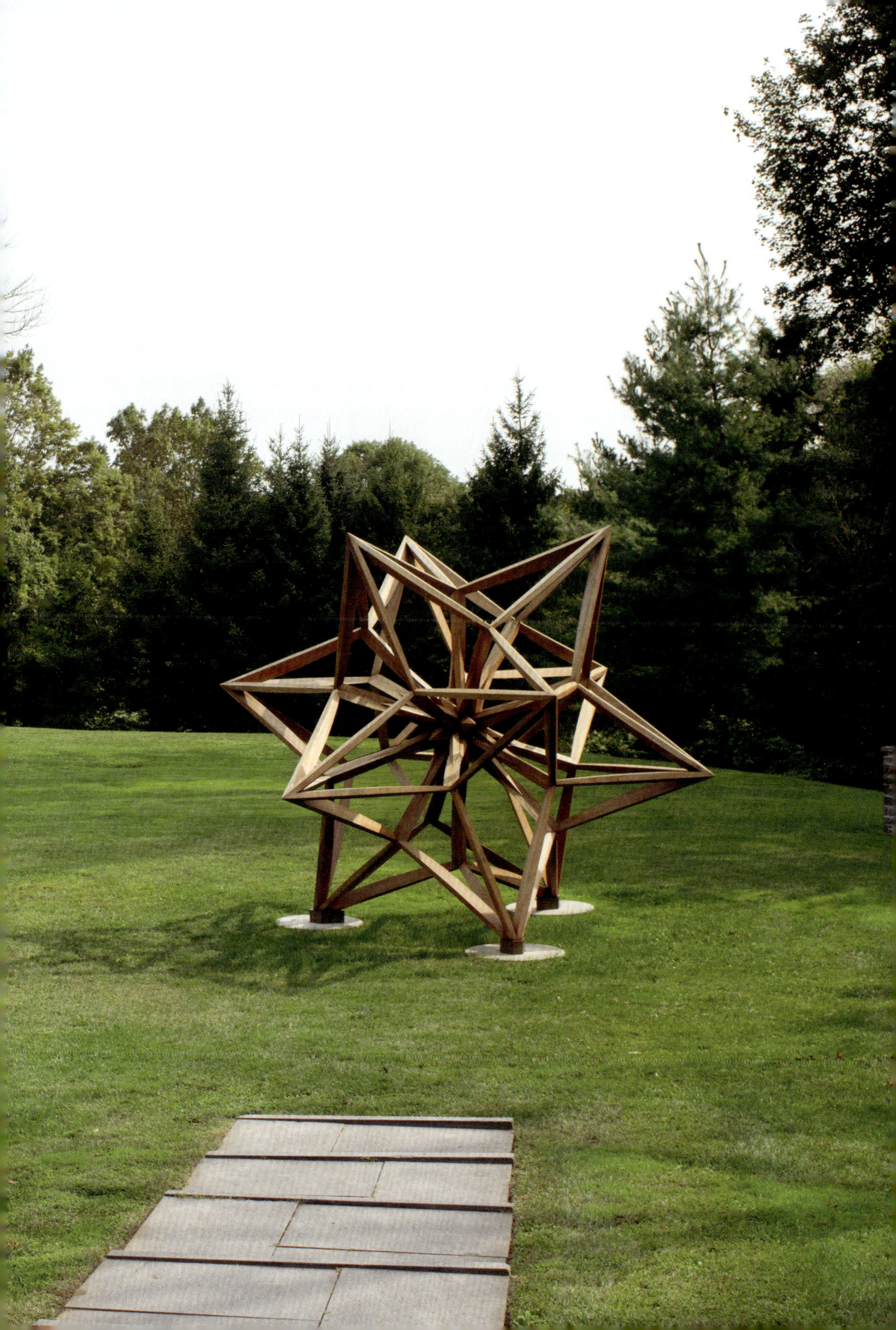

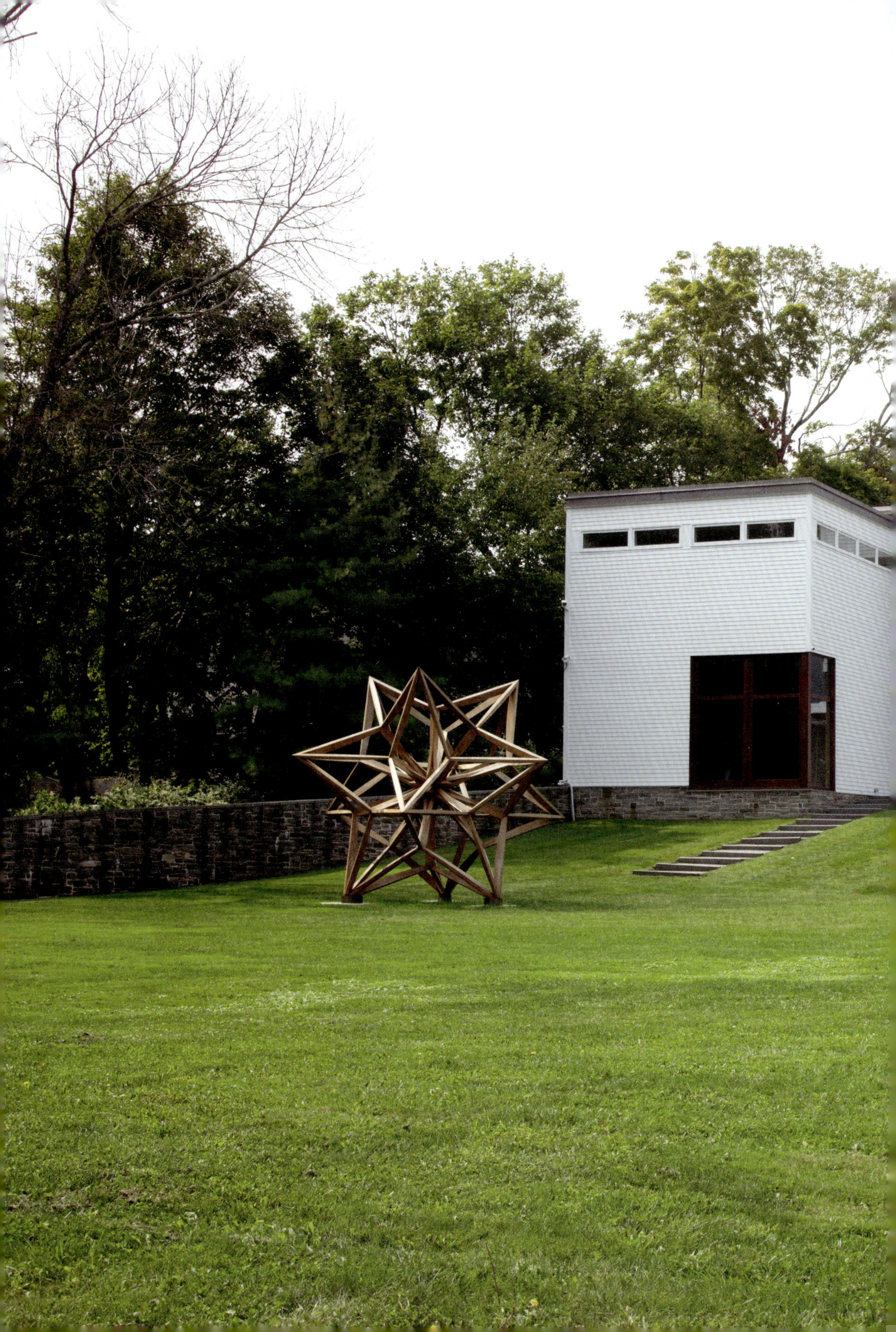

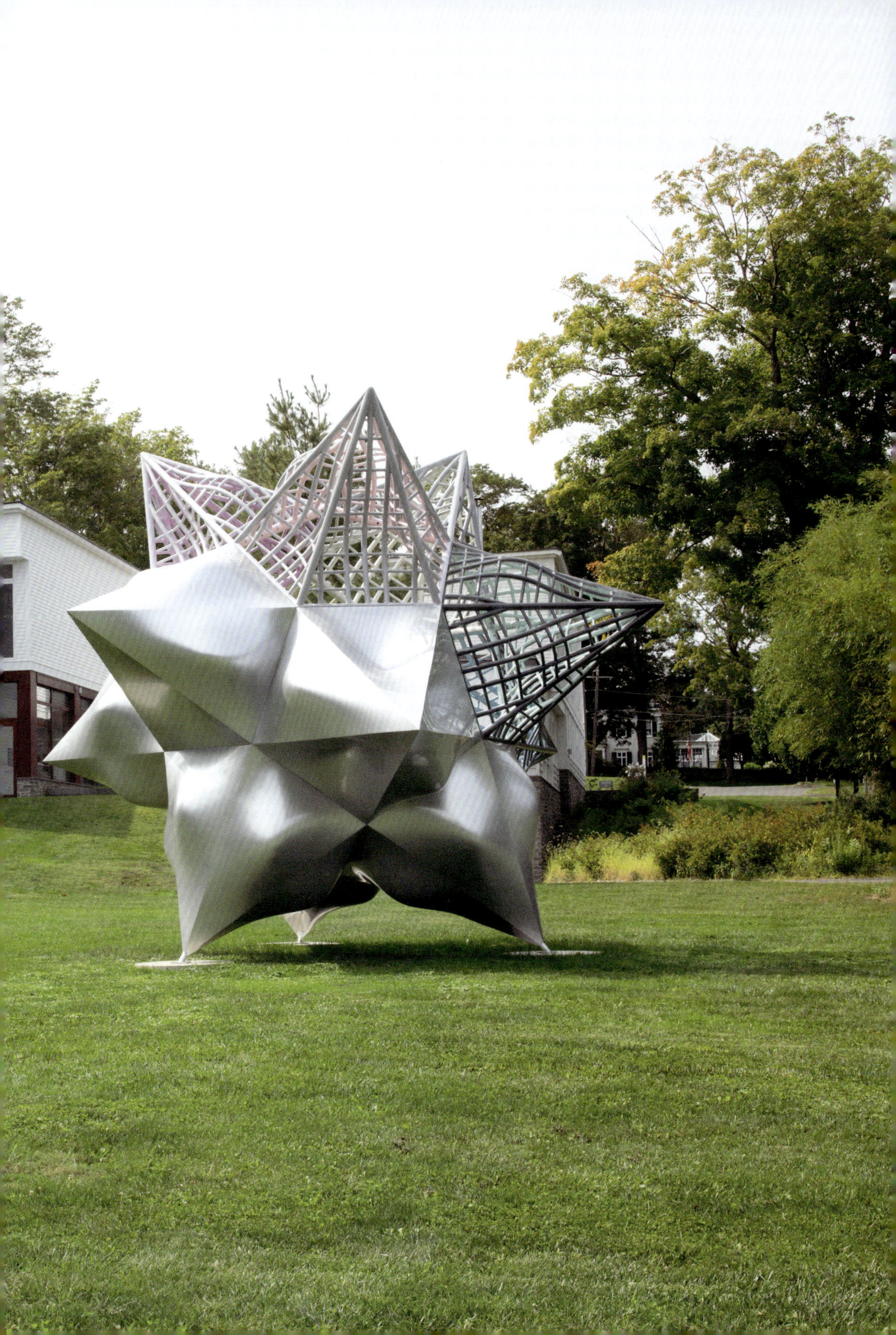

Stainless split star with truss segments, 2016
Stainless steel
88 x 67 x 84
(FS2016.081)

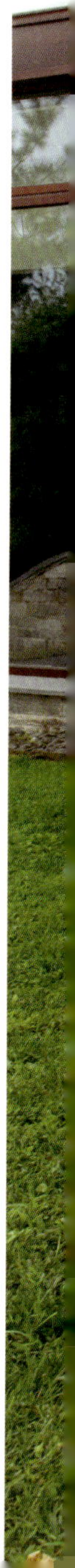

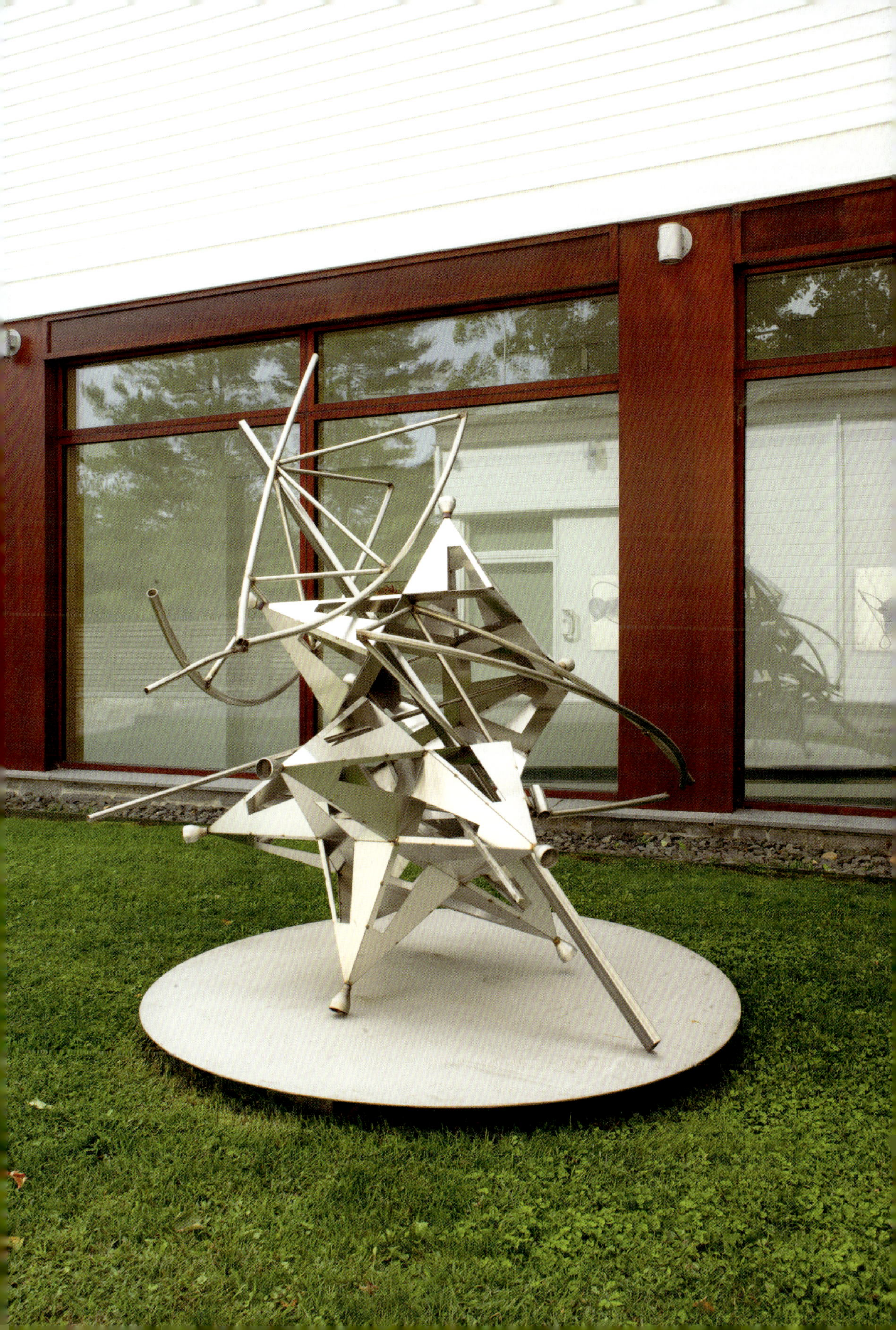

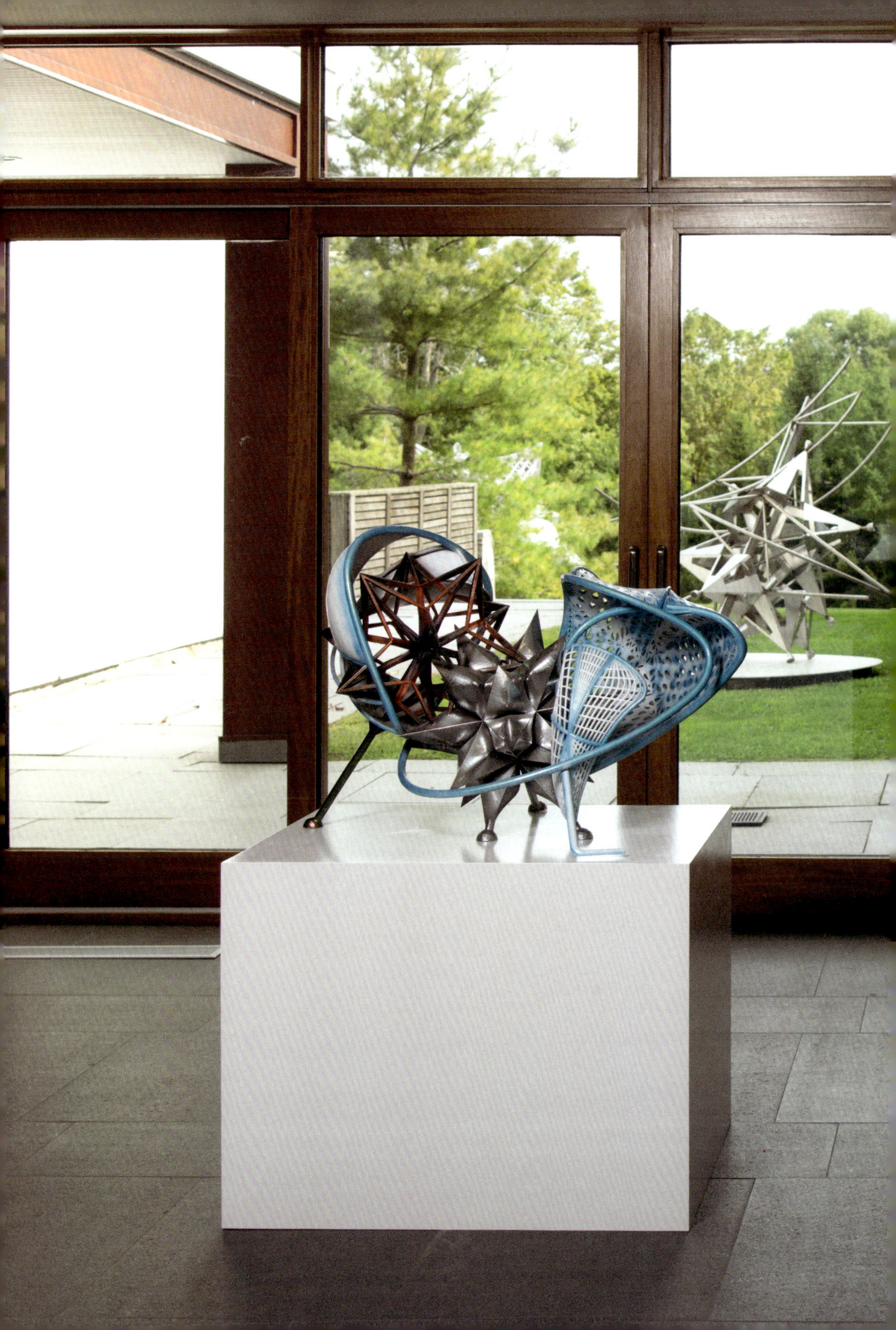

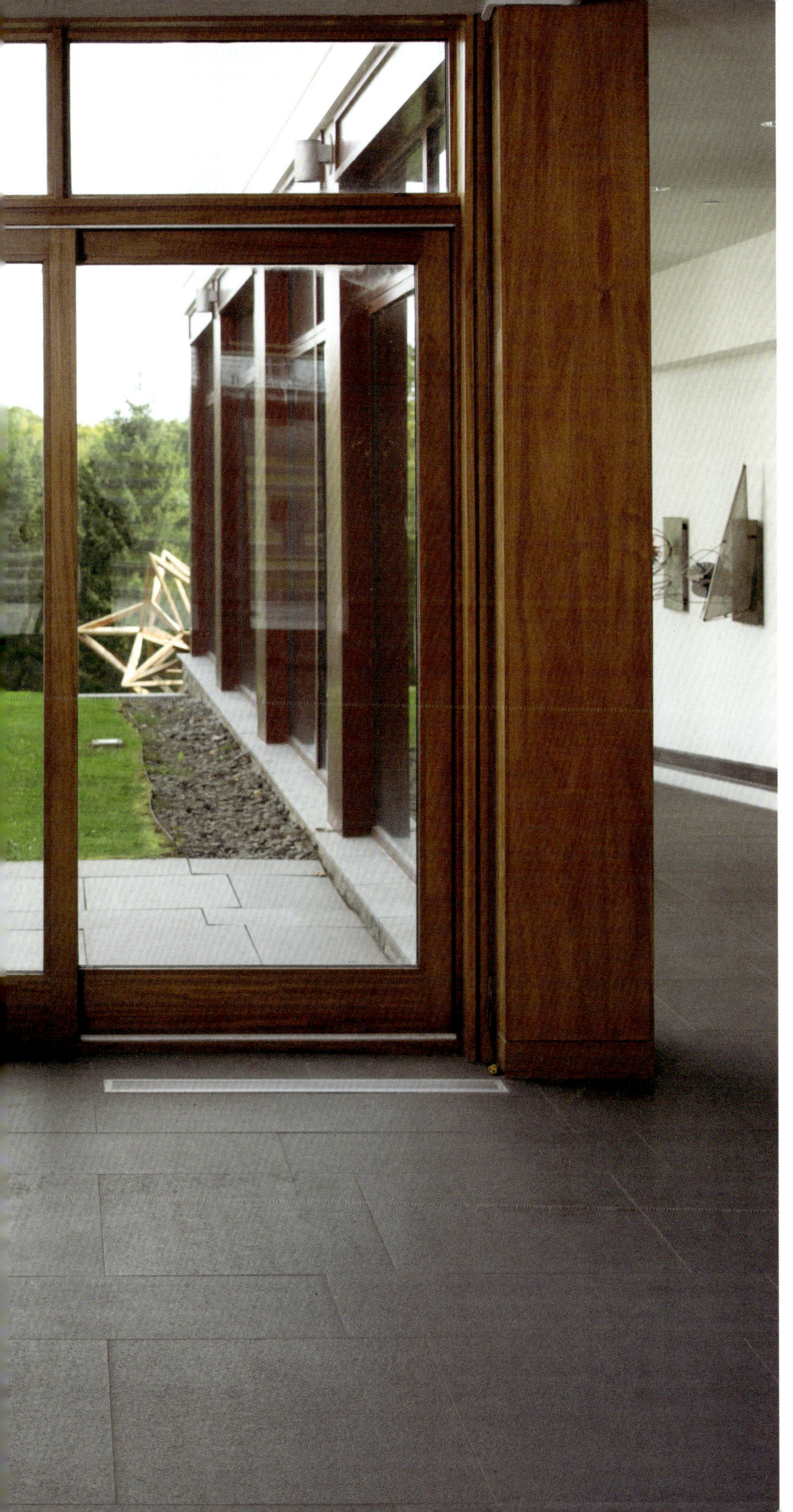

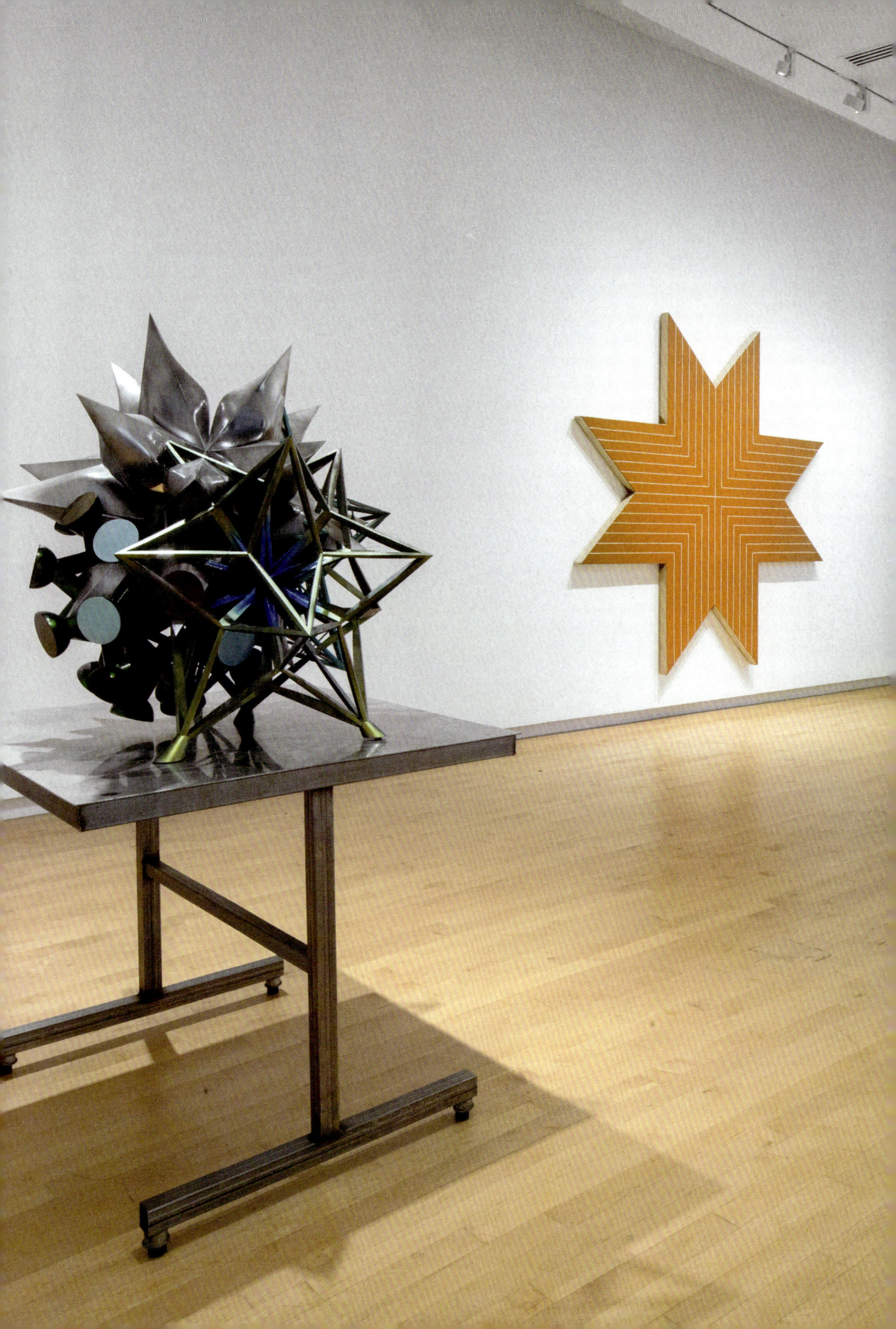

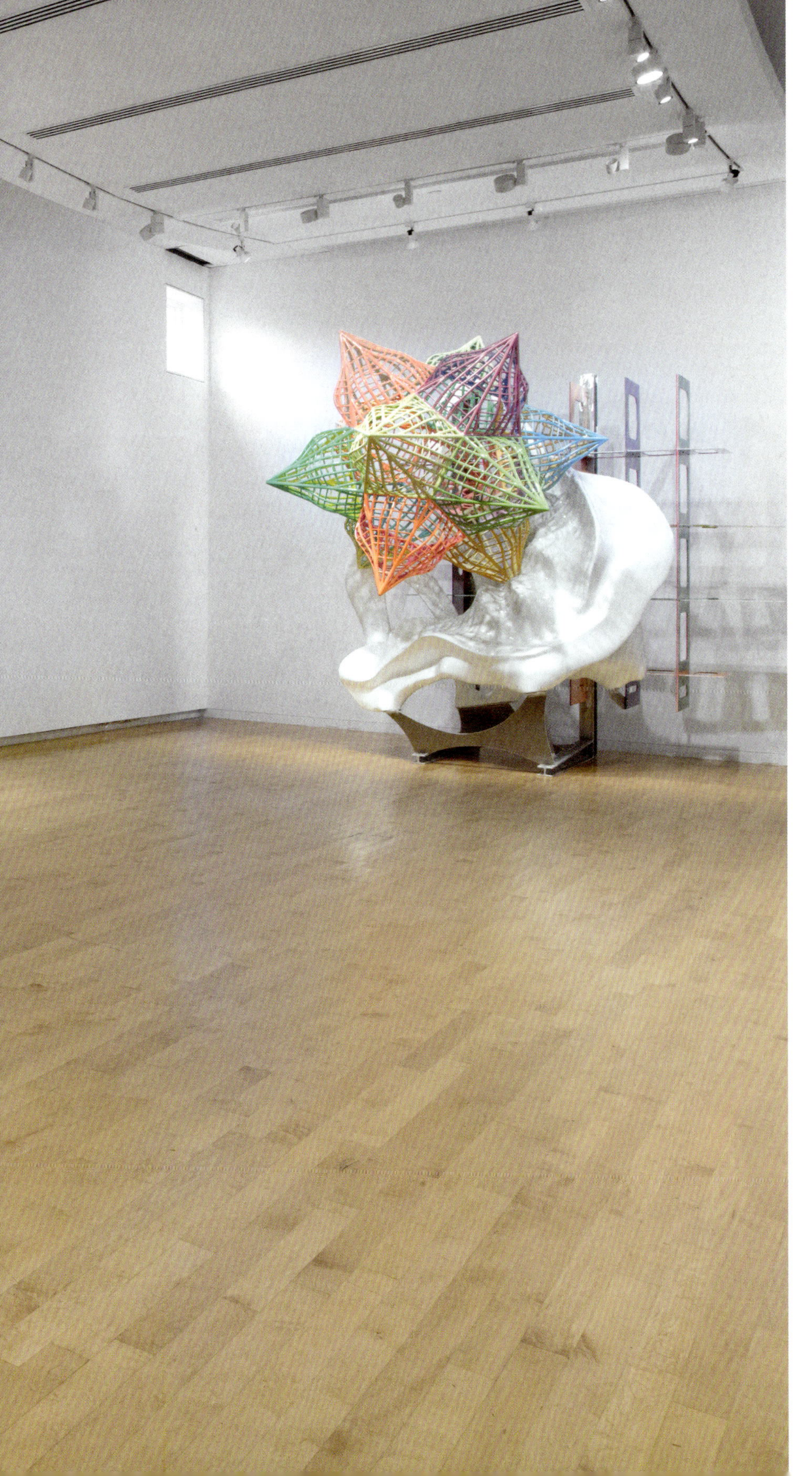

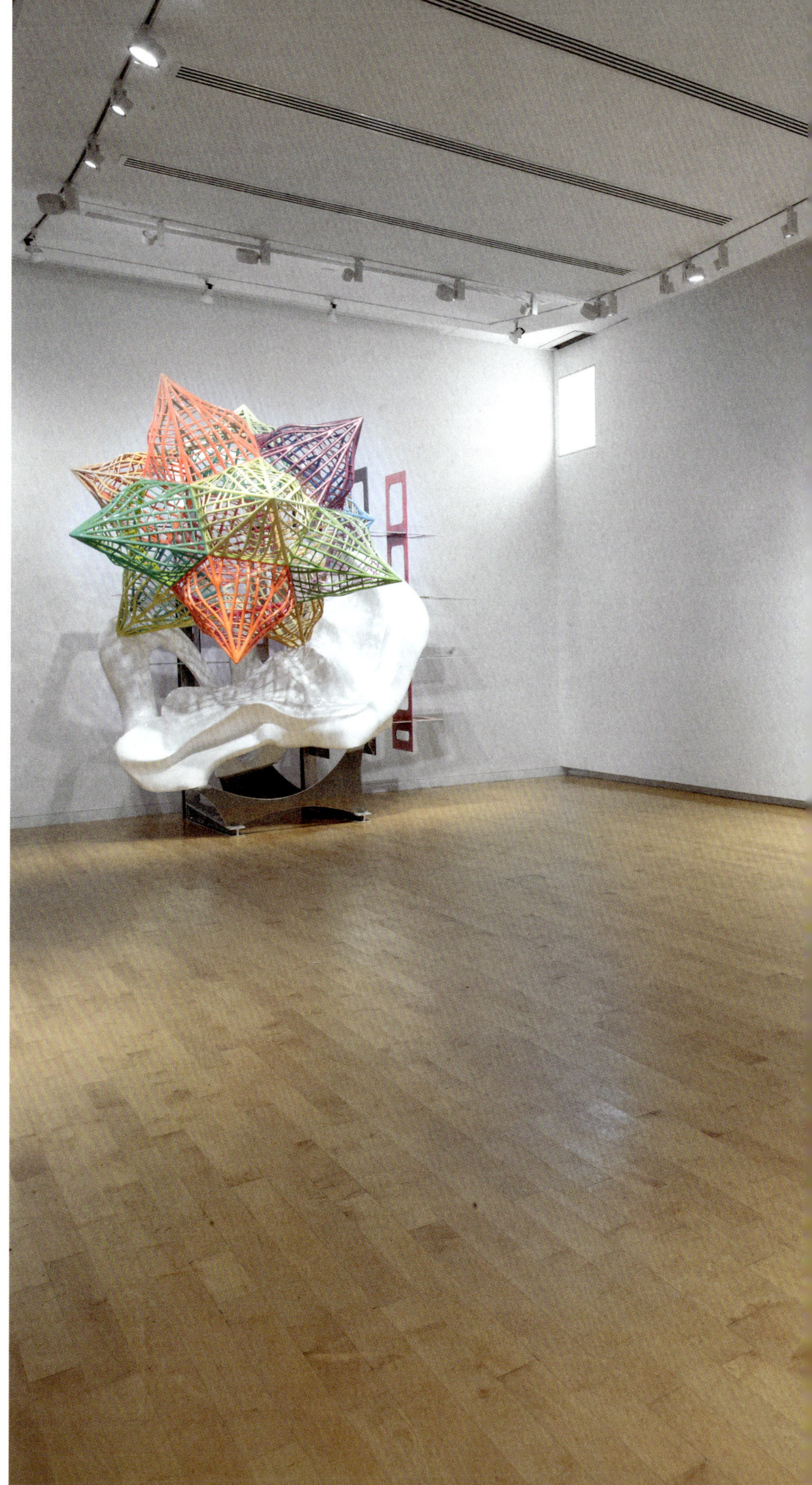

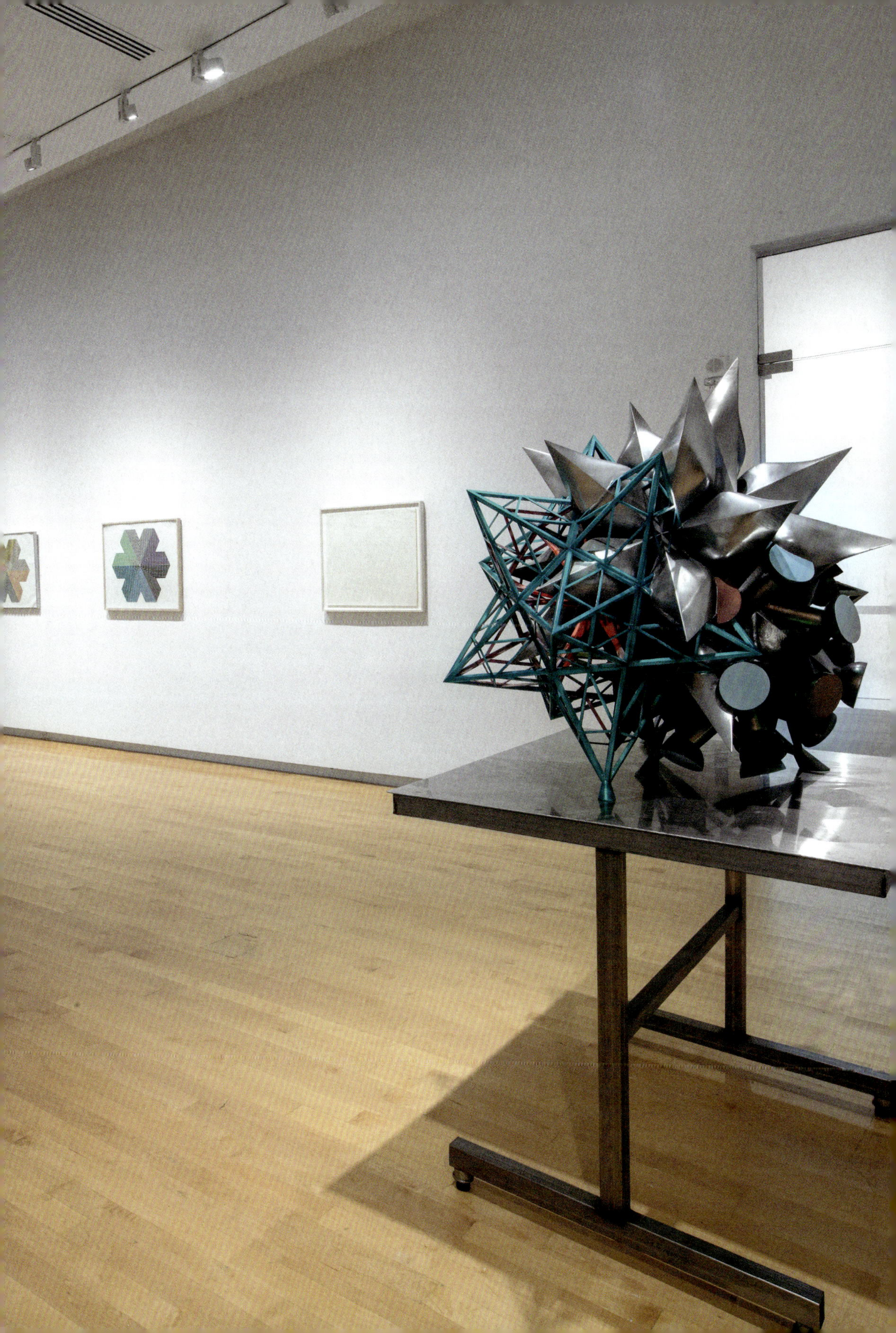

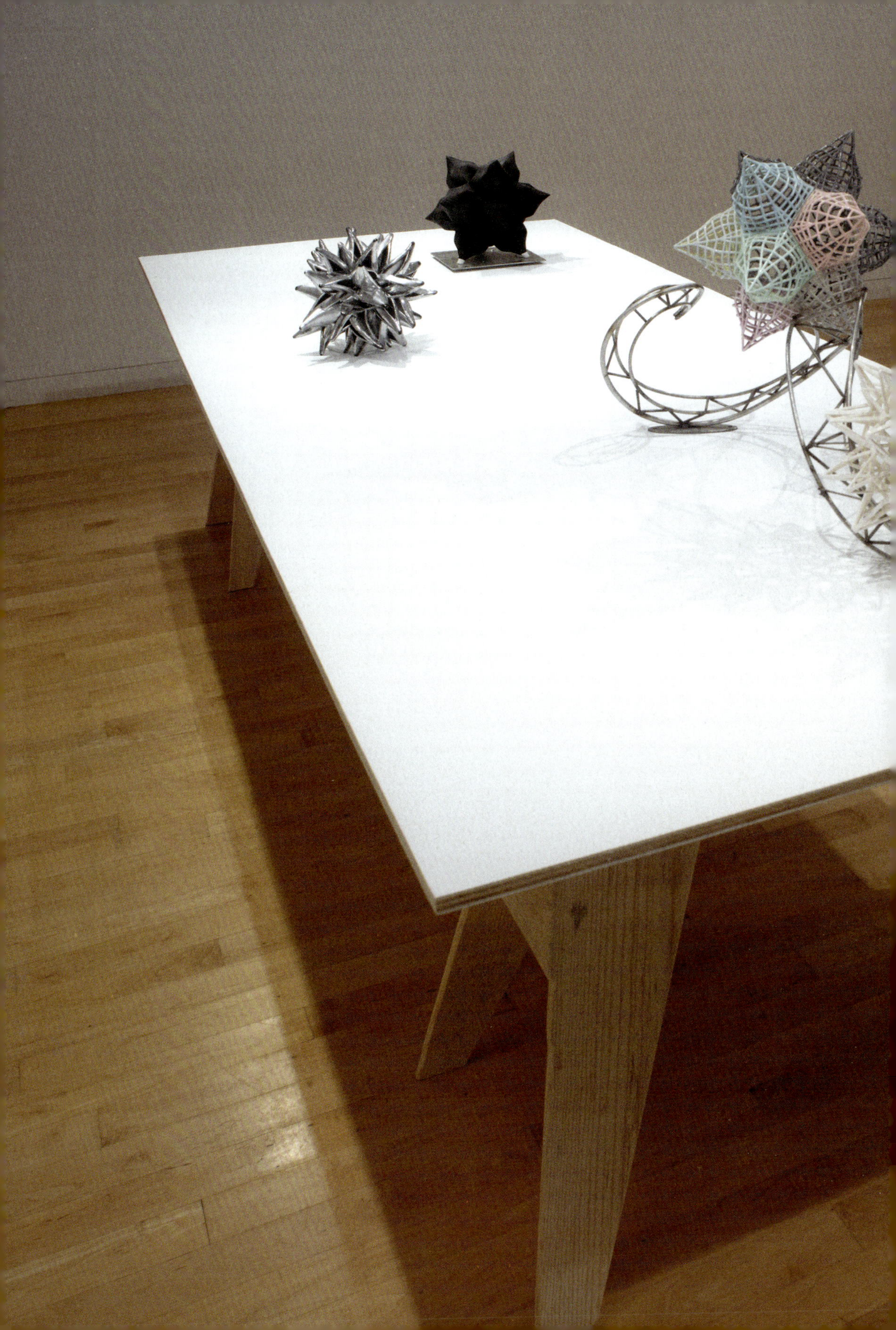

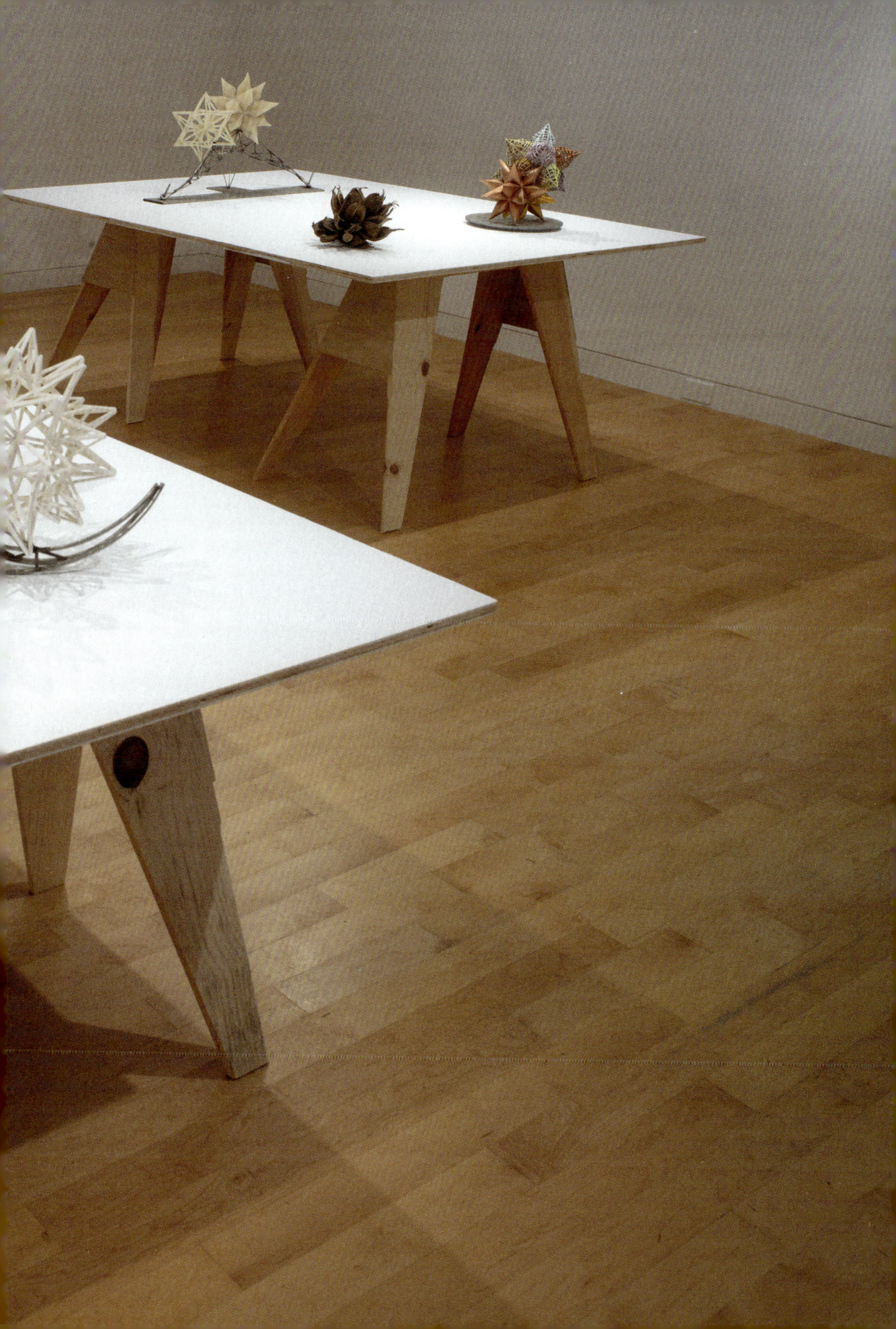

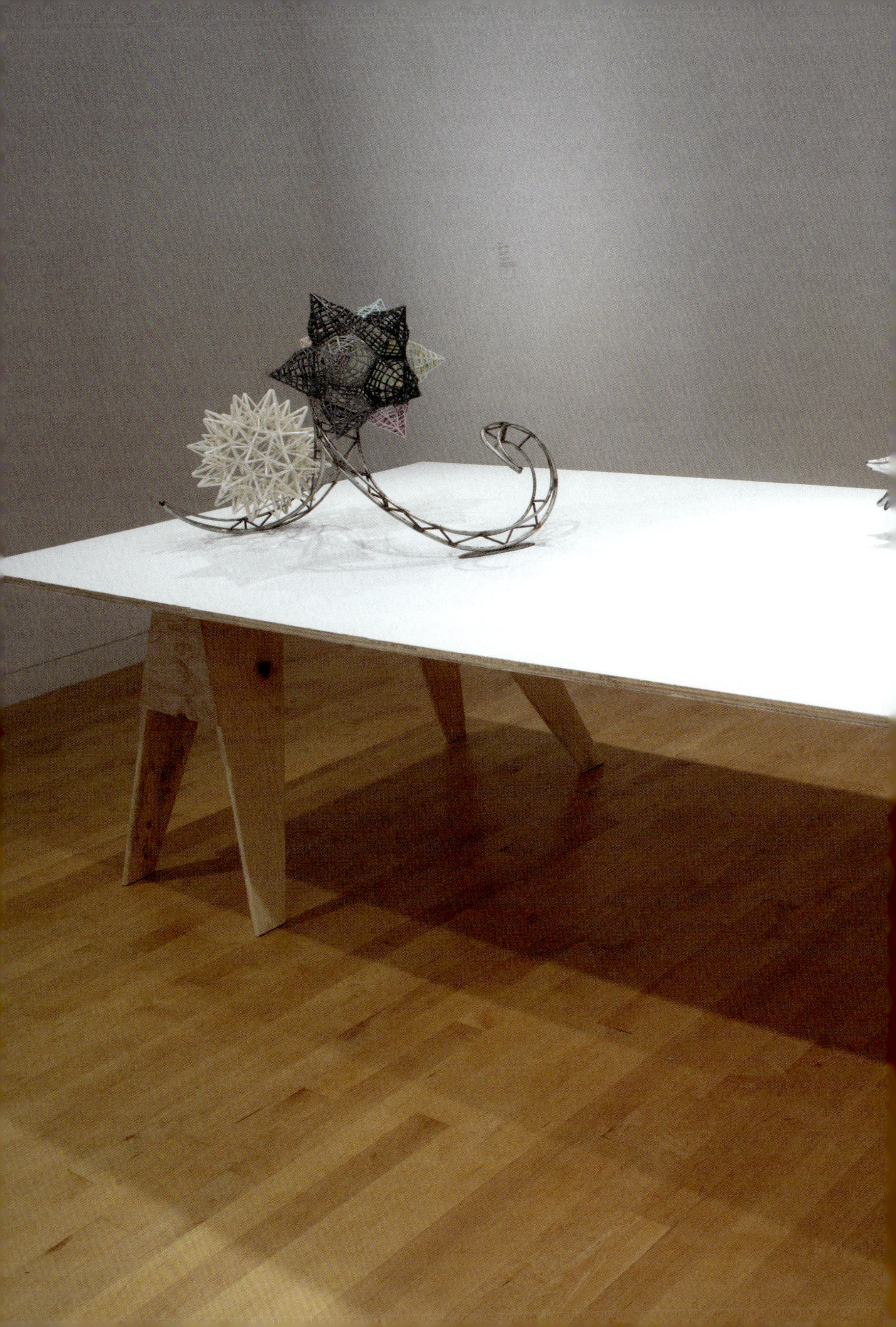

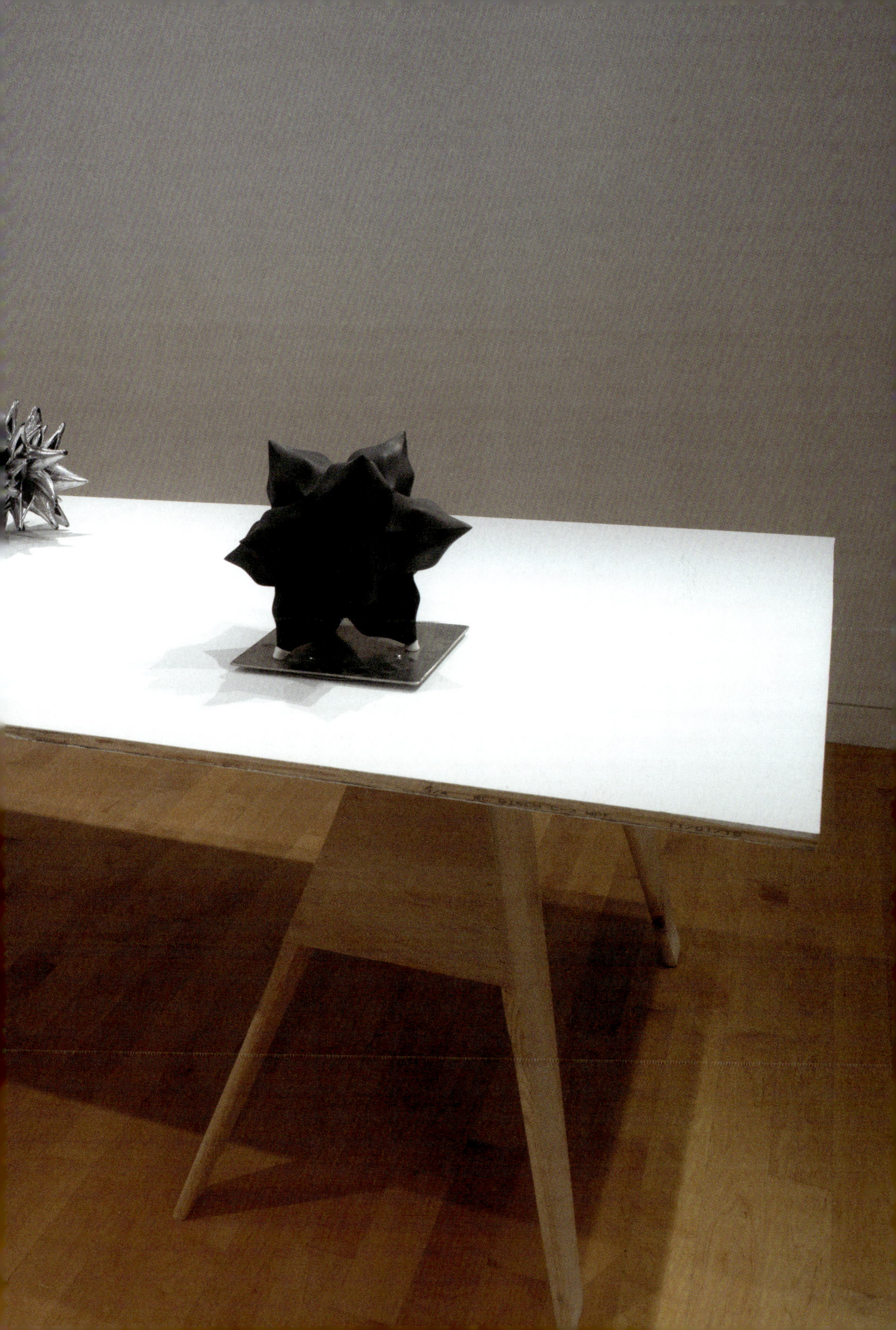

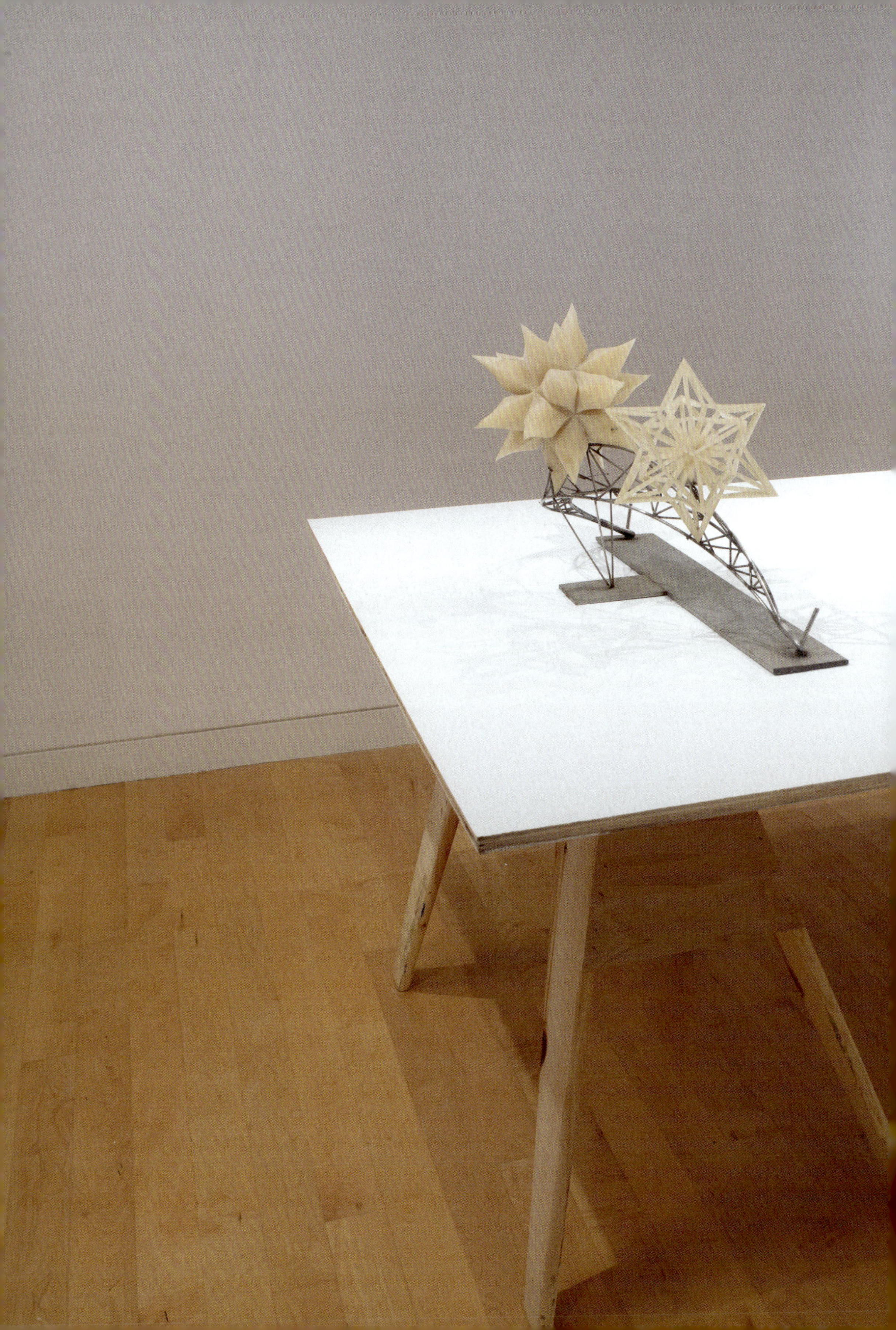

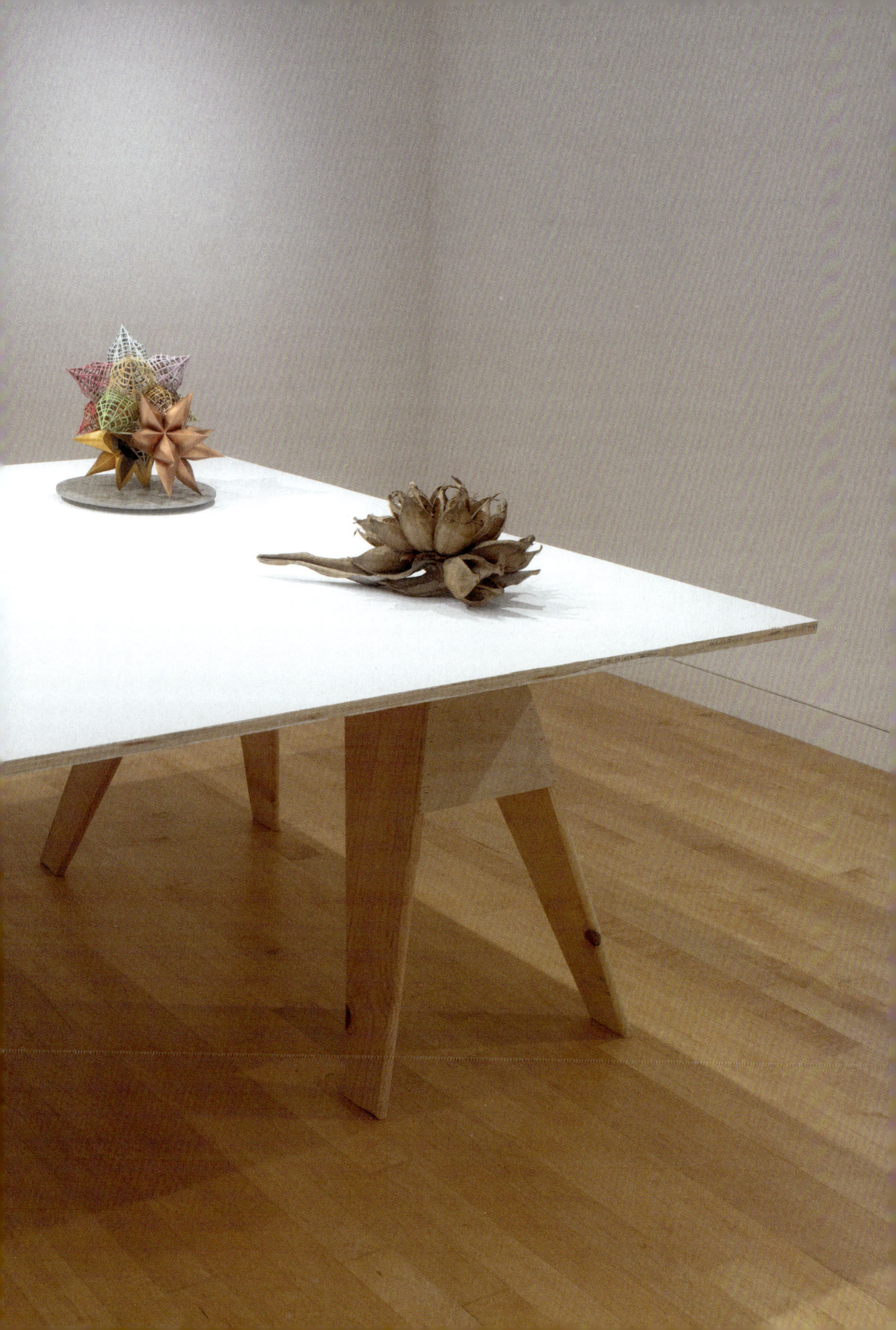

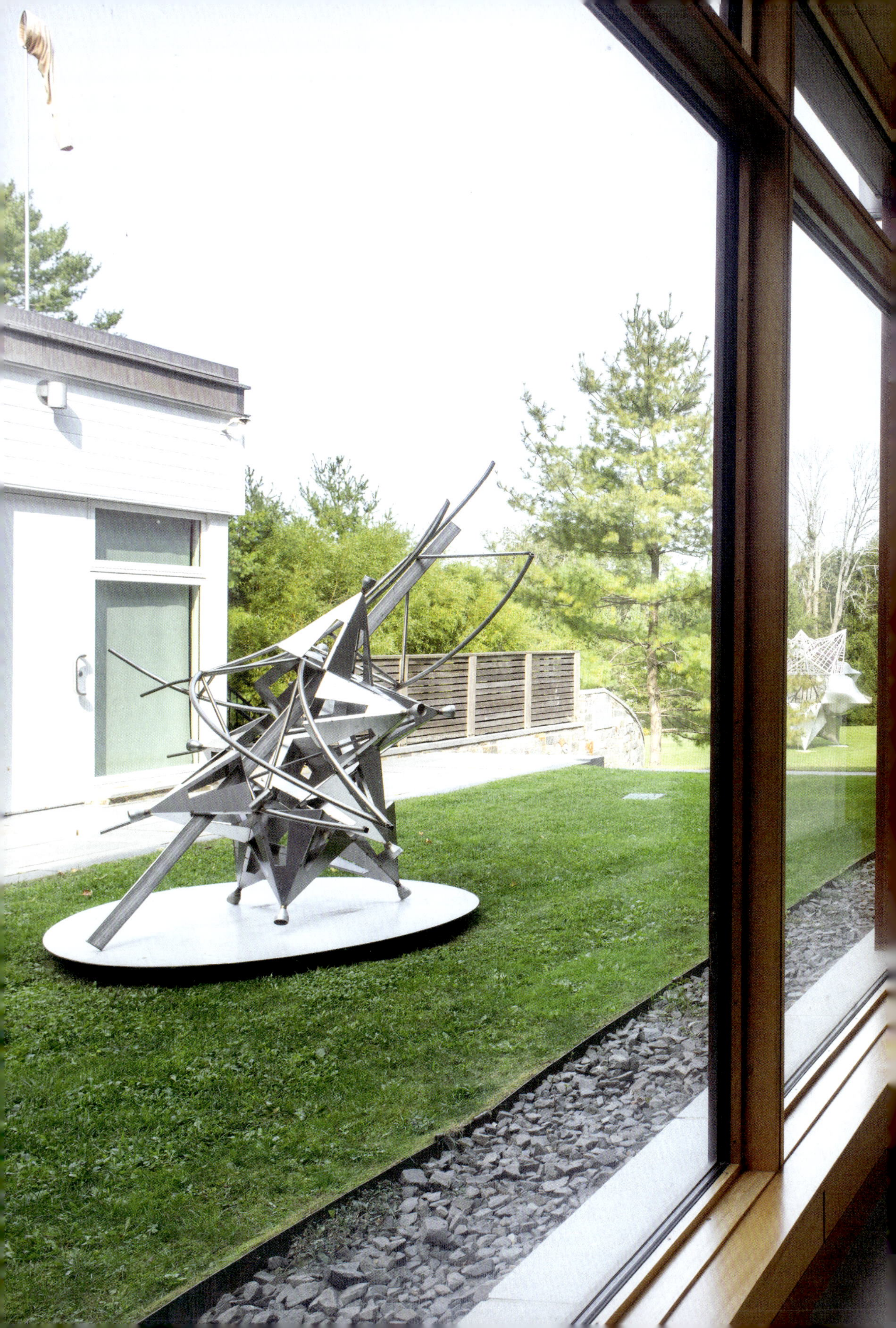

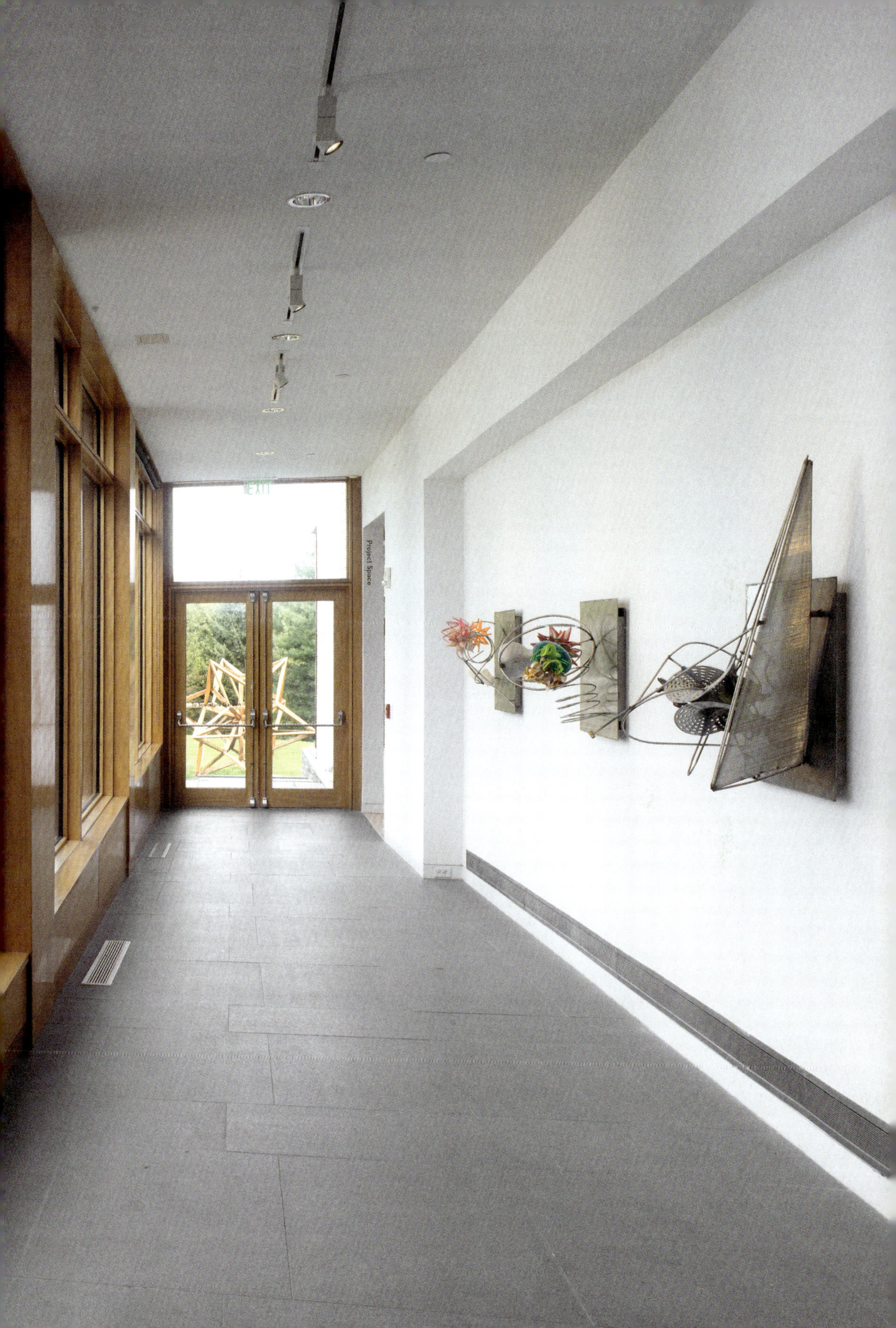

Project Space

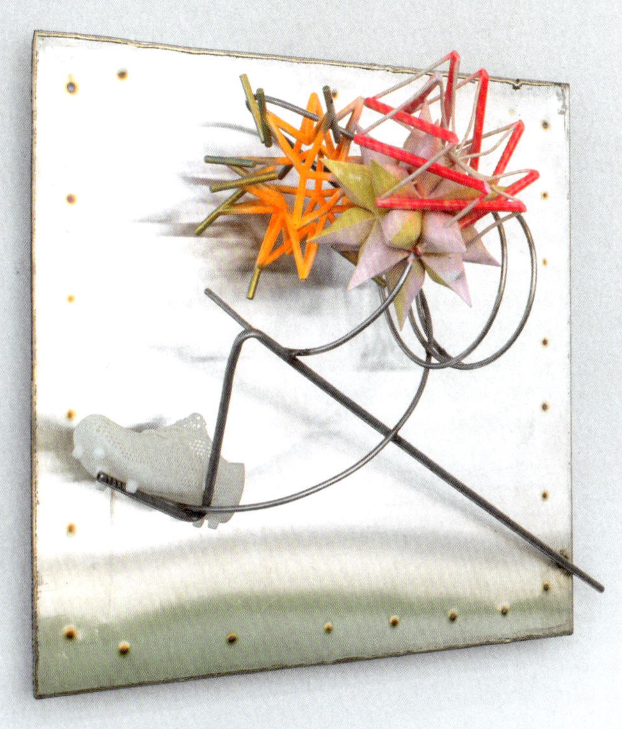

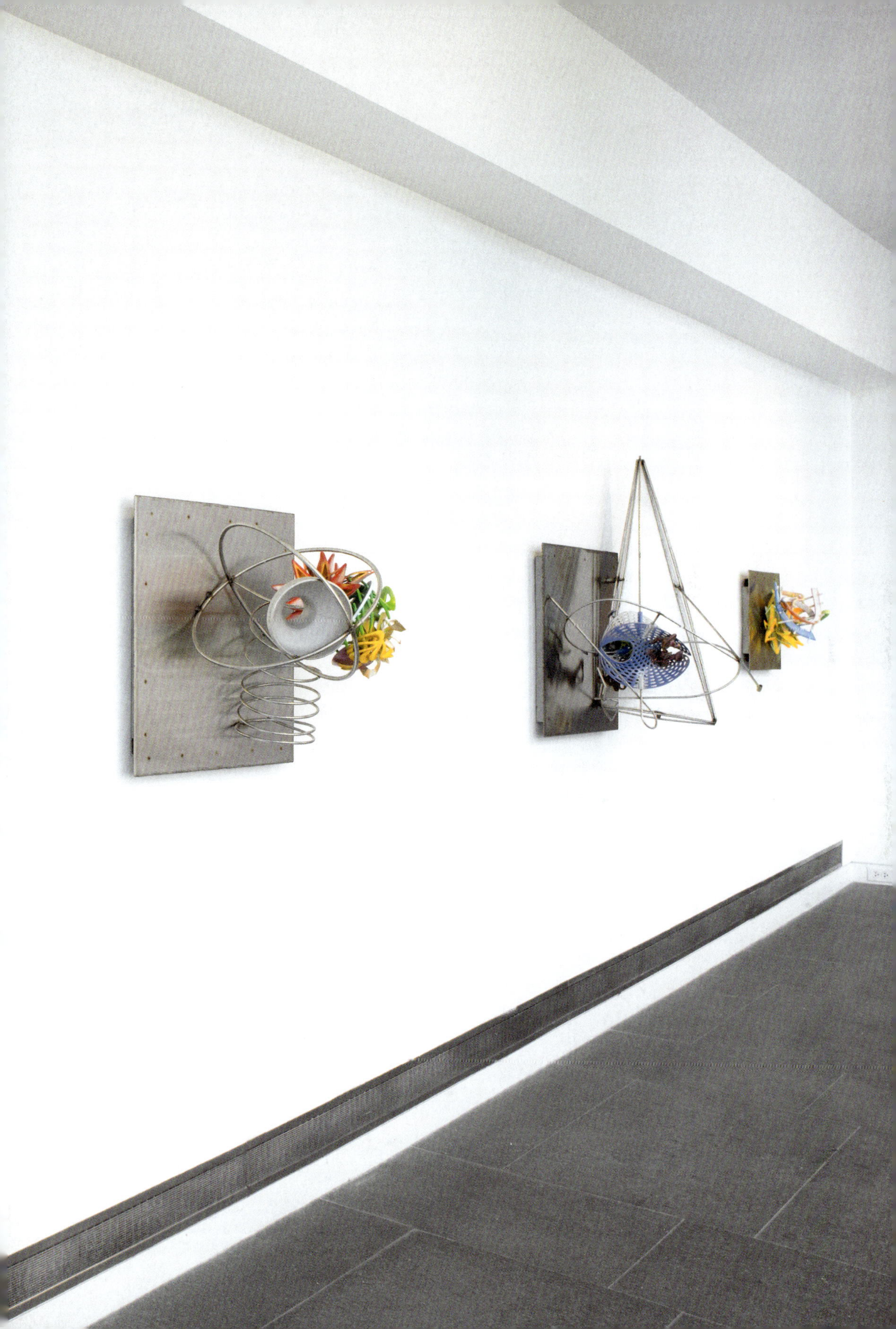

Fat 12 Point Carbon Fiber Star, 2016
Carbon fiber
252 x 252 x 204
(FS2016.033)

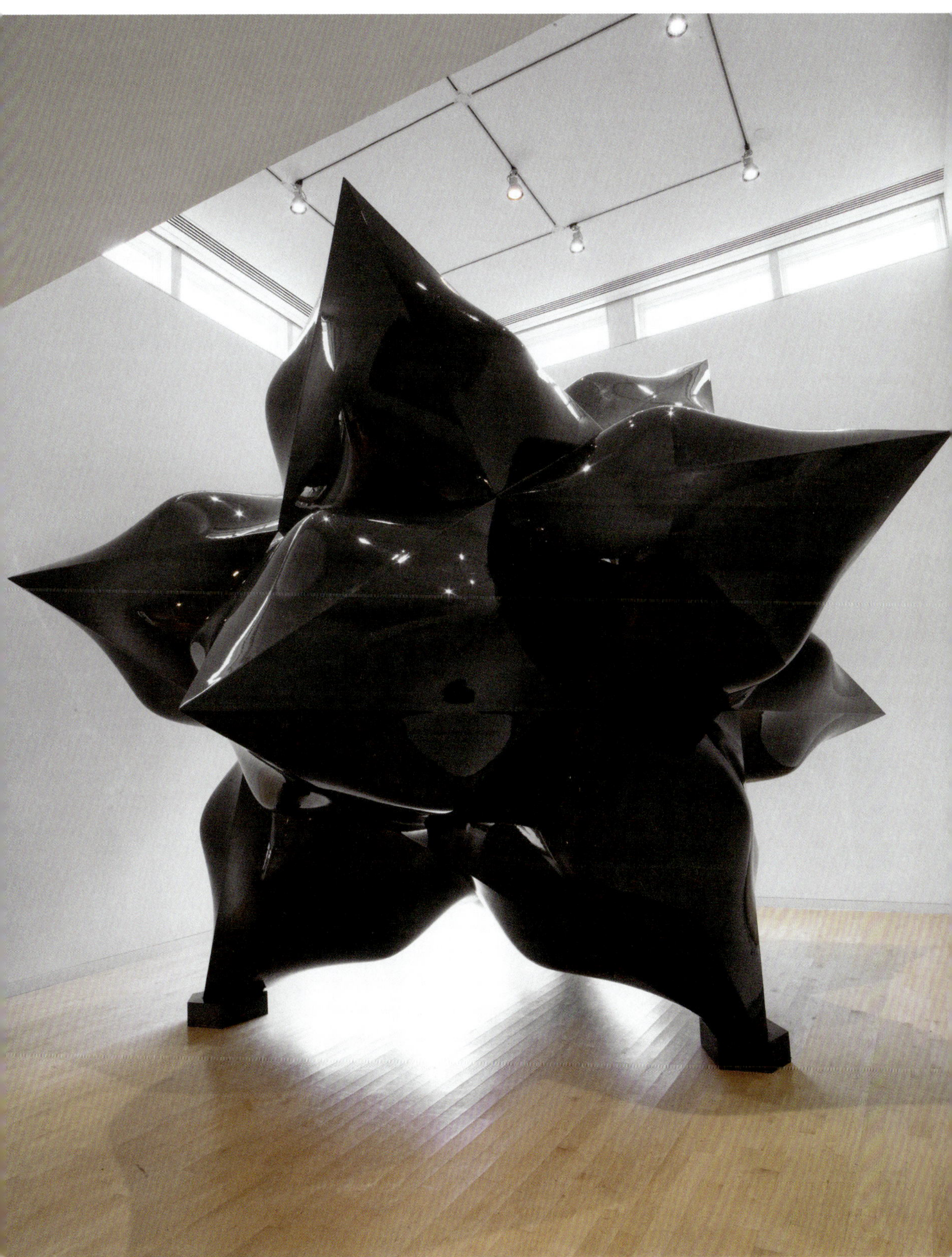

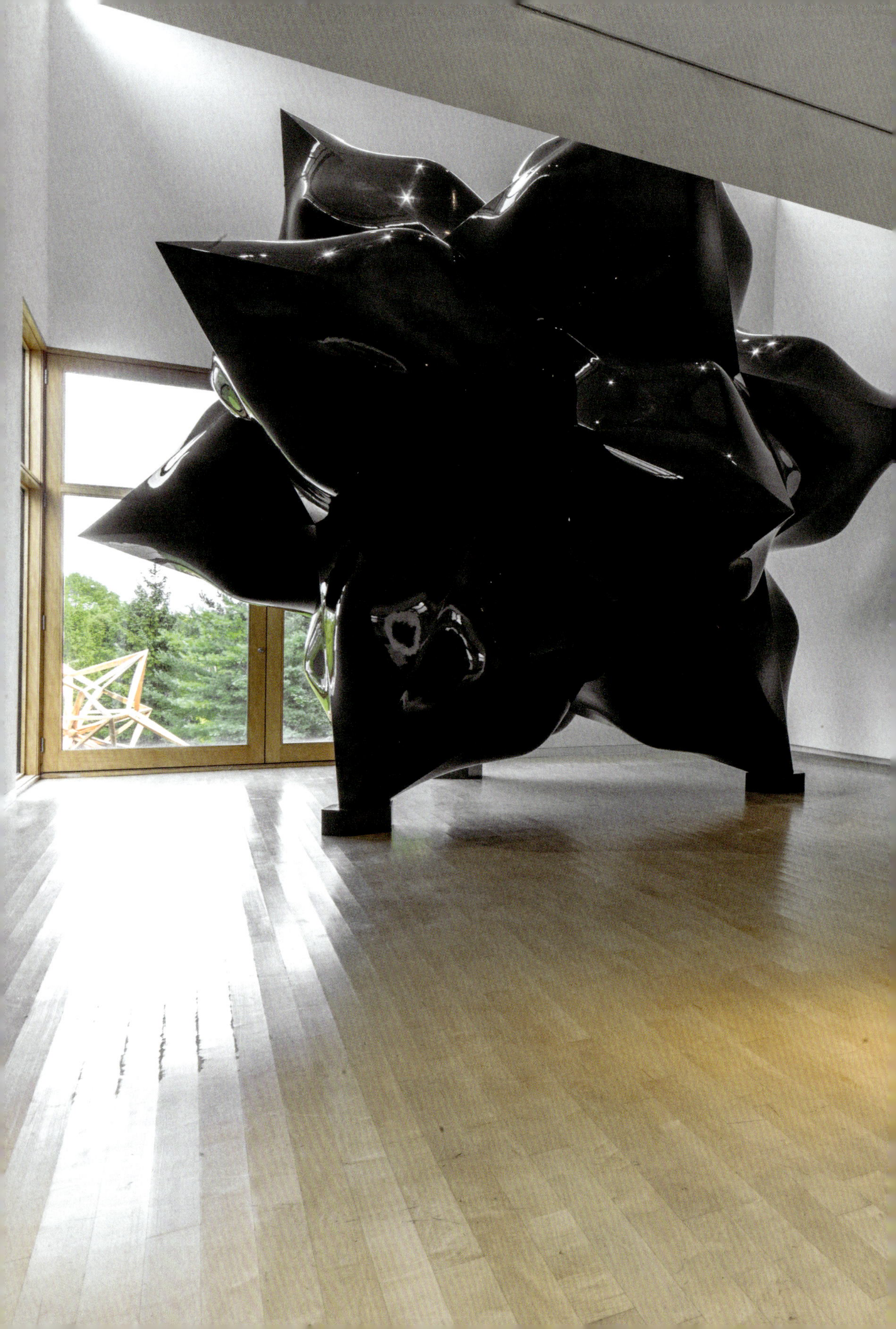

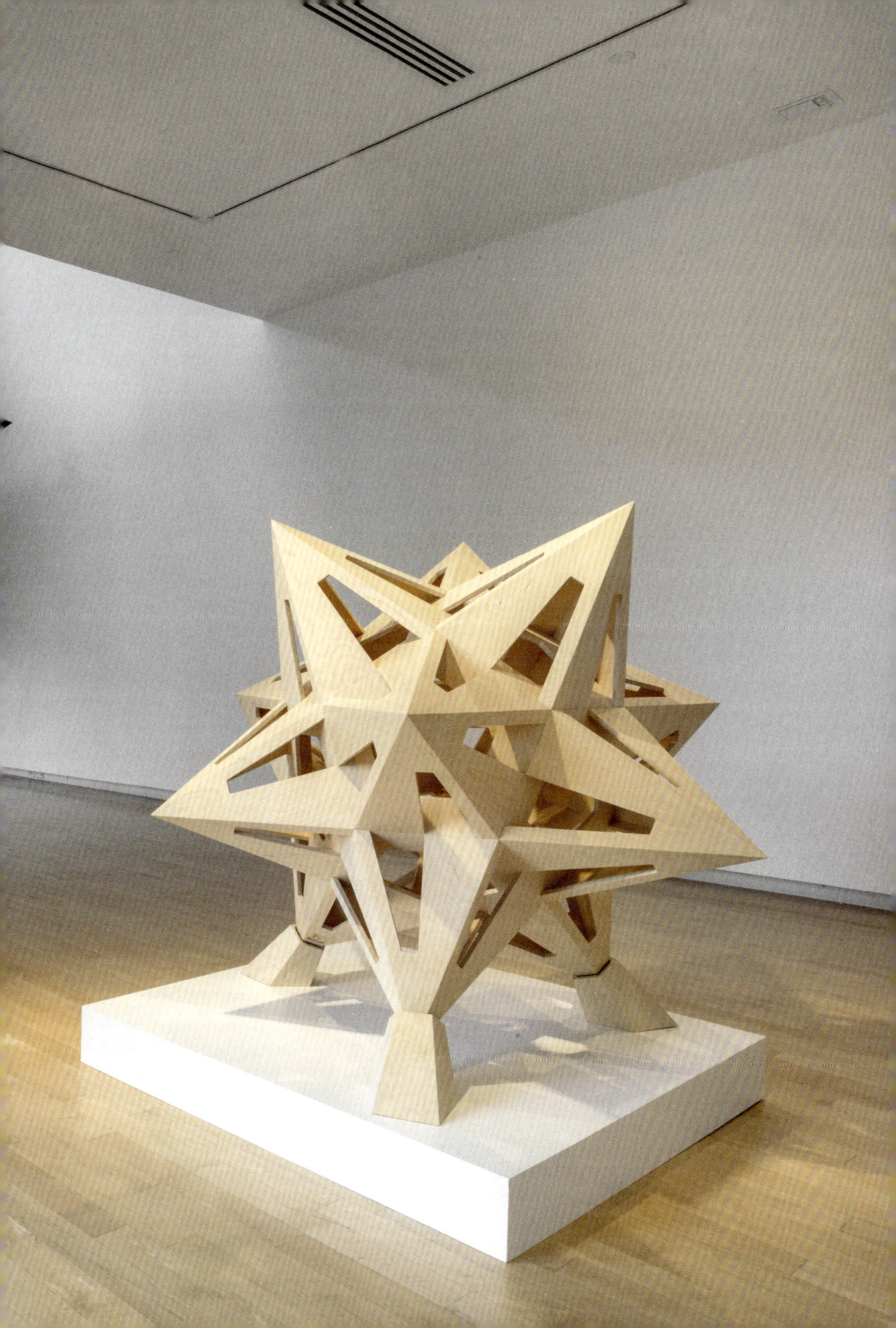

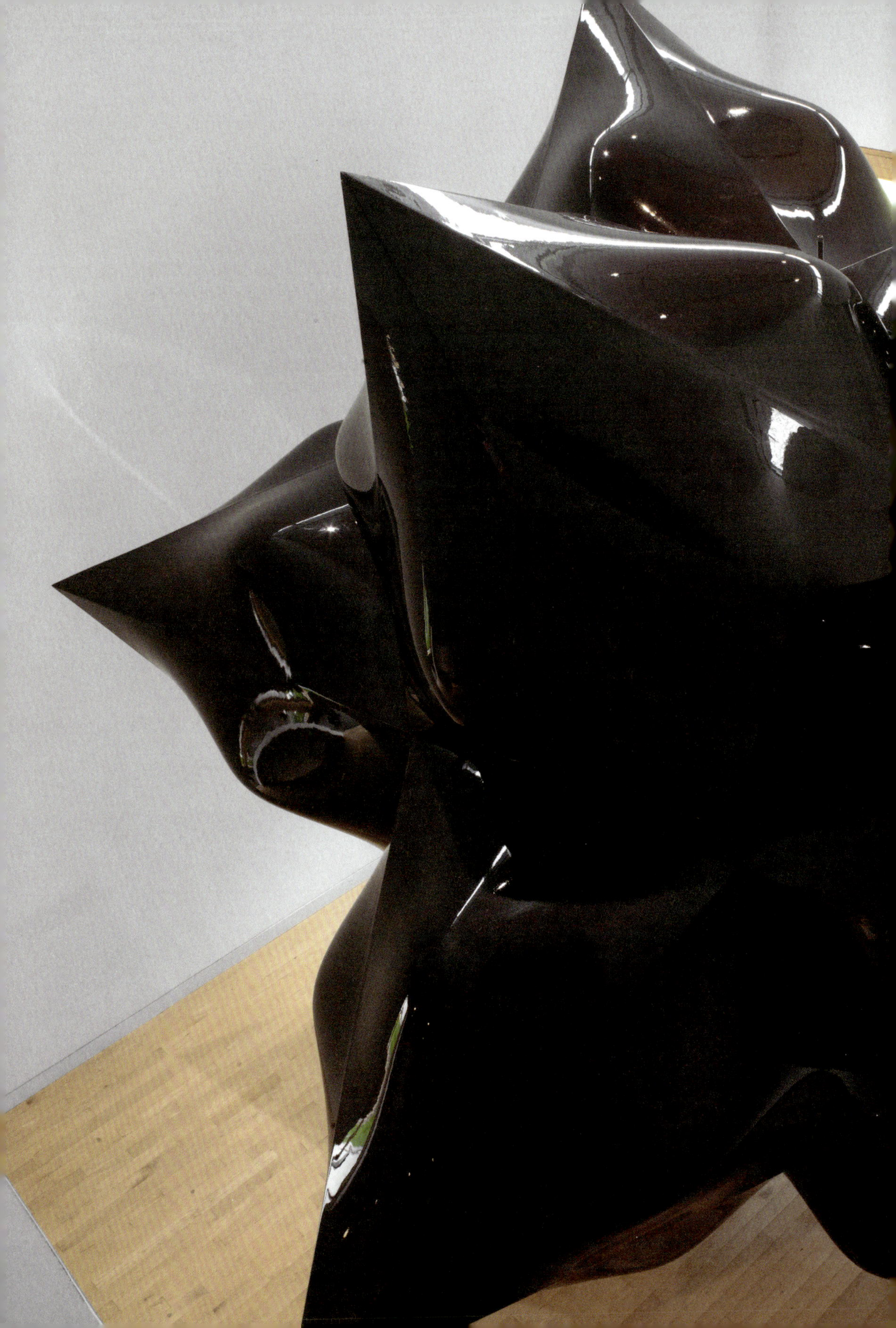

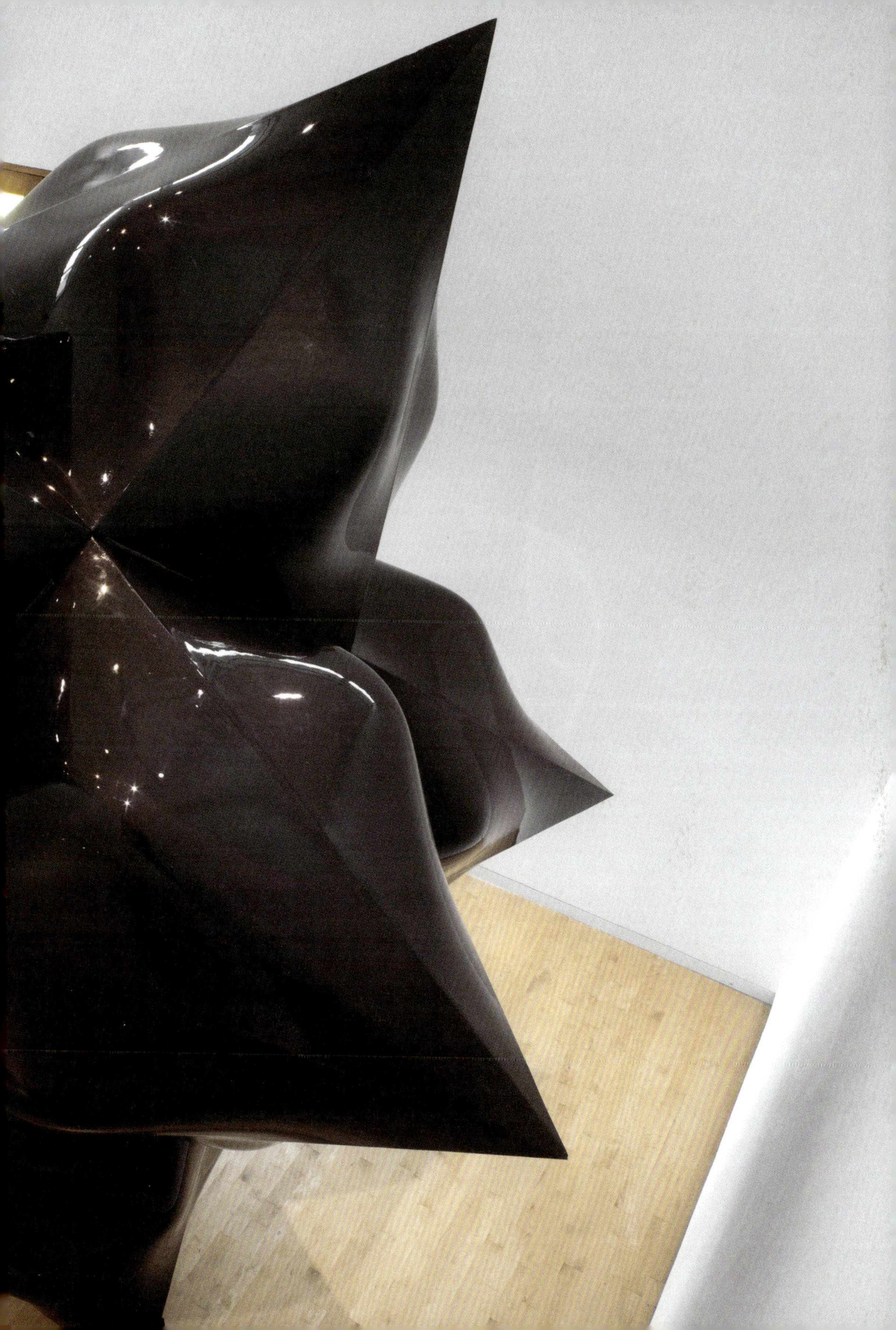

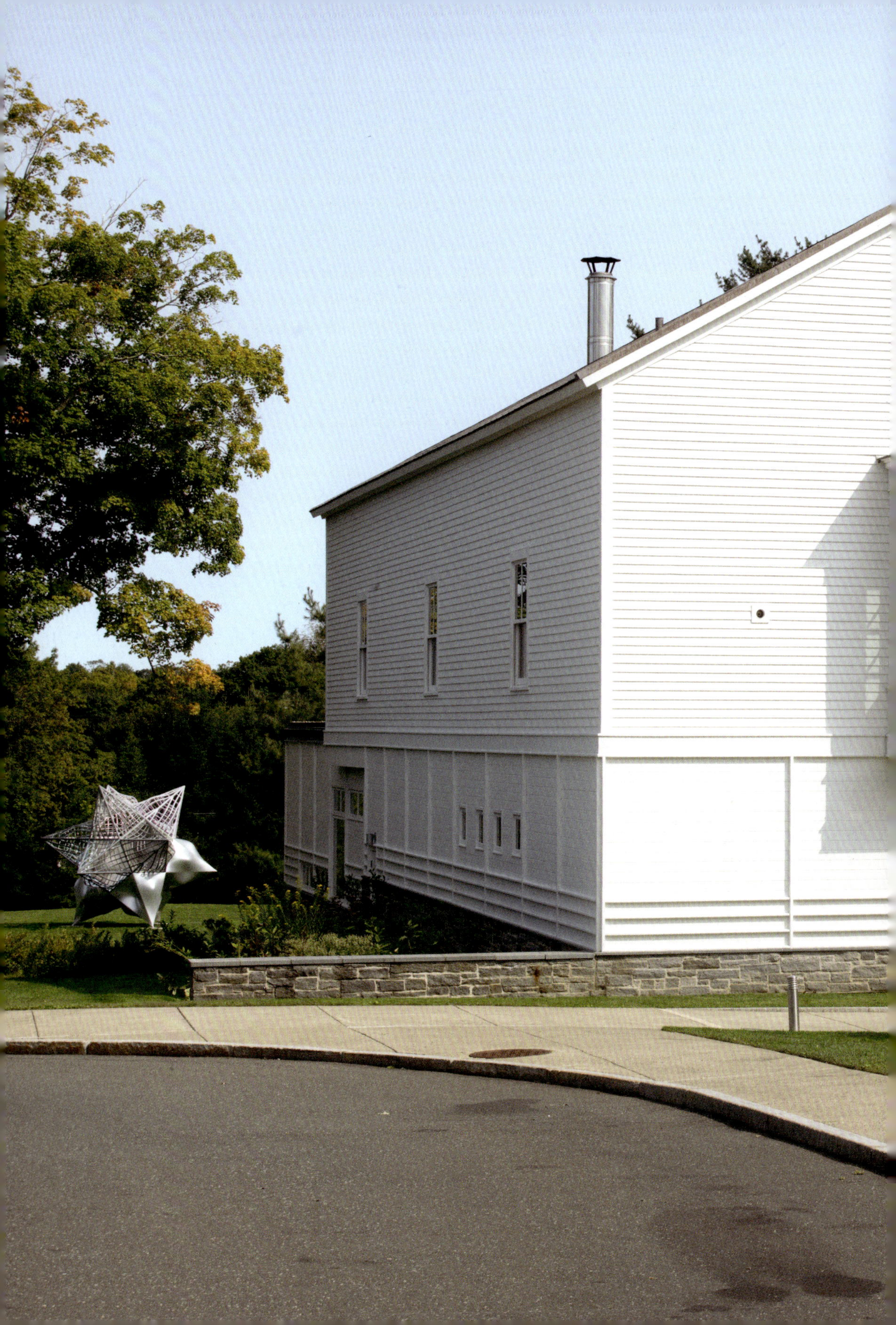

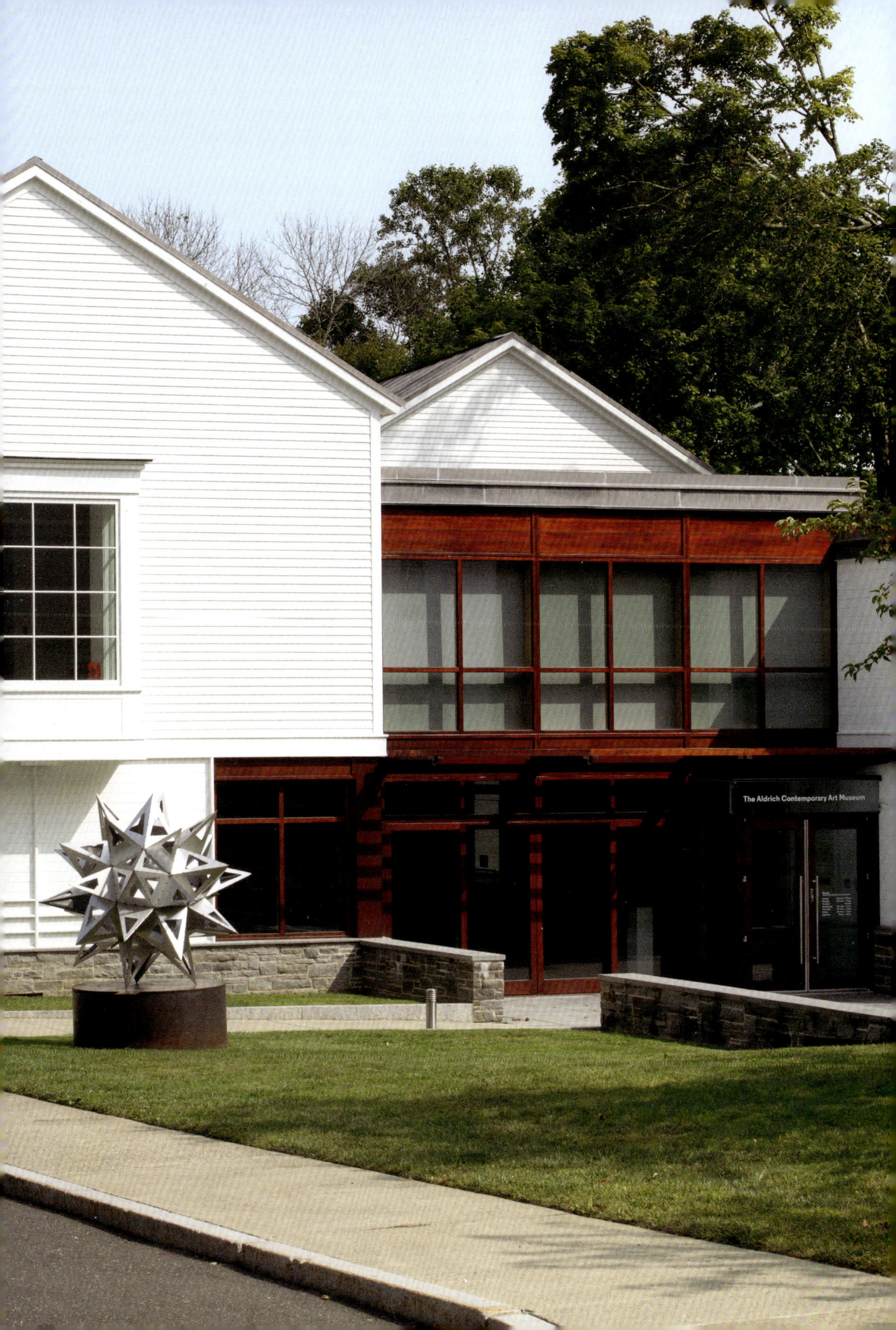
The Aldrich Contemporary Art Museum

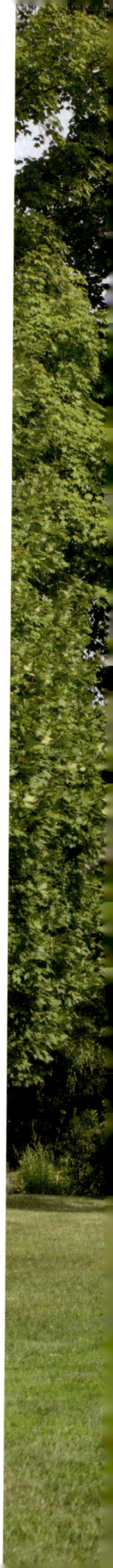

Jasper's Split Star, 2017
Aluminum
202 x 257 x 249
(FS2017.007)

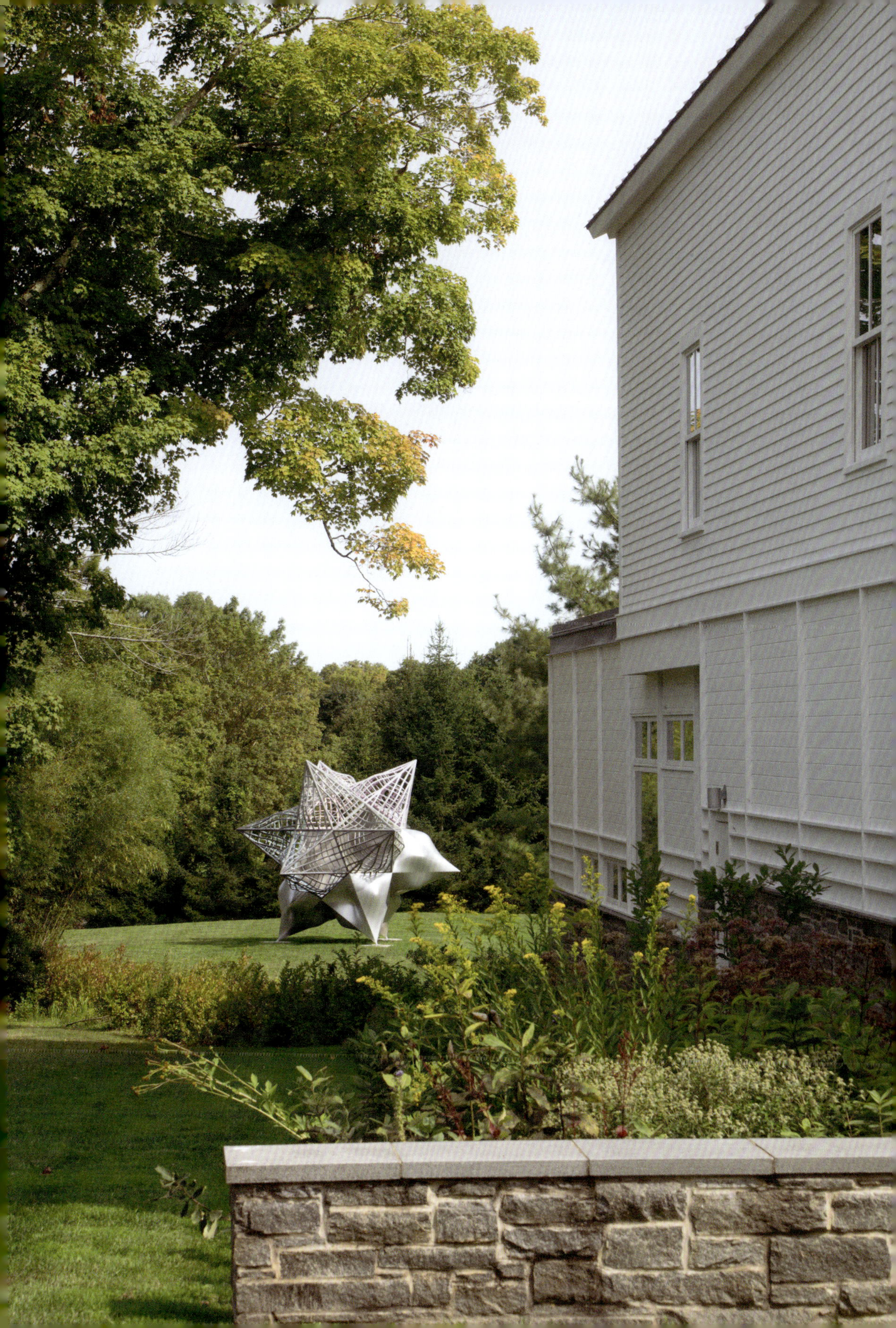

Jay's Star, 2017
Stainless steel
75 x 85 x 85
(FS2017.023)

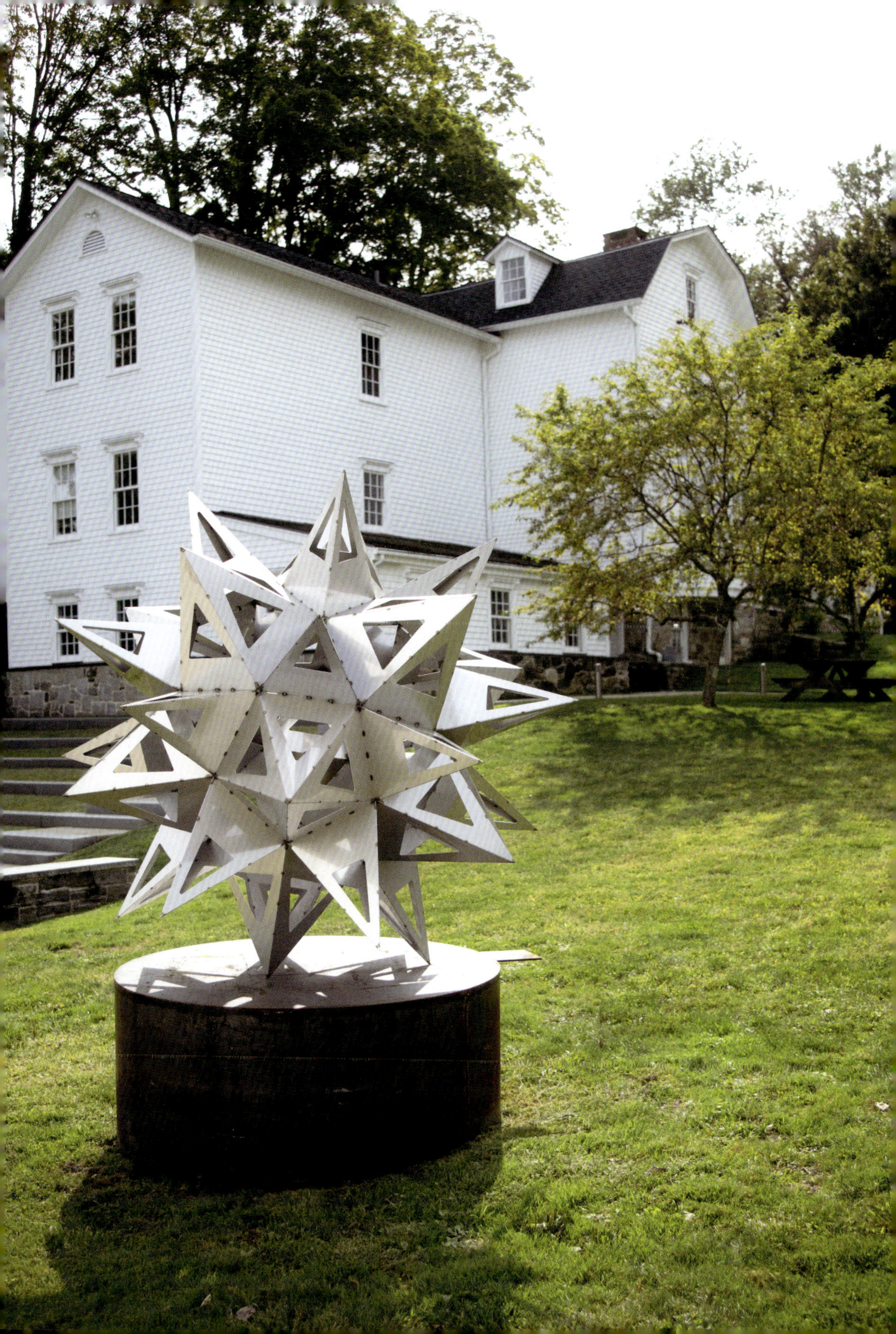

(background)
Jasper's Split Star, 2017
Aluminum
202 x 257 x 249
(FS2017.007)

(middle ground)
Jay's Star, 2017
Stainless steel
75 x 85 x 85
(FS2017.023)

(foreground)
Star with Square Tubing, 2016
Stainless Steel
46 x 46 x 46
(FS2016.001)

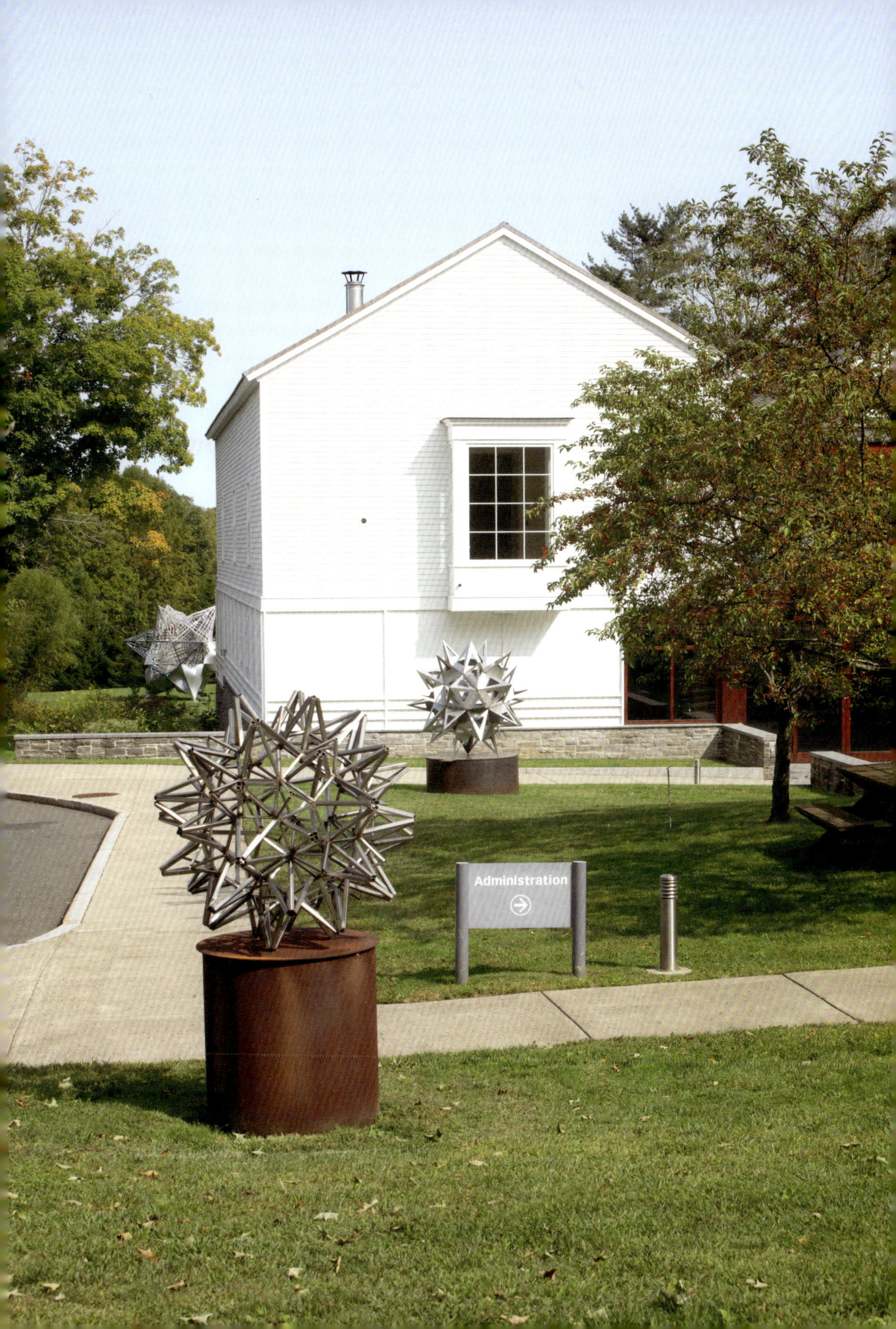

Administration

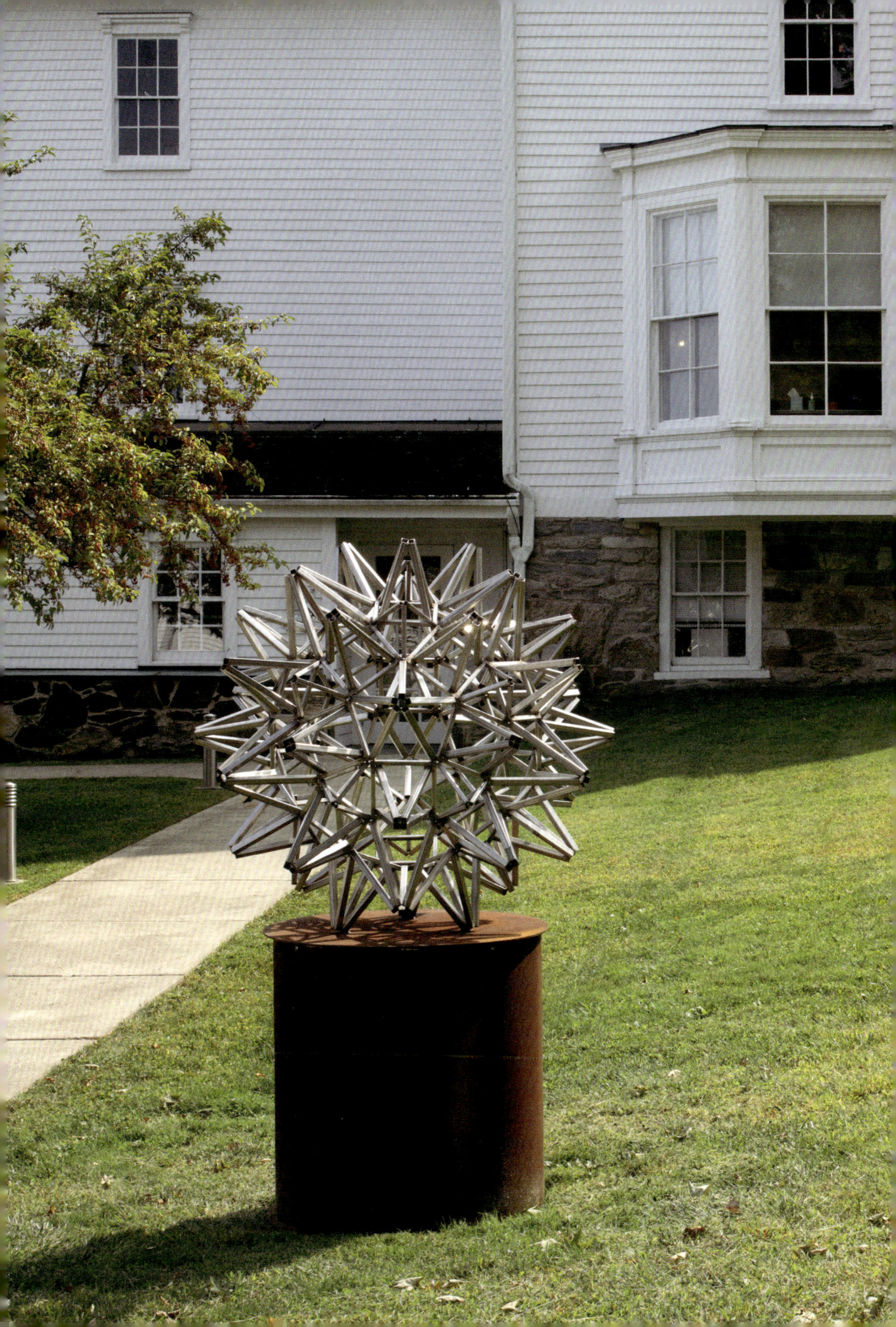

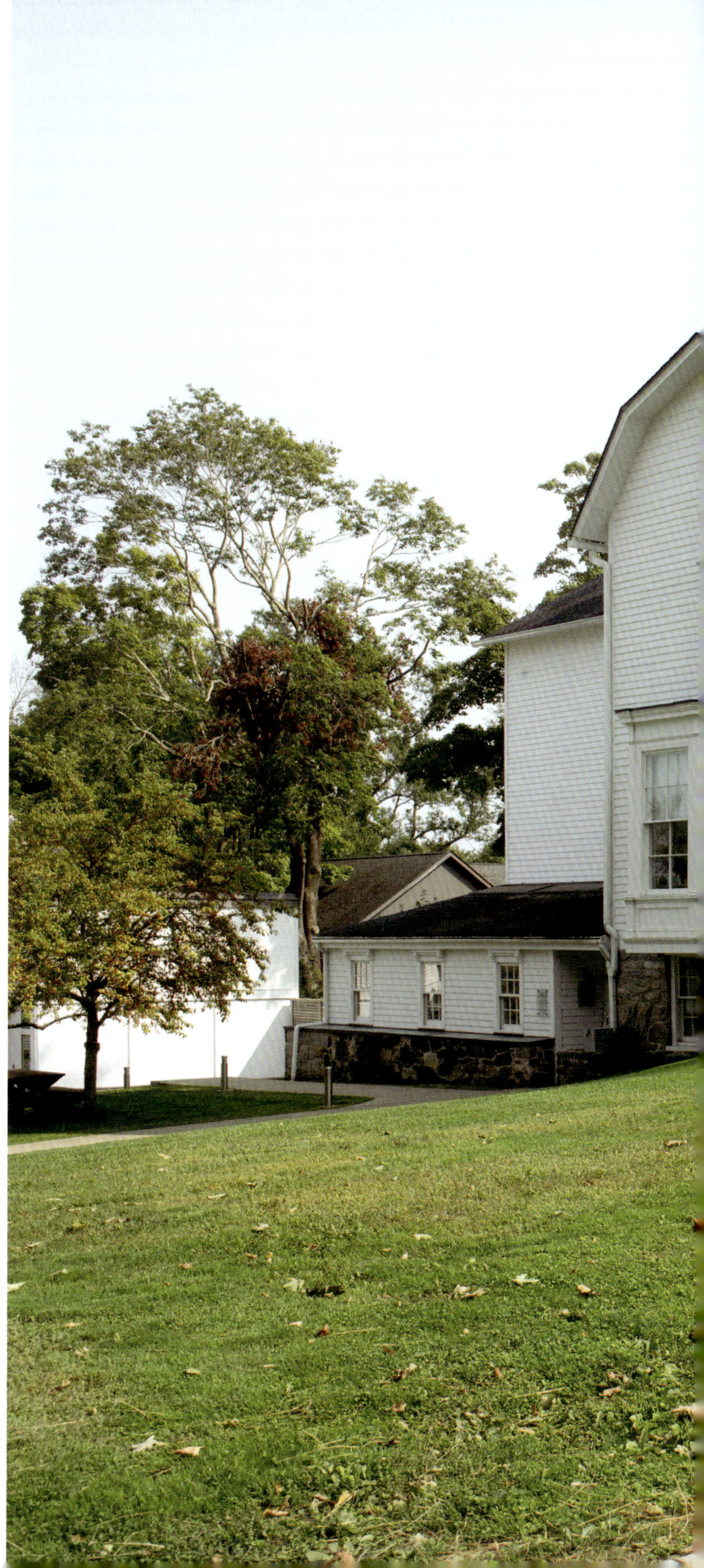

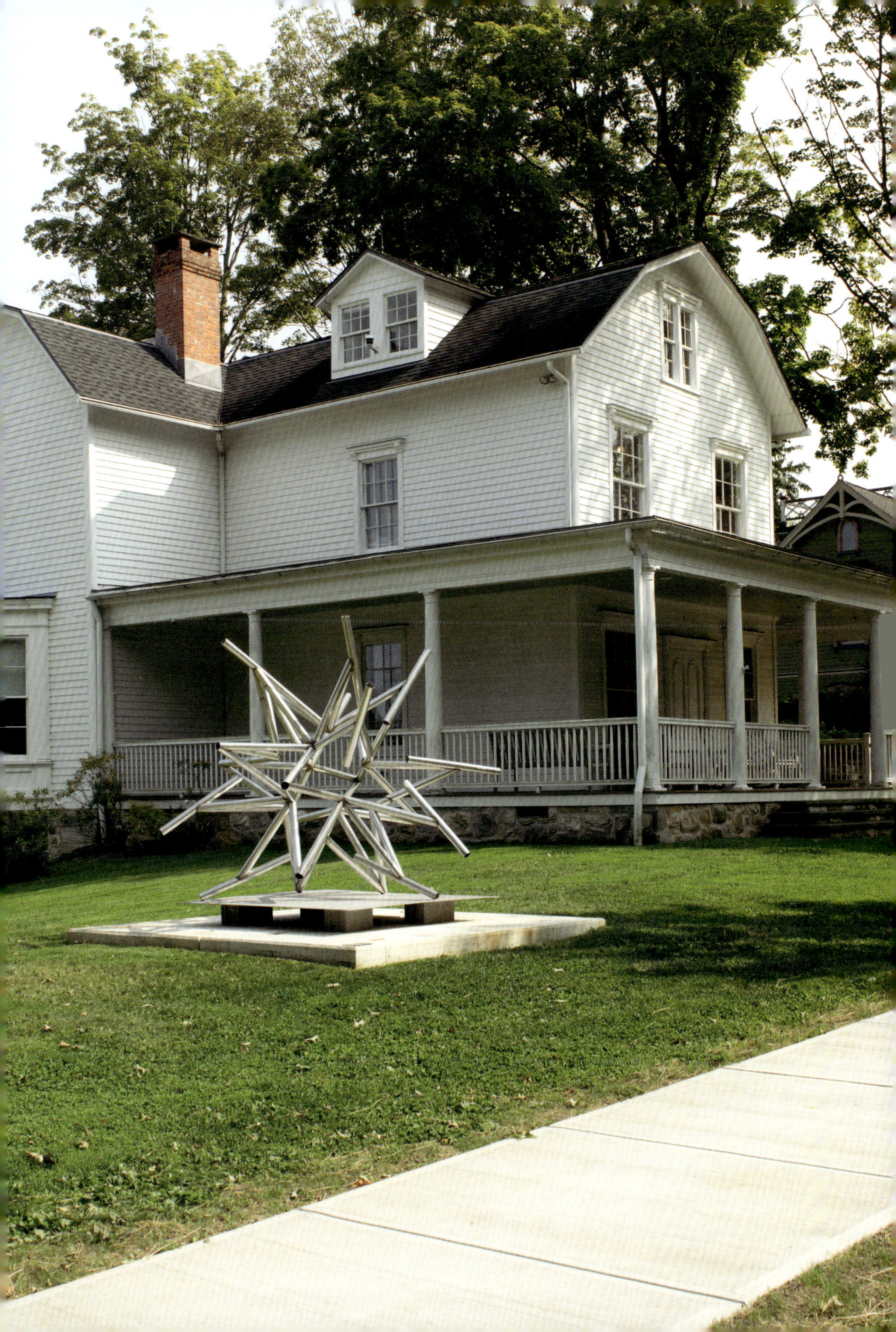

Stick Star, 2017
Stainless steel
106 x 96 x 96
(FS2017.013)

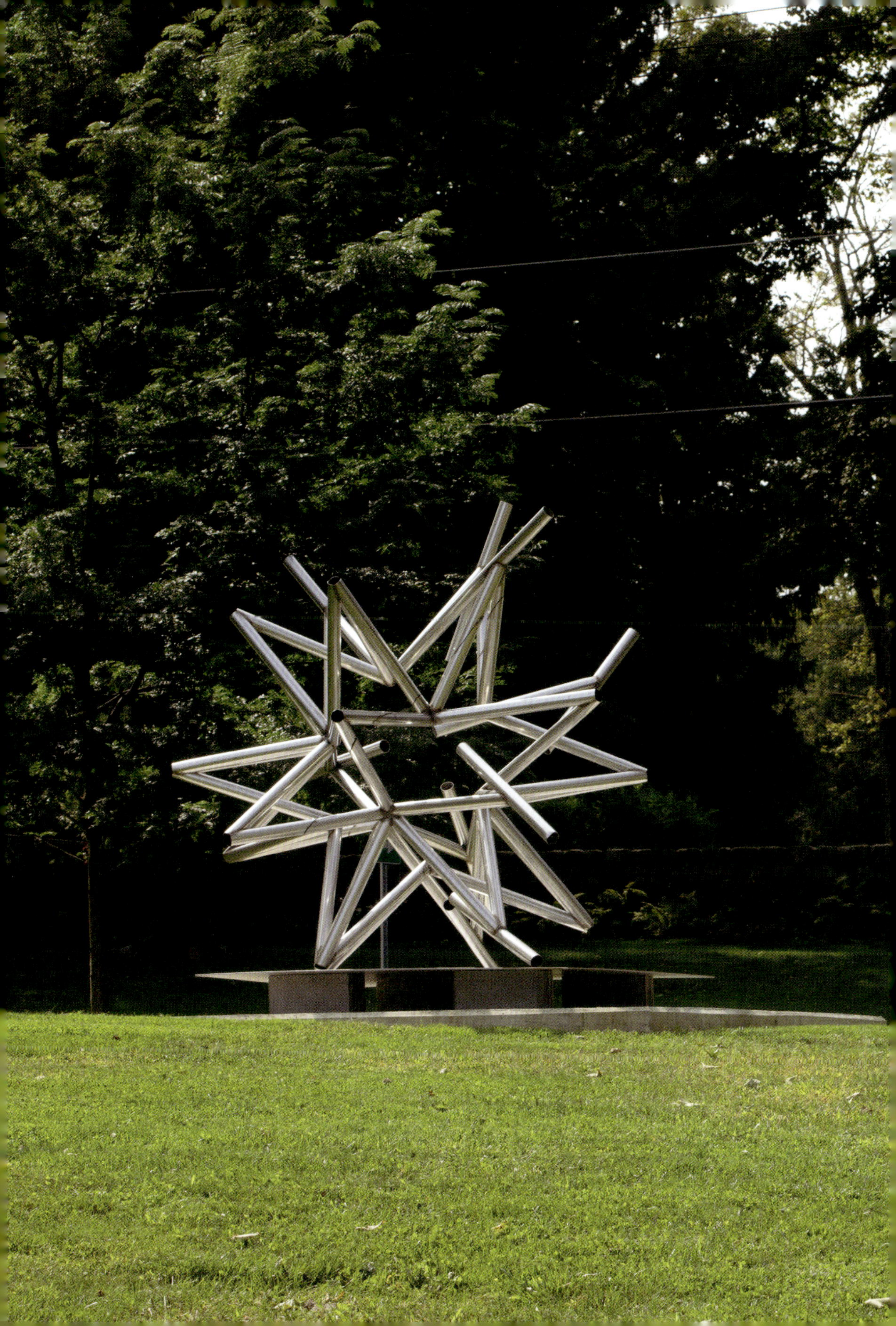

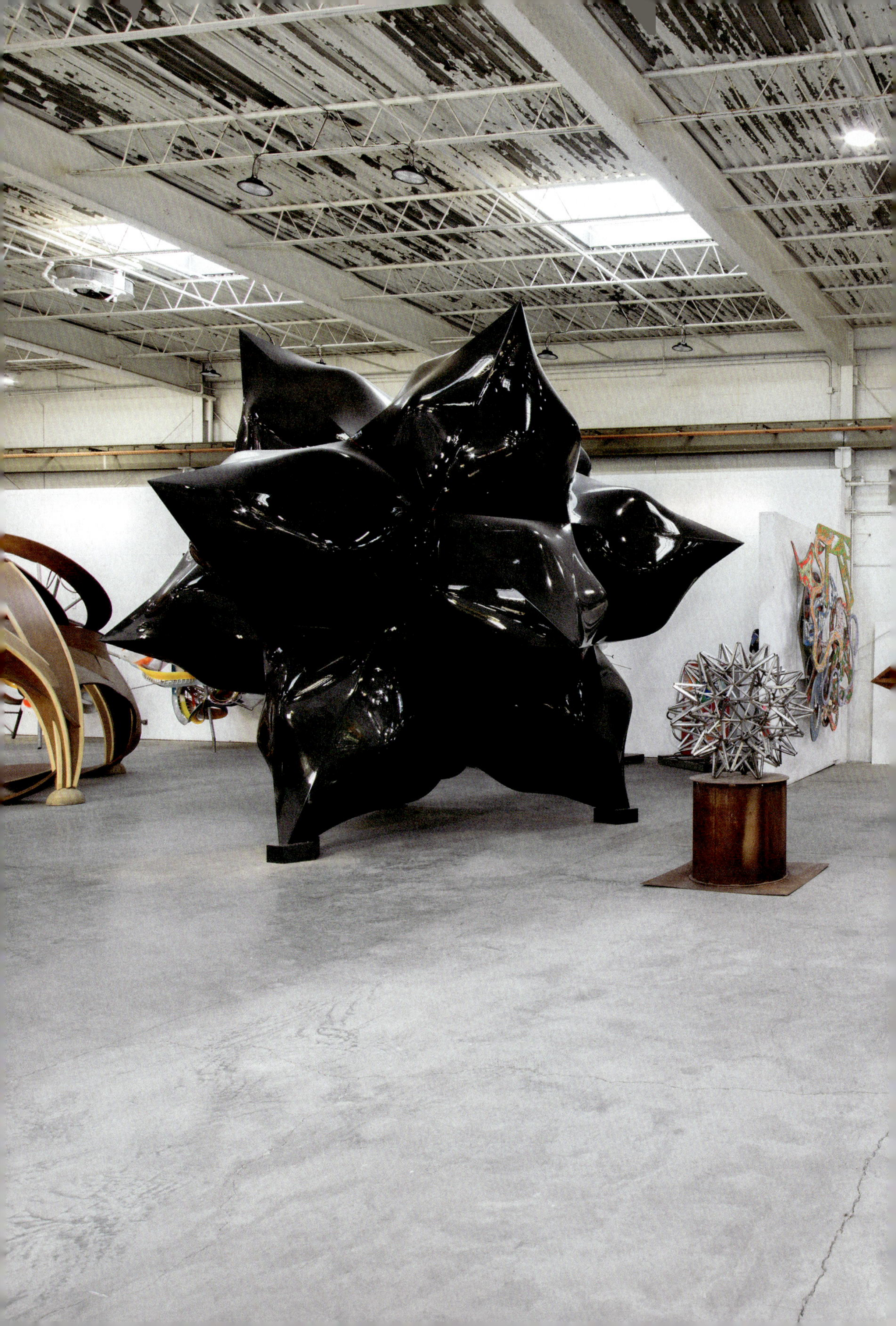

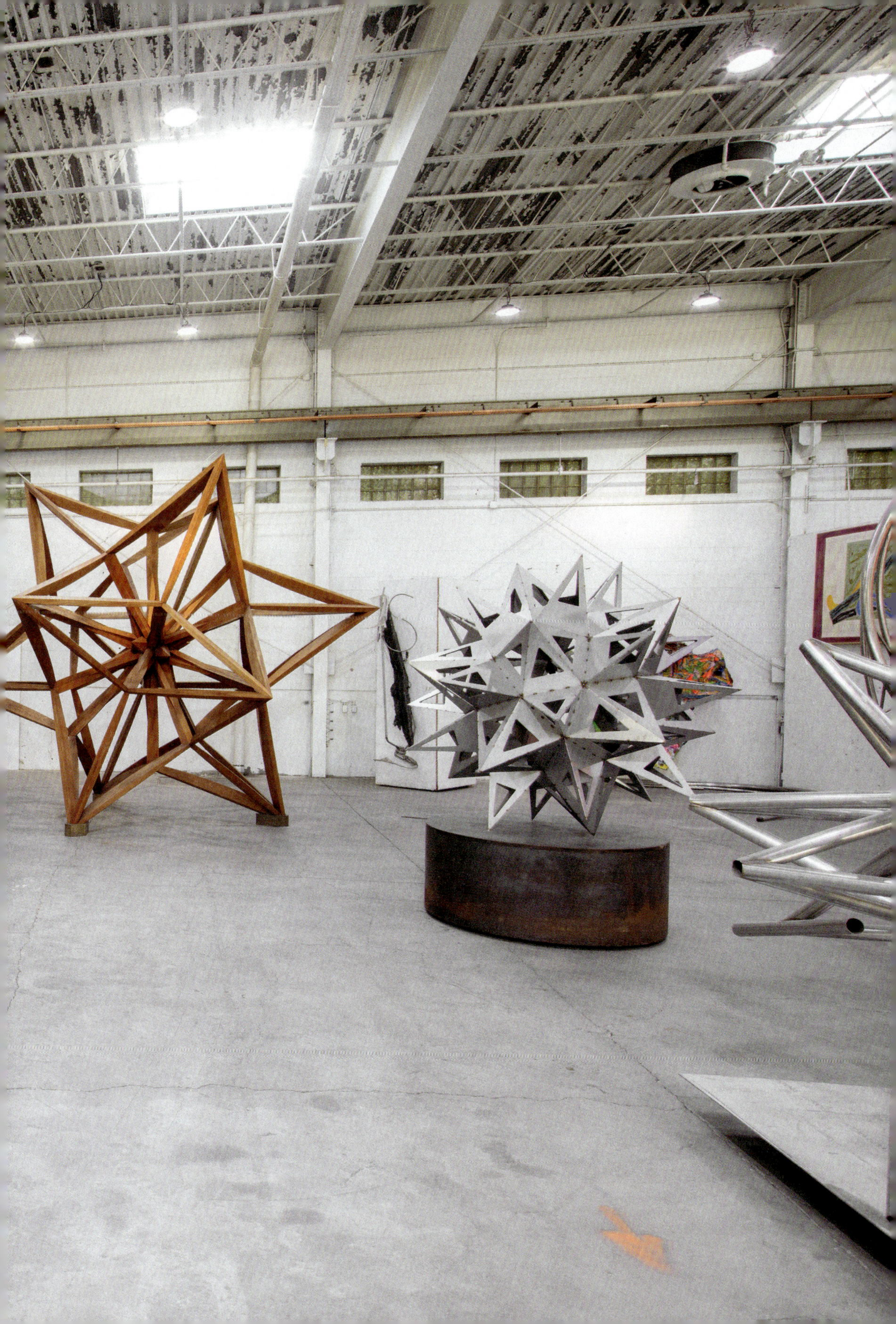

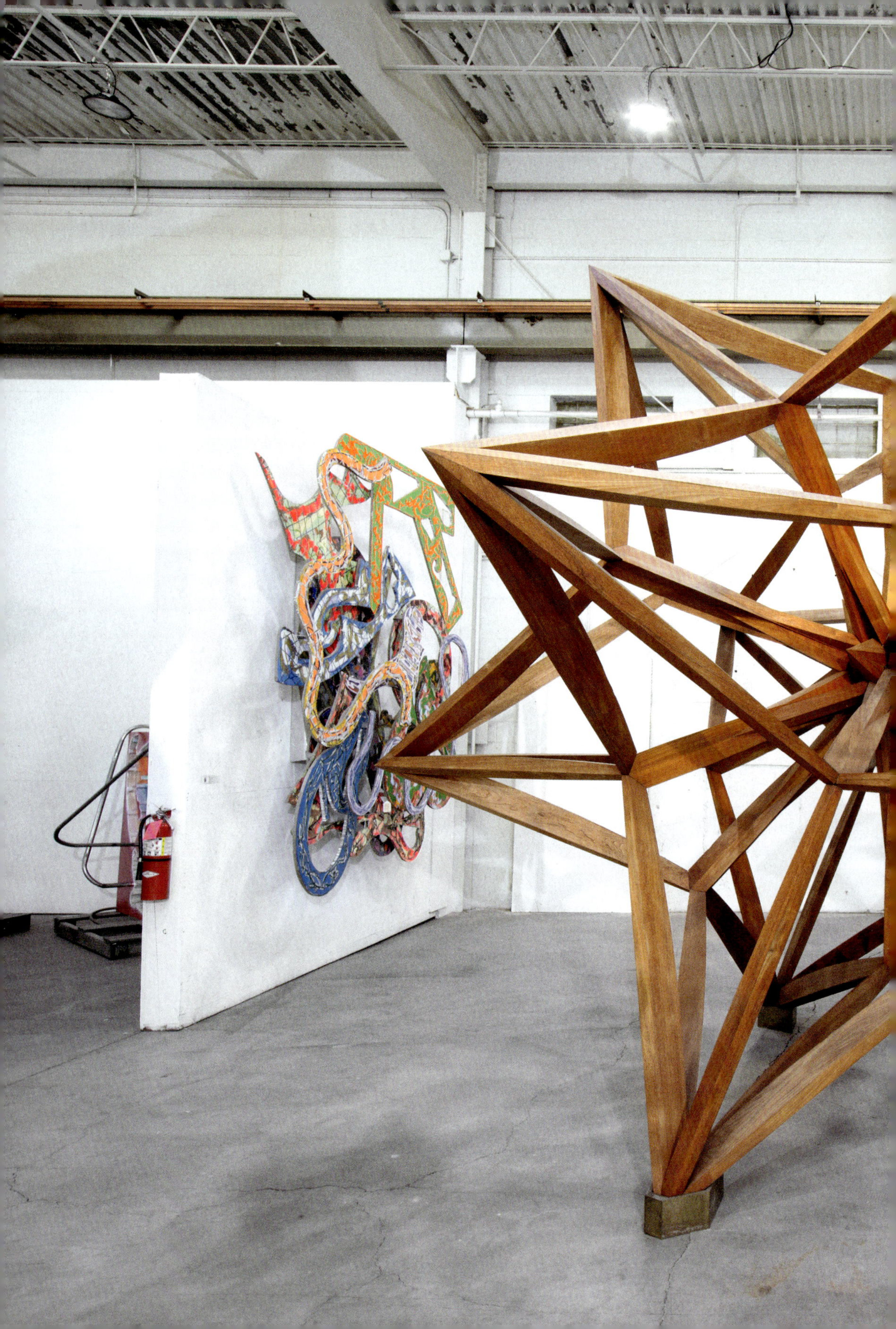

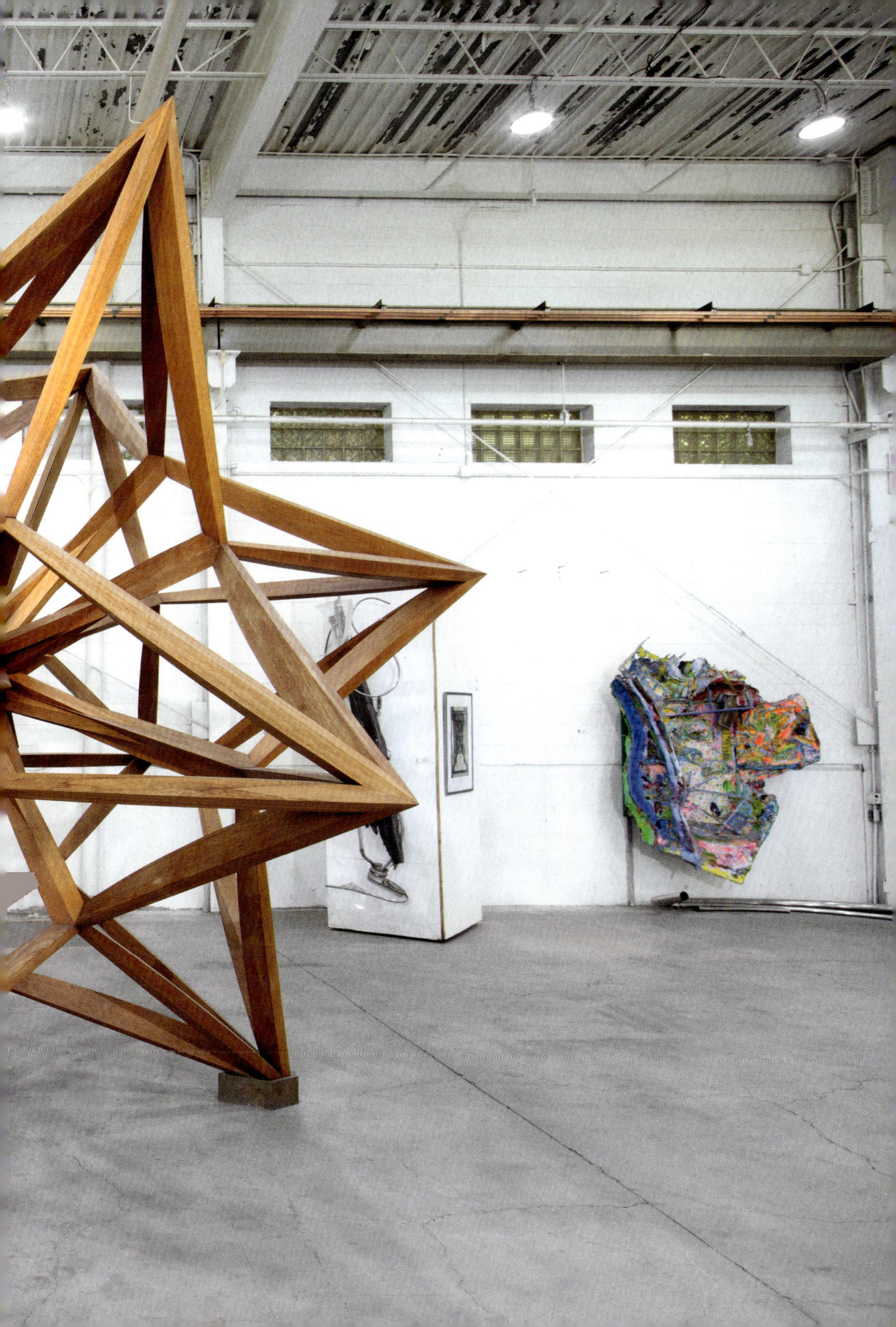

Stick Star, 2017
Stainless steel
106 x 96 x 96
(FS2017.013)

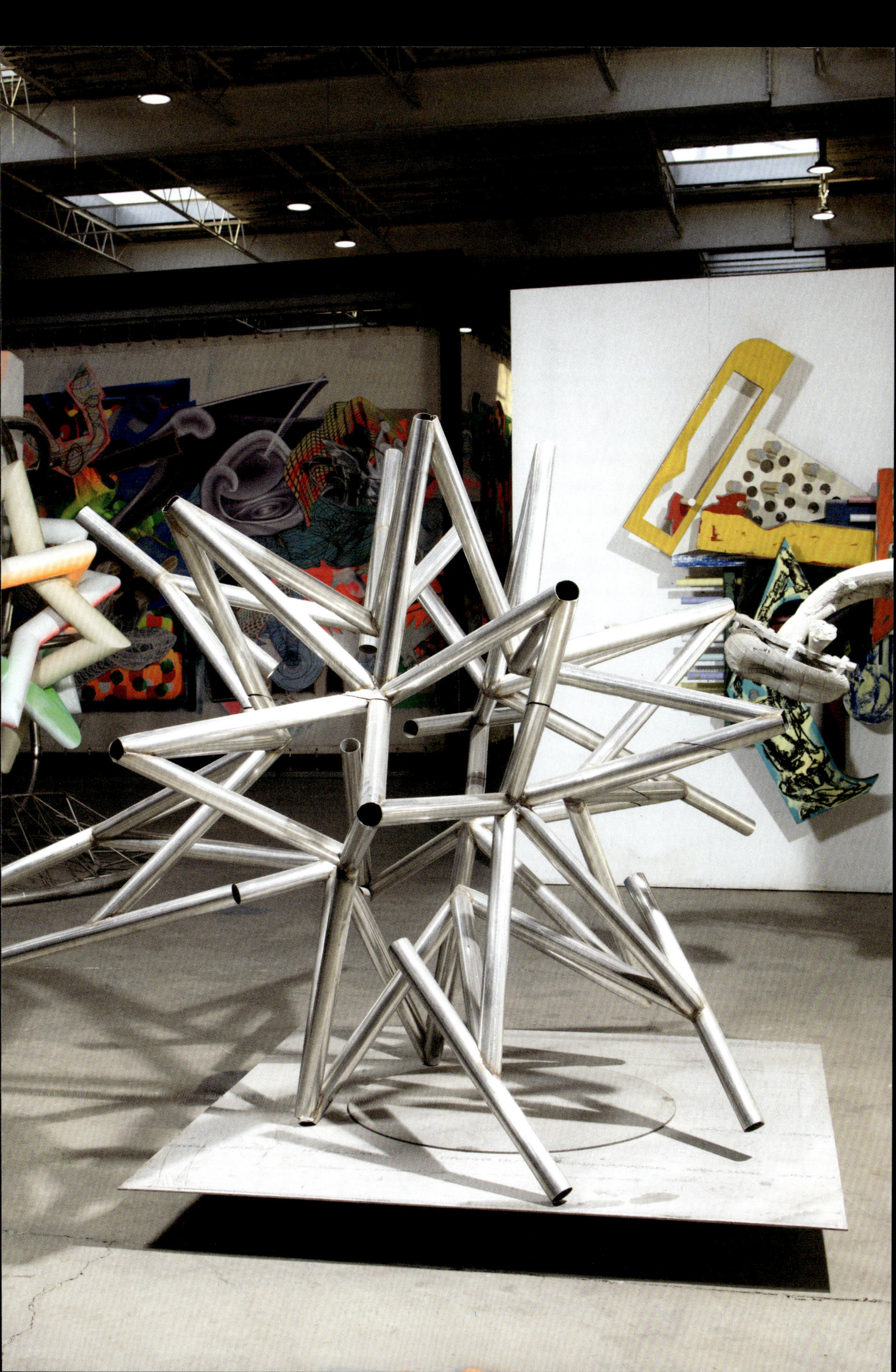

Jay's Star, 2017
Stainless steel
75 x 85 x 85
(FS2017.023)

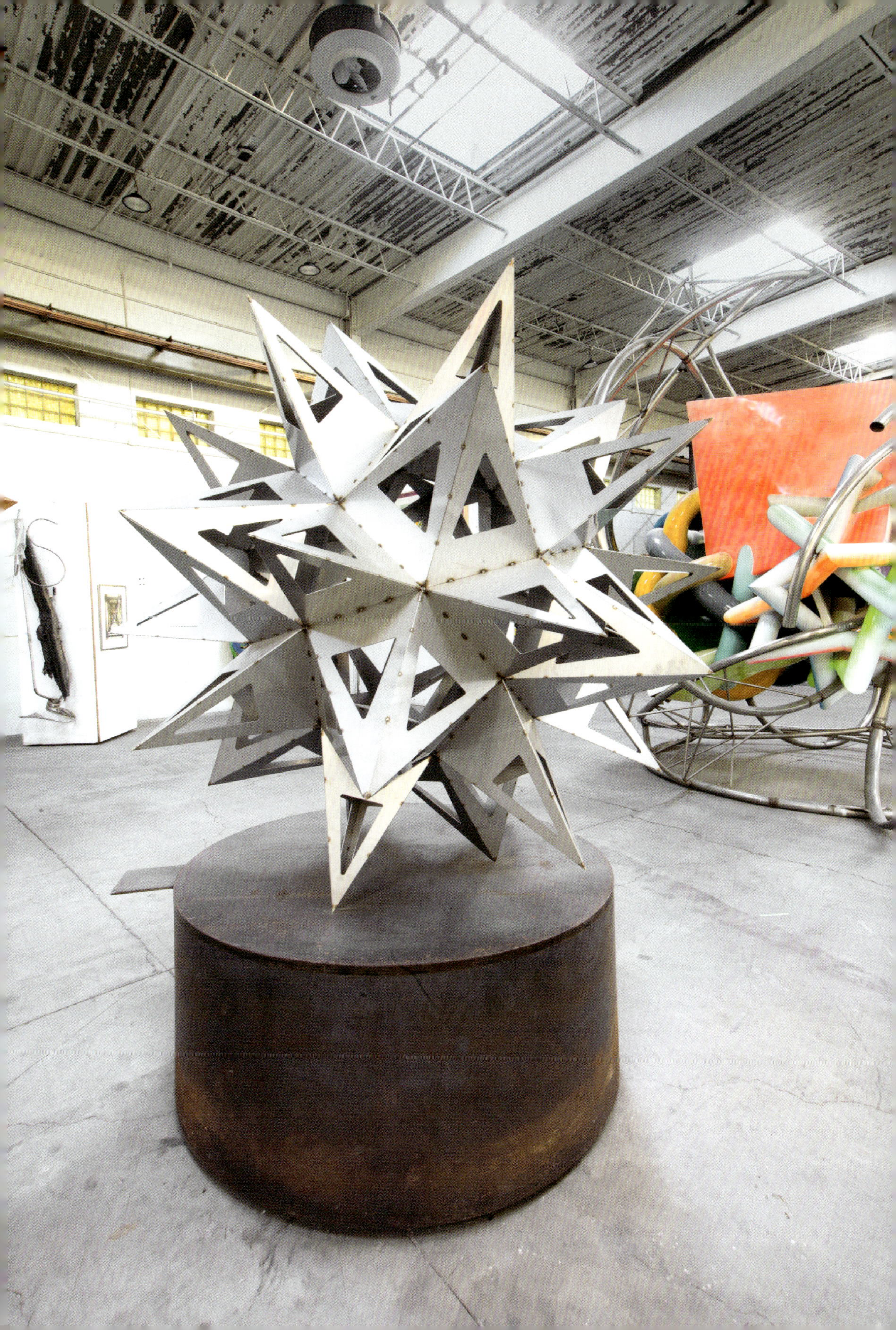

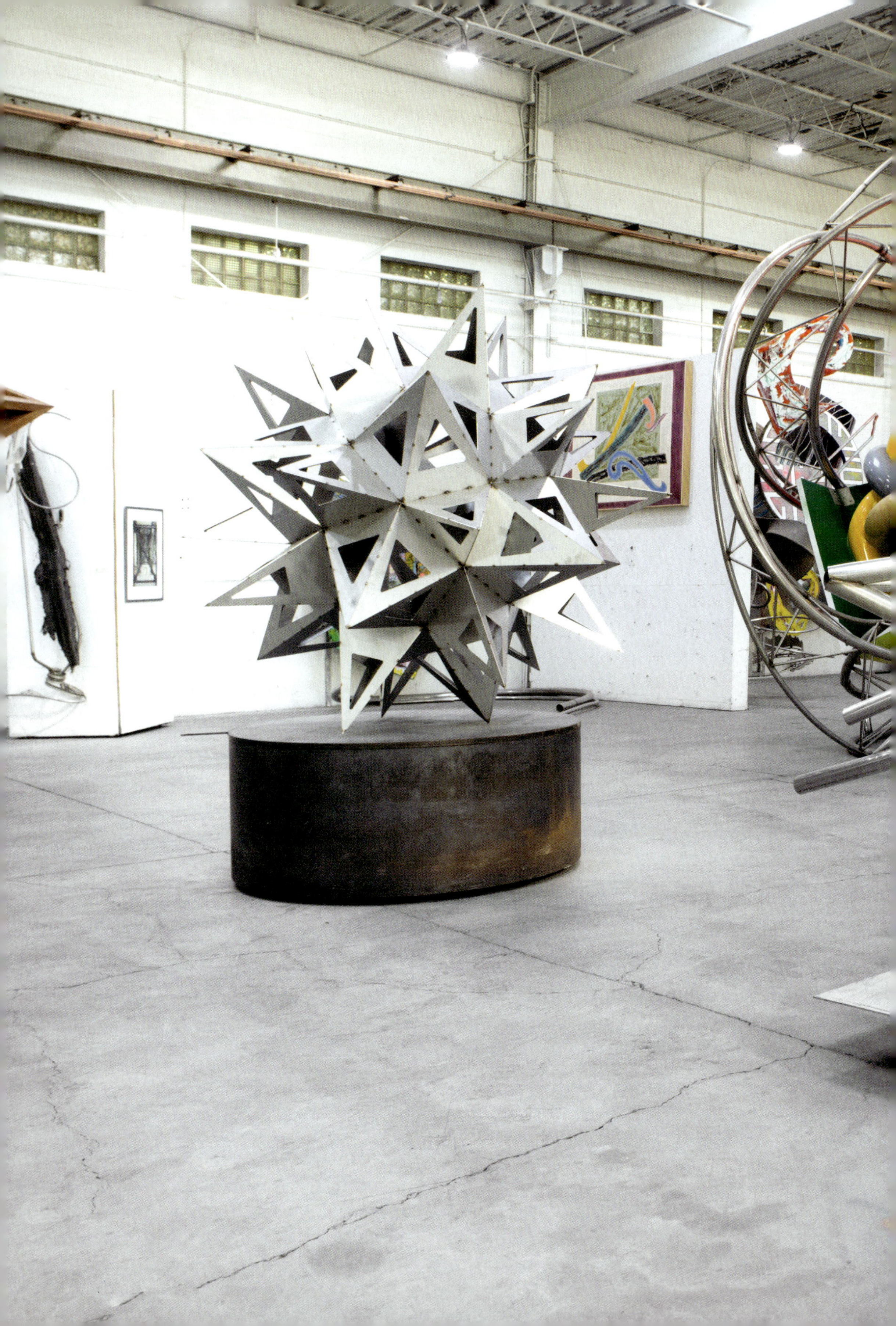

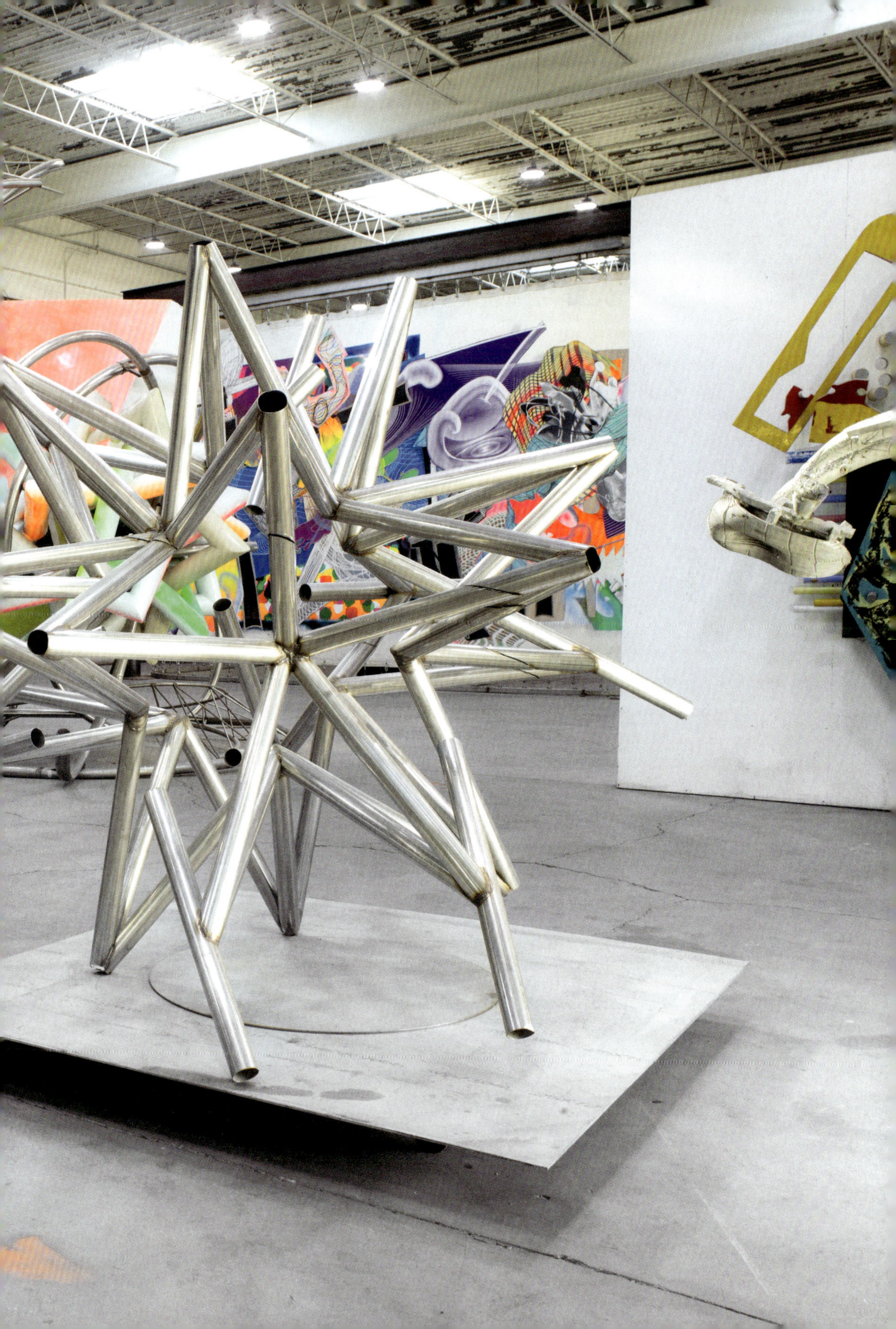

Star with Square Tubing, 2016
Stainless Steel
46 x 46 x 46
(FS2016.001)

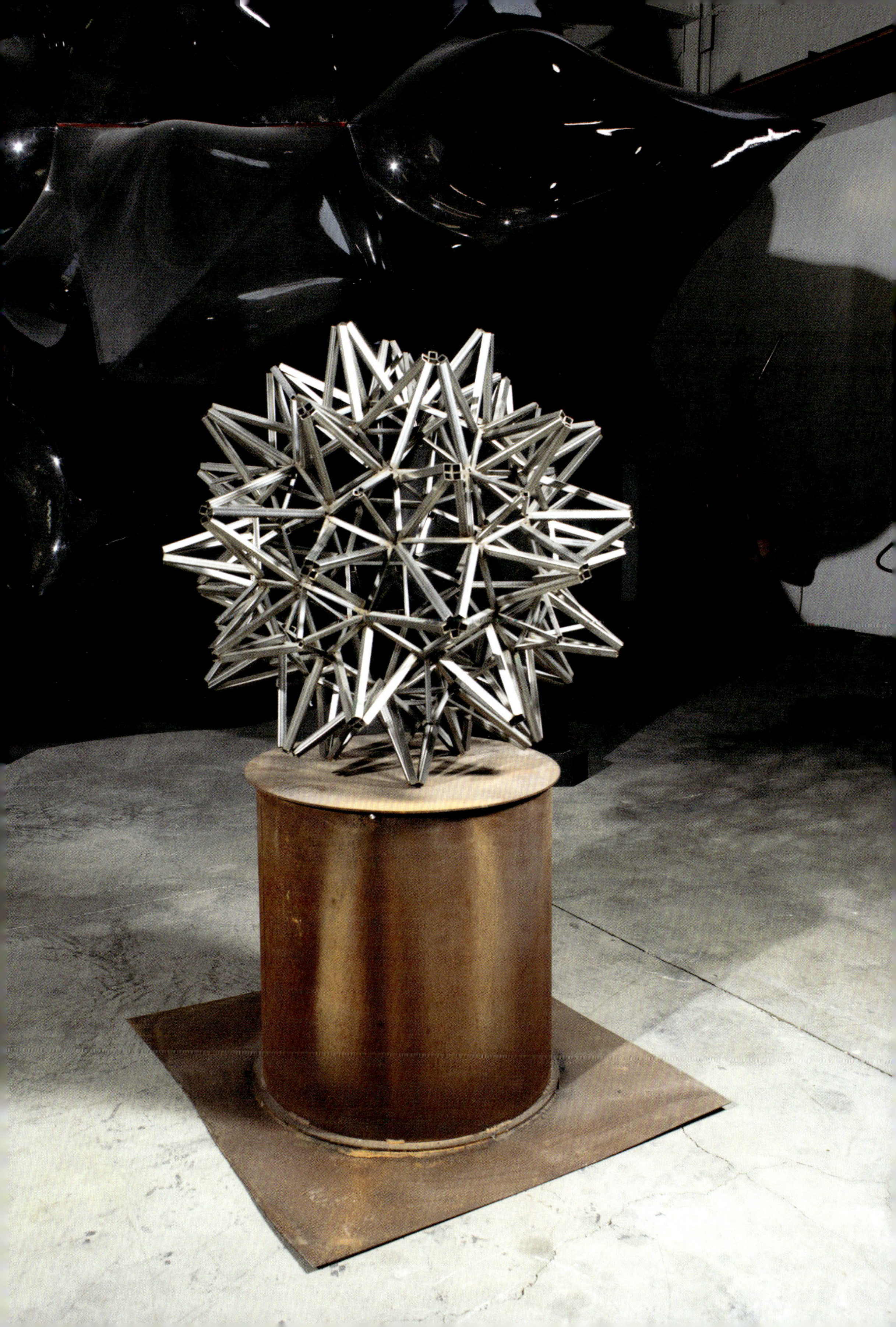

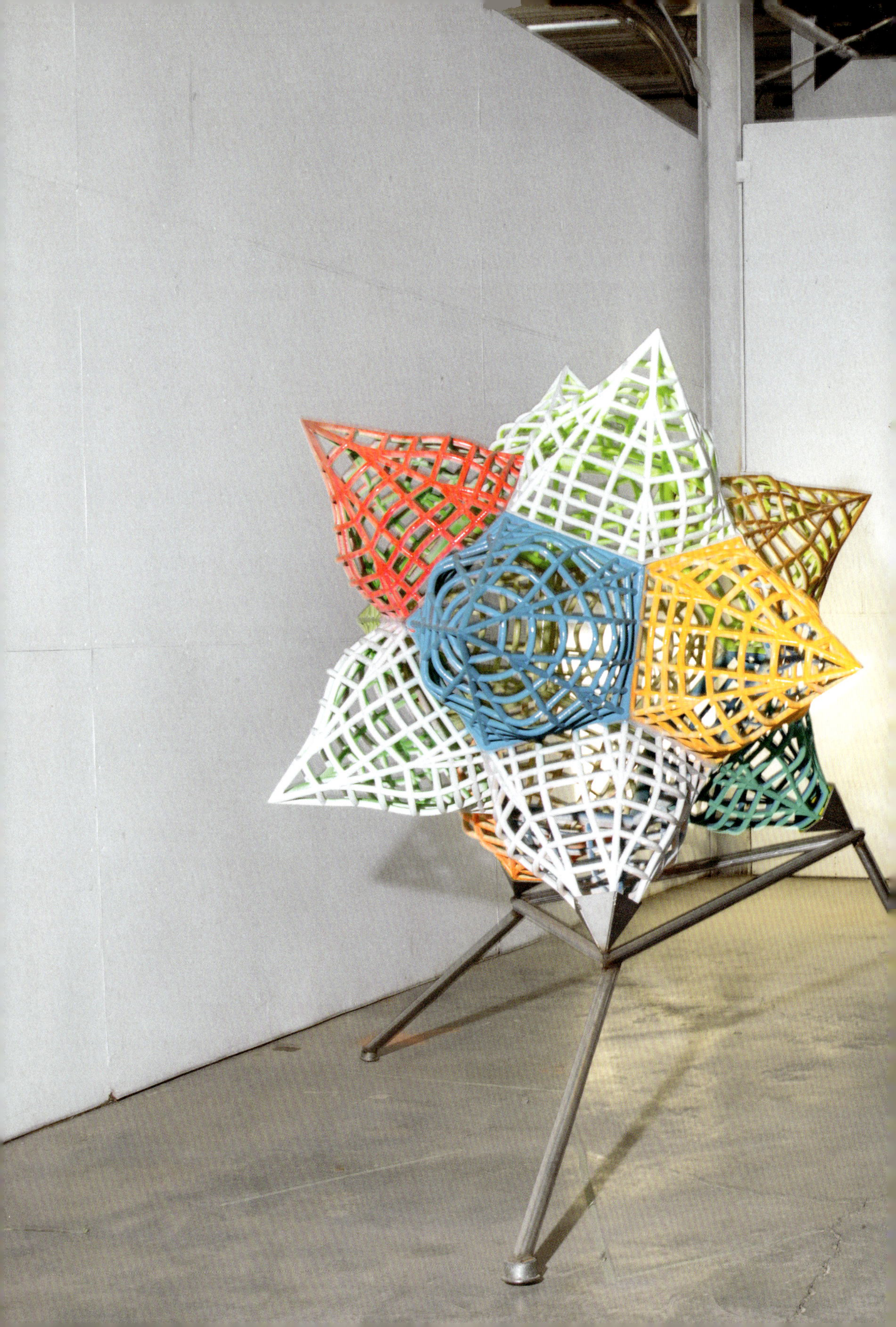

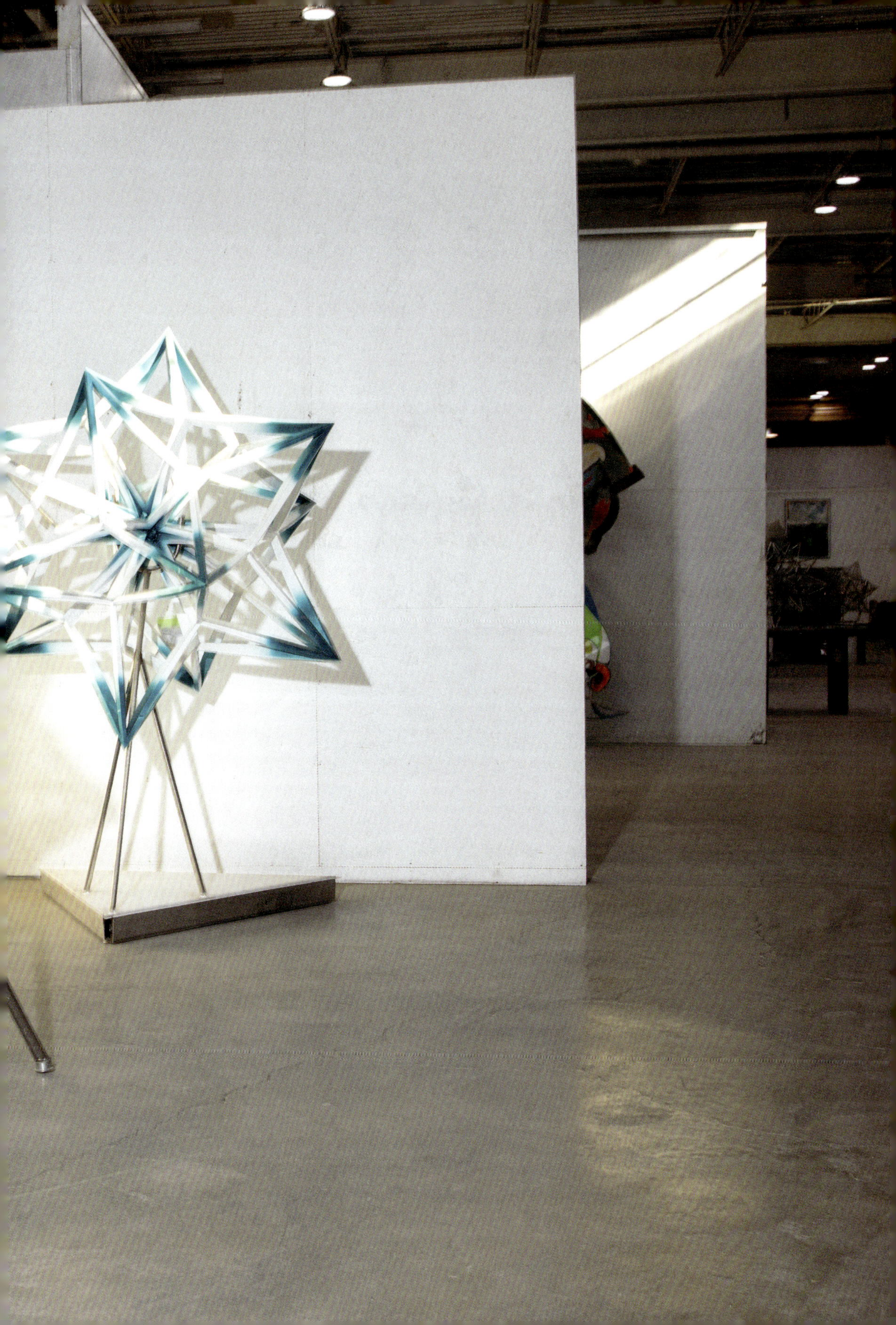

(background)
Nessus and Dejanira, 2017
Aluminum and fiberglass
143 x 139 x 118
(FS2017.011)

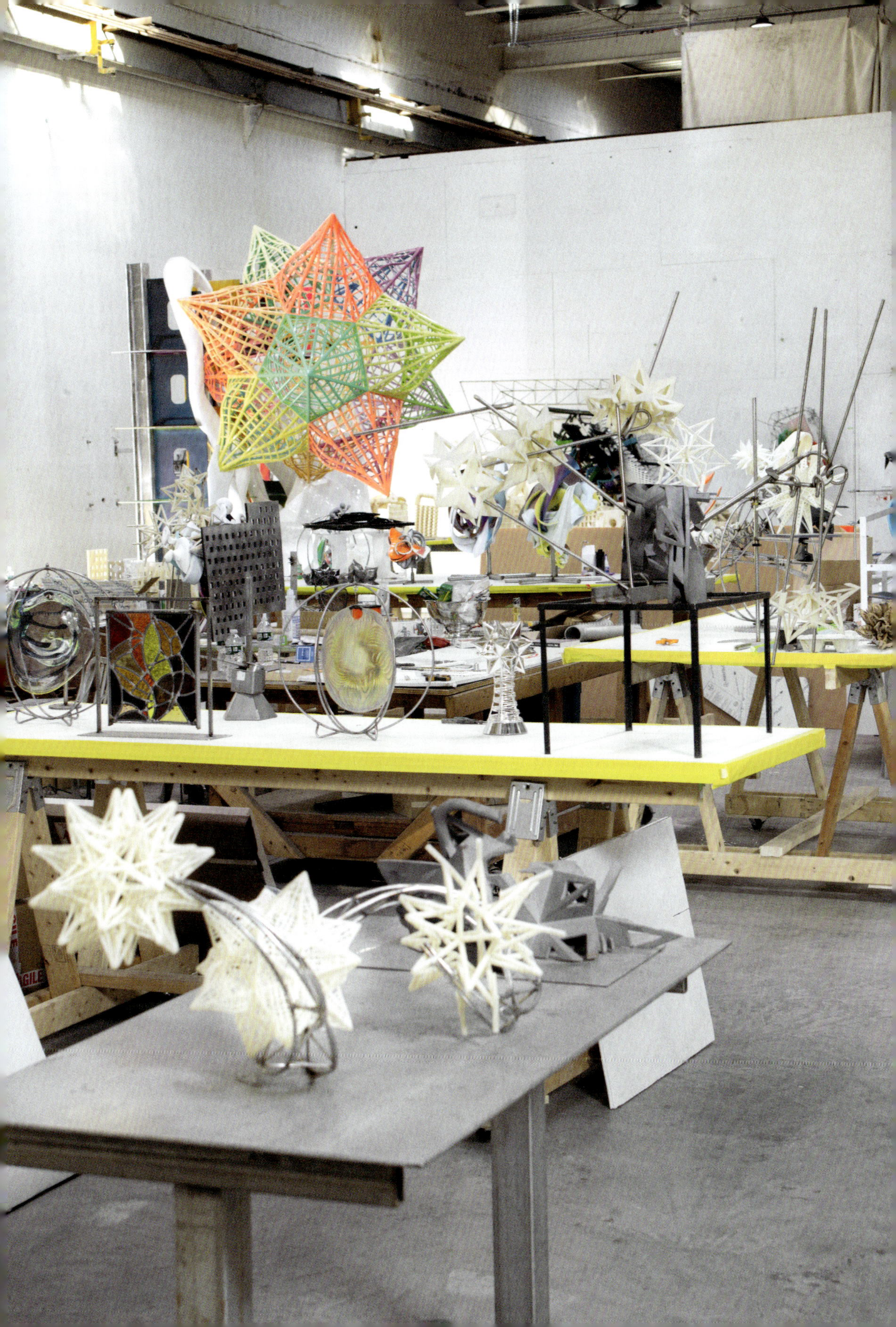

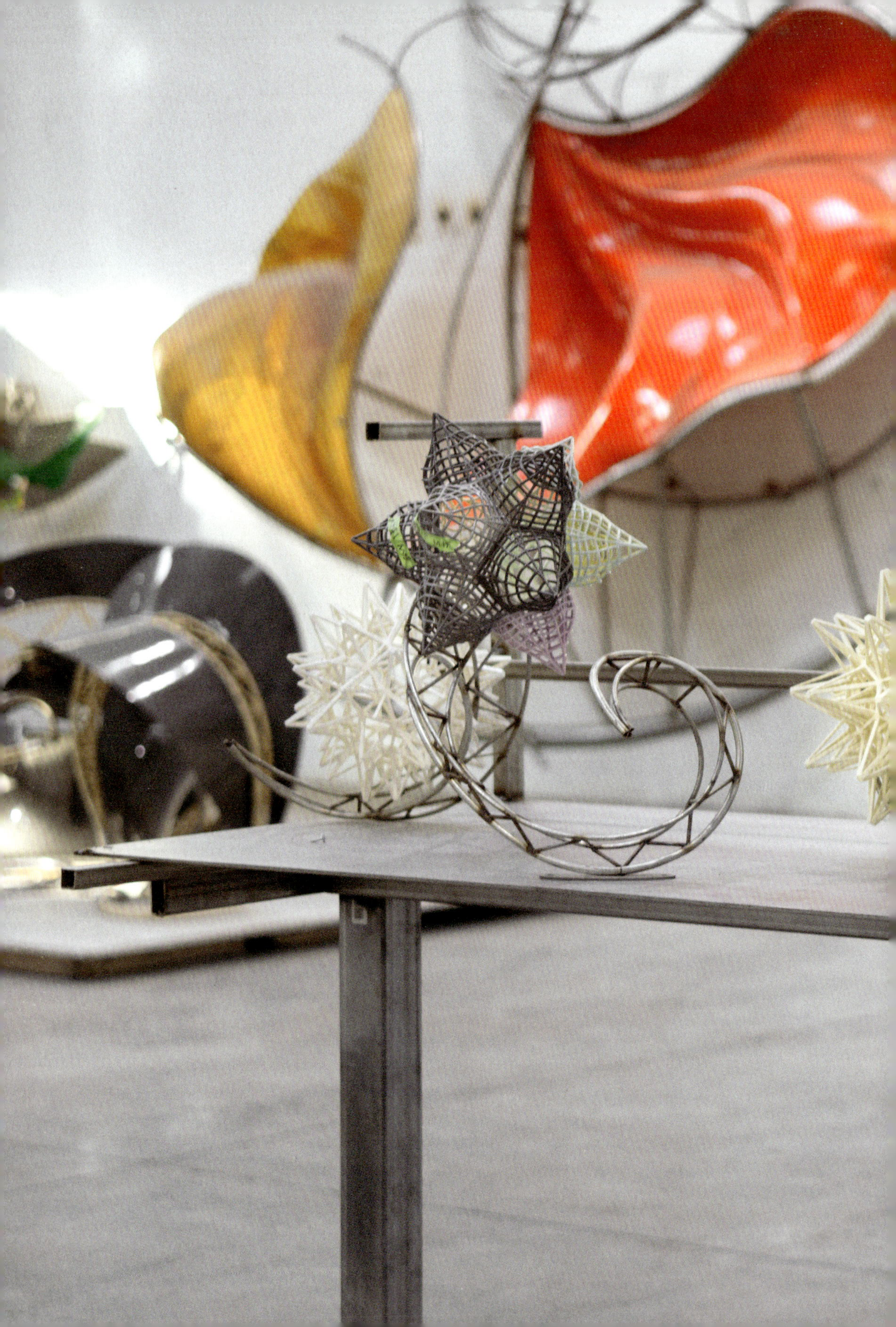

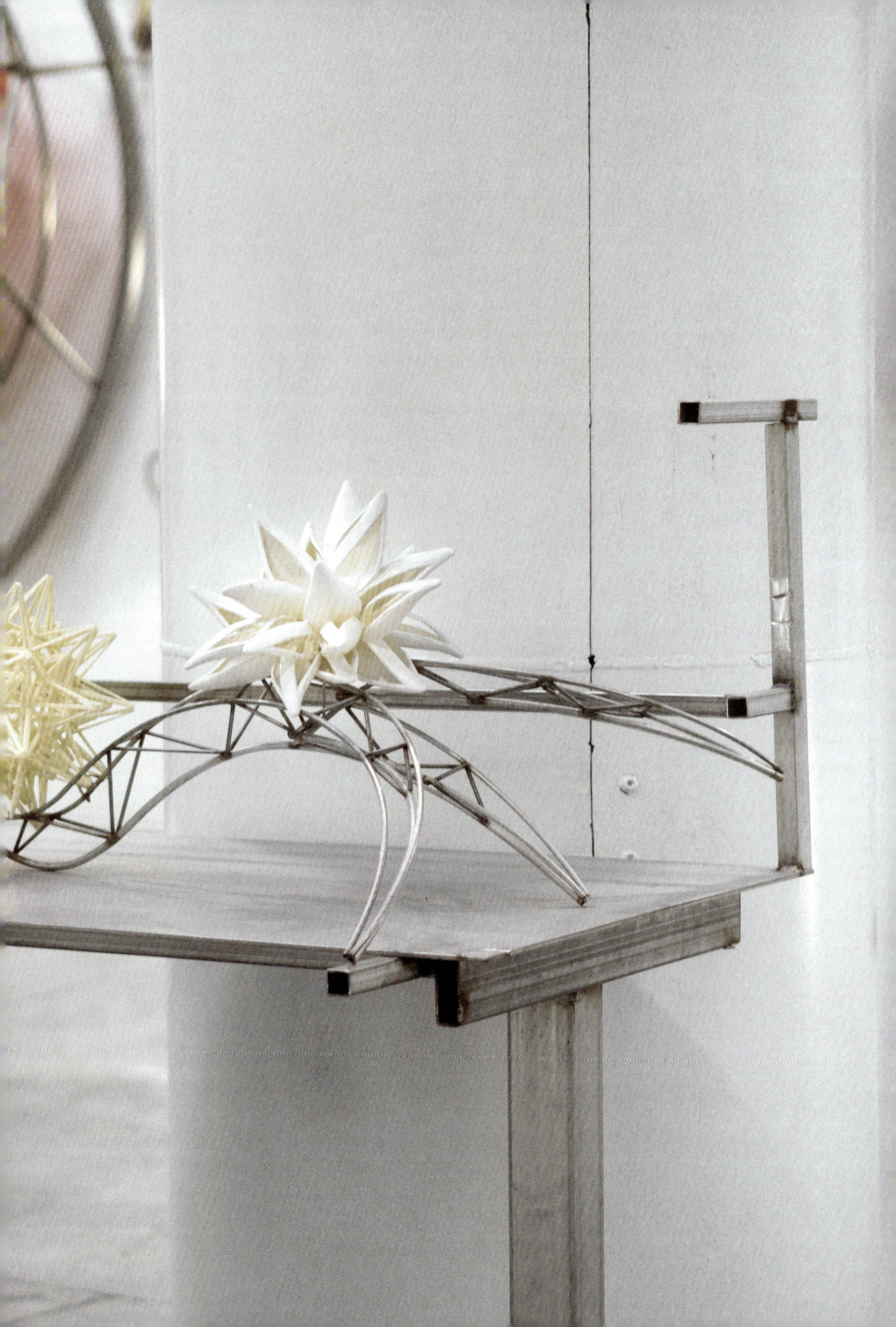

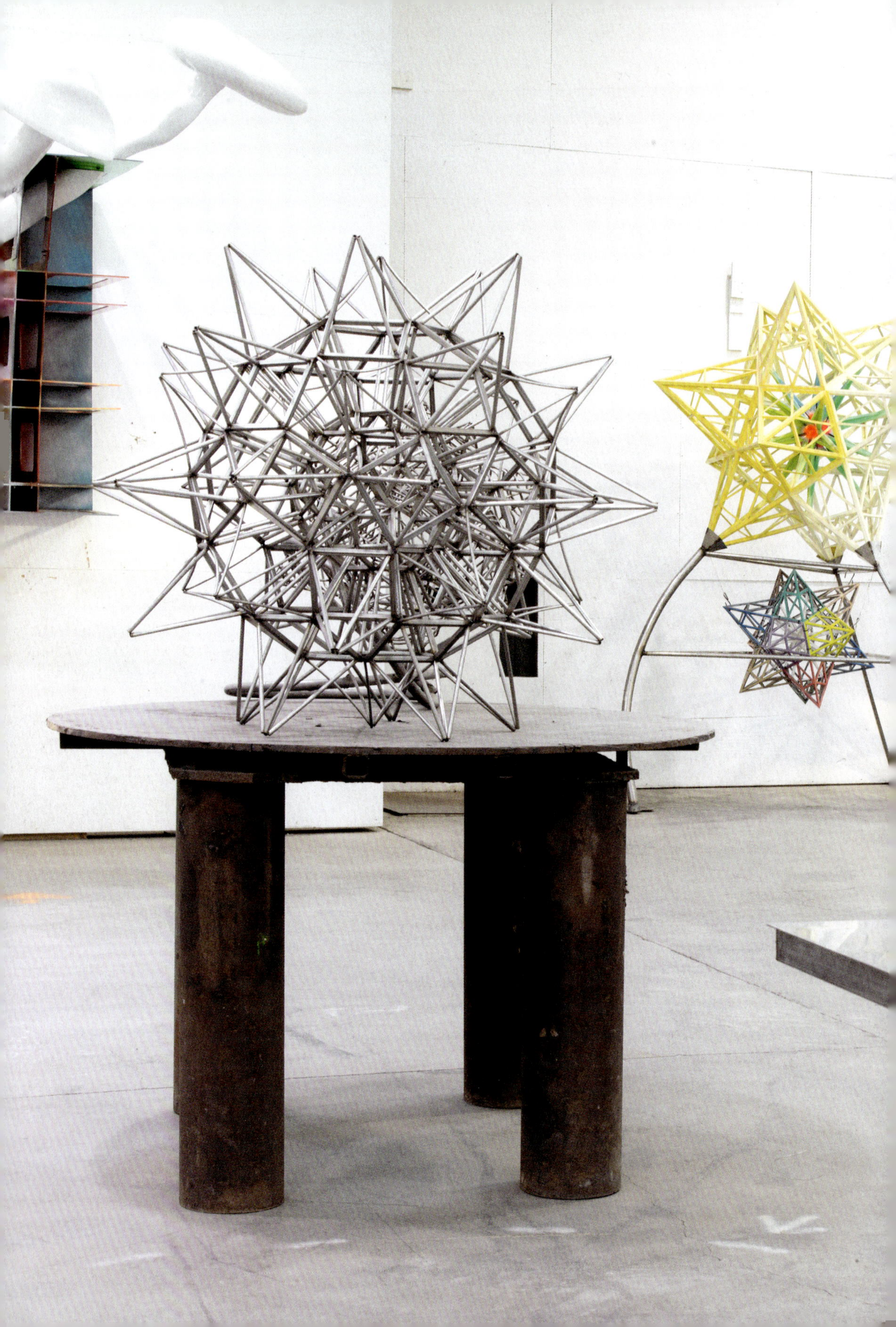

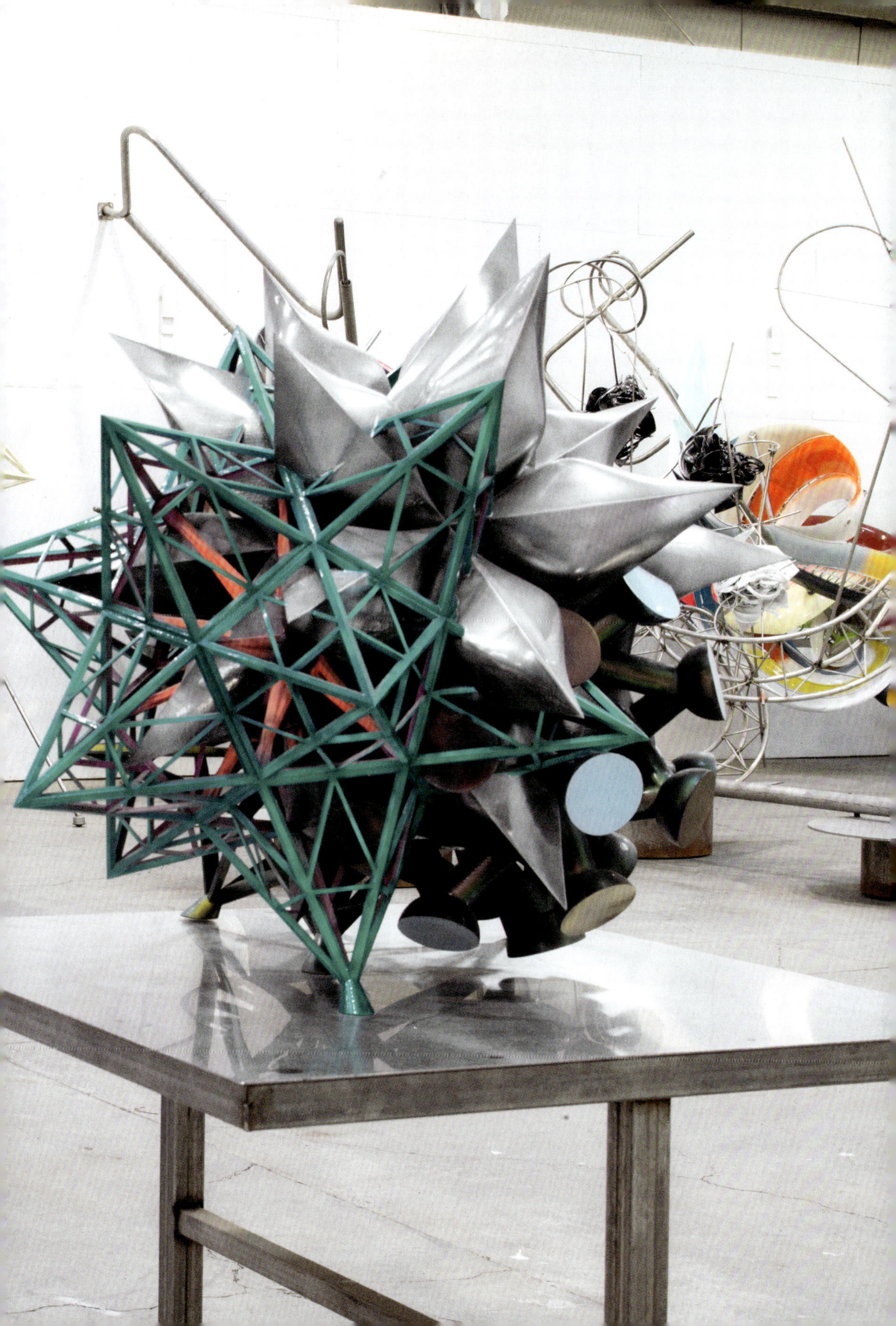

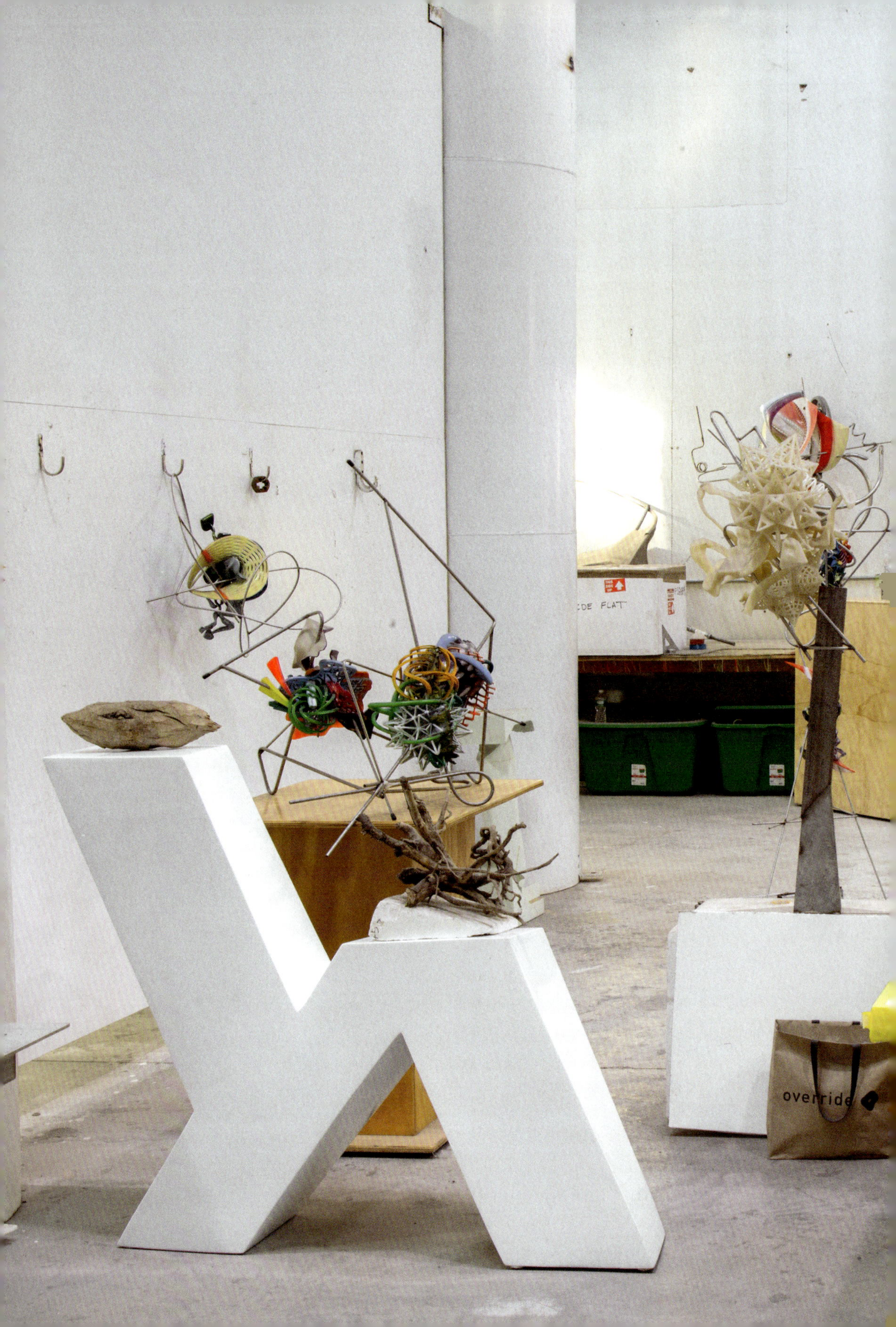

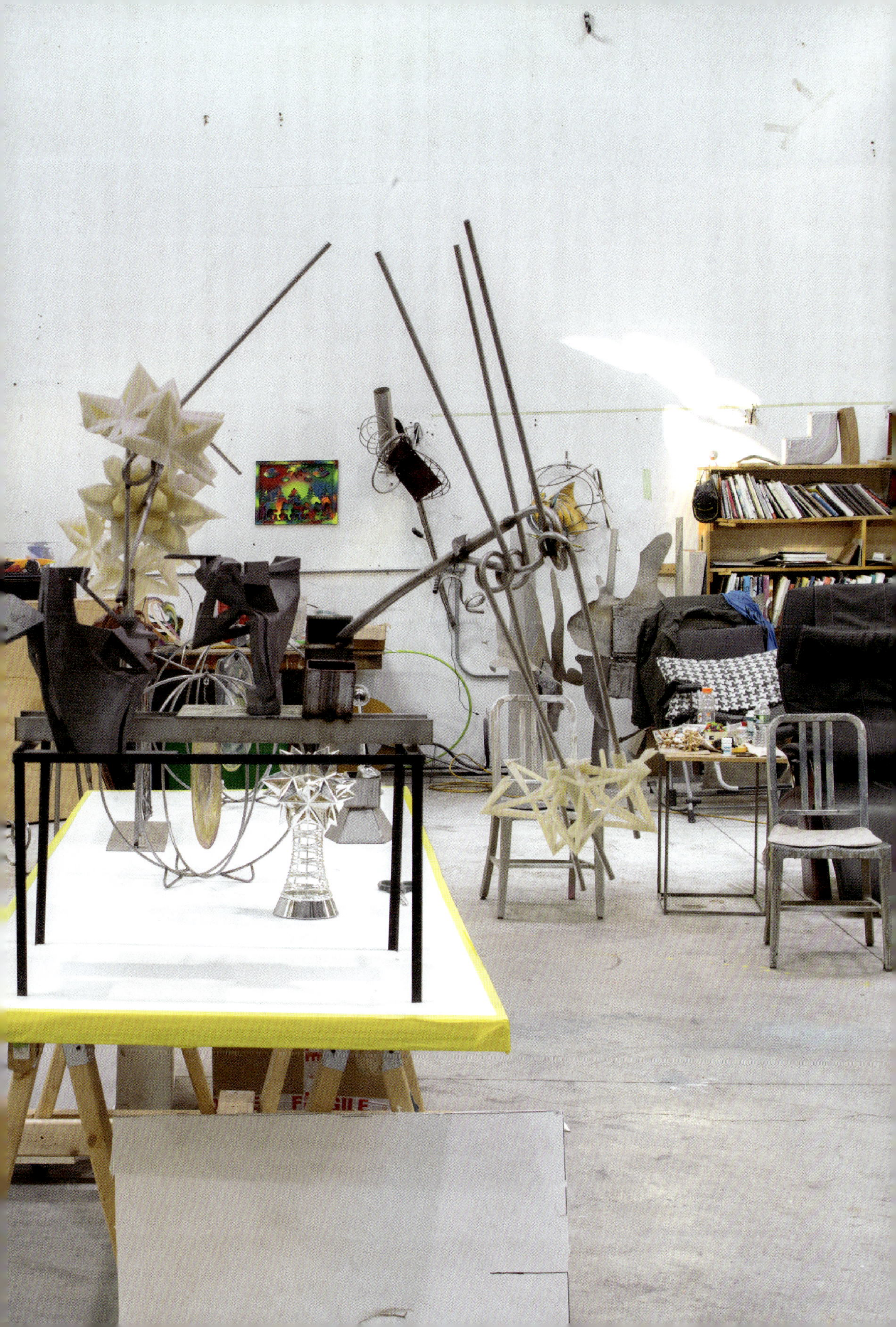

ABOUT THE ARTIST

Born on May 12, 1936, in Malden, Massachusetts, Frank Stella has spent the last six decades producing a remarkable body of work spanning sculpture, painting, printmaking, installation, and public art. He attended Phillips Academy in Andover, Massachusetts, where he participated in a studio art program under the tutelage of abstract painter Patrick Morgan. Stella then continued his studies at Princeton University, dabbling in multidisciplinary courses in history and art history with renowned art historian William Seitz and practical work with artist Stephen Greene. After graduating in 1958 with a Bachelor of Arts degree in History, Stella moved to New York, where his career commenced with a bang—his canonical *Black Paintings* challenged the gestural expression of the Abstract Expressionists of the 1950s, skyrocketing his work into the critical discourse of art history. He had his first solo show at the Leo Castelli Gallery in New York in 1960, and his work has been included in numerous significant historical exhibitions such as *Sixteen Americans* (Museum of Modern Art, New York, 1959), *Geometric Abstraction in America* (Whitney Museum of American Art, New York, 1962), *The Shaped Canvas* (Solomon R. Guggenheim Museum, New York, 1964), and *Documenta 4* (Kassel, Germany, 1968). He has had several major retrospectives at notable institutions, including the Museum of Modern Art, New York (1970 and 1987), where he continues to hold the record for the youngest artist to have a retrospective at age thirty-three; the Museo Nacional Centro de Arte Reina Sofia, Madrid (1995); the Kunstmuseum Wolfsburg (2012); the Whitney Museum of American Art (2015); and the NSU Art Museum, Fort Lauderdale (2017). Impressively traversing time and artistic styles, Stella's contributions to the art world are unparalleled. He is the recipient of several prestigious awards, including the Skowhegan Award for Painting (1981), New York City Mayor's Award for Arts and Culture (1981), Ordre des Arts et des Lettres from the French government (1989), Honorary Royal Academician (1993), and National Medal of Arts from President Barack Obama (2009). Based in New York City, Stella has maintained a studio in Rock Tavern, New York, since 2005. A cavernous, industrial space, once an old cement factory, aptly houses the artist's immense appetite for experimentation and production.

Caitlin Monachino

LIST OF WORKS

All dimensions h x w x d in inches

P. 24
boeta, 2004
Stainless steel tubing and
carbon fiber
74⅝ x 53⅛ x 41
FS2004.009

PP. 15 & 37
Plant City, 1963
Zinc chromate and oil on
canvas
102½ x 102½
Philadelphia Museum of Art
Gift of Agnes Gund
in memory of Anne
d'Harnoncourt, 2008
(Rubin 211)

P. 39
Port Tampa City, 1963*
Red lead on canvas
102 x 102
Courtesy of the artist and
Mnuchin Gallery, New York
(Rubin 215)

P. 41
Untitled, 1964
Pencil and crayon on graph
paper
17 x 21⅞
Gift of the artist
The Museum of Modern Art,
New York, NY

P. 43
Star of Persia, 1967*
Graphite on graph paper
24½ x 27
FS67.178

P. 45
Star of Persia I, 1967*
Lithograph on English Vellum
Graph paper
Edition #14 of 92
26 x 31
Pizzuti Collection
FS67.110
(Axsom/Kolb 1)

P. 6 & 47
Star of Persia II, 1967*
Lithograph on English Vellum
Graph paper
Edition #8 of 92
26 x 31
Collection of Jordan D.
Schnitzer
FS67.111
(Axsom/Kolb 2)

LIST OF WORKS

P. 49
Irving Blum Memorial Edition,
1967
Lithograph on English Vellum
Graph paper
26 x 32
Courtesy National Gallery of
Art, Washington, DC
Gift of Gemini G.E.L.
and the artist
FS67.159
(Axsom/Kolb 3)

P. 51
K.109, 2006
Stainless steel tubing, nylon
RPT, spray paint
19 x 17 x 10
FS2006.043

PP. 52–53
K.161a, 2011
Nylon and lacquer paint
20 x 20 x 20
FS 2011.017

PP. 54–55
K.162, 2011
Nylon and lacquer paint
22 x 22 x 24
FS2011.002

P. 57
K.432, 2013
ABS RTP and stainless steel
59 x 56 x 52
FS2013.011

PP. 58–59
K.159, 2013*
Polyamide (laser-sintered
prototype part)
41 x 49 x 45
FS2013.015

P. 61
October Maquette No. 3,
2014
Elasto plastic, honeycomb
aluminum, Kevlar
13 x 11½ x 11¼
FS2014.060

PP. 34, 62–63
K.359, 2014*
ABS RPT
27½ x 40 x 24
FS2014.017

P. 65
K.140, 2008, 2014
Tusk RPT with stainless steel
tubing
45 x 62 x 36
FS2008.002

P. 67
Puffed Net Star (Smoke I),
2014
Painted RPT with metal
21 x 12 x 11
FS2014.070

P. 69
Puffed Star II, 2014
Polished aluminum
224½ x 224½ x 224½
FS2014.043

PP. 70–71
Black Star, 2014
Carbon fiber
224½ x 224½ x 224½
FS2014.041

P. 73
Frank's Wooden Star, 2014*
Teak wood
157¼ x 157¼ x 157¼
FS2014.047

PP. 74–75
K.374 (Tower with Porcupine),
2015
Elasto plastic
13 x 12 x 8½
FS2015.021

PP. 76–77
*K.505 on Stainless
Background,* 2015*
Elasto plastic, stainless steel
37 x 24 x 24
FS2015.009

PP. 78–79
*Bell Piece on Stainless
Background,* 2016*
Elasto plastic RPT,
stainless steel
24 x 24 x 18
FS2016.066

PP. 80–81
*Shoe Piece on Stainless
Background,* 2016*
Elasto plastic RPT,
stainless steel
24 x 25½ x 17½
FS2016.064

PP. 82–83
Truss with Stars I, 2016*
Nylon RPT with stainless steel
17¾ x 31½ x 13½
FS2016.052

P. 85
Fat Puffed Star Model, 2016*
Nylon RPT
11 x 14 x 13
FS2016.043

LIST OF WORKS

PP. 12 & 87
*Fat 12 Point Carbon Fiber
Star*, 2016*
Carbon fiber
252 x 252 x 204
FS2016.033

P. 89
Alu Truss Star, 2016
Milled aluminum
168 x 168 x 168
FS2016.056

P. 91
Jay's Carbon Fiber Star, 2016
Carbon fiber and RPT joints
111 x 94 x 94
FS2016.071

P. 93
*Stainless split star with truss
segments*, 2016*
Stainless steel
88 x 67 x 84
FS2016.081

P. 95
Star with Square Tubing,
2016*
Stainless Steel
46 x 46 x 46
FS2016.001

PP. 96–97
Pavillion, 2016
Carbon fiber roof, painted
steel base with three
aluminum stars
300 x 552 x 552
FS2016.058

P. 99
Flat Pack Star, 2016*
Coated Baltic birch plywood
48 x 48 x 48
FS2016.061

P. 101
Corian Star, 2017
Corian
47 x 47 x 47
FS2017.012

P. 103
Jay's Star, 2017*
Stainless steel
75 x 85 x 85
FS2017.023

P. 105
Stick Star, 2017*
Stainless steel
106 x 96 x 96
FS2017.013

P. 107
Jasper's Split Star, 2017*
Aluminum
202 x 257 x 249
FS2017.007

P. 18 & 109
Maquette for Star, 2017*
Strong flexible RPT
10 x 12 x 12
FS2017.035

P. 111
Nessus and Dejanira, 2017*
Aluminum and fiberglass
143 x 139 x 118
FS2017.011

PP. 112–13
Truss with Stars II, 2018*
Elasto plastic, paint, steel
21½ x 38 x 16½
FS2018.025

PP. 114–15
Botanical Star on Stainless Background, 2018*
Elasto plastic, paint, stainless steel
16½ x 16½ x 10½
FS2018.033

P. 32 & 117
Model for the Phoenix Suns I, 2019*
Elasto plastic and paint
13 x 13 x 12
FS2019.031

Also included in the exhibition:

P. 19
Natural pod star, no date*
Seedpod of the Travelers Palm, *Phenakospermum guyannense*
7 x 17 x 10
FS2019.064

PP. 118–65
Frank Stella's Stars, A Survey, The Aldrich Contemporary Art Museum, September 21, 2020 to May 9, 2021 (installation views)

PP. 2–3, 10, 22–23, 166–87
Frank Stella's Studio, Rock Tavern, NY

*Works on view in *Frank Stella's Stars, A Survey,* September 21, 2020 to May 9, 2021, The Aldrich Contemporary Art Museum.

All works courtesy of the artist and Marianne Boesky Gallery, New York and Aspen, unless otherwise noted. All works © 2020 Frank Stella / Artists Rights Society (ARS), New York.

PHOTOGRAPHY CREDITS

Christopher Burke Studio:
P. 65

Frank Stella Studio: PP. 18,
32, 109, 112–13, 117

Jason Mandella: PP. 2–3, 10,
19, 22–23, 43, 73, 85, 166–87,
118–65, Front cover, Back
cover

Digital Image © The Museum
of Modern Art / Licensed by
SCALA / Art Resource, NY:
P. 41

Object Studies: PP. 21,
76–77, 78–79, 80–81, 93, 99,
101, 107, 111, 114–15

Bill Orcutt: PP. 61, 74–75,
82–83

Tom Powel Imaging: P. 39

Ralphoto Studios, Alan Geho:
P. 45

Steven Sloman: PP. 24, 51

Strode Photographic: PP. 6,
47

Robert Wedemeyer: P. 105

Bruce White: PP. 52–53,
54–55, 67

Jason Wyche: PP. 12, 34,
62–63, 69, 71, 87, 89, 91, 95,
96–97

Guillaume Ziccarelli: PP. 57,
58–59

P. 8
Frank Stella
Manteneia III, 1968
Acrylic on canvas
Overall: 60 x 240
*Highlights of the 1967–1968
Art Season* (installation view),
The Aldrich Contemporary Art
Museum, 1968

P. 13
Frank Stella
Louisiana Lottery Co., 1962 (left)
Synthetic polymer and pencil on
canvas
85 x 85
Botafogo I, 1975 (right)
Lacquer and oil on aluminum
86 x 130
Changes (installation view),
The Aldrich Contemporary Art
Museum, 1983

P. 13
Frank Stella
Die Fahne hoch!, 1959
Enamel on canvas
Overall: 121 5/8 x 72 13/16
Gift of Mr. and Mrs. Eugene
M. Schwartz and purchase,
with funds from the John I.
H. Baur Purchase Fund; the
Charles and Anita Blatt Fund;
Peter M. Brant;
B. H. Friedman; the Gilman
Foundation, Inc.; Susan
Morse Hilles; The Lauder
Foundation; F. Inv. N.: 75.22,
Whitney Museum of American
Art, New York, NY
Digital image © Whitney
Museum of American Art
/ Licensed by Scala / Art
Resource, NY
(Rubin 35)

P. 14
Frank Stella
*Untitled (list of "Copper
Paintings," 1960–61, and
"Purple Paintings," 1961)*,
1961
Pencil on yellow lined paper
10¾ x 8½
Kunstmuseum Basel
Photo: Martin P. Buhler

P. 20
Frank Stella
Jasper's Dilemma, 1962
Alkyd on canvas
77 x 154
Collection of Irma and
Norman Braman
Photo: Kevin Todora
(Rubin 178)

P. 27
Johannes Kepler, *Mysterium
Cosmographicum* (Tubingen,
Austria: University of
Tubingen, 1597, 2nd ed.
1621), 24
Photo: Courtesy of the
Archives, California Institute
of Technology

P. 28
Johannes Kepler, *Harmonices
Mundi* (Linz, Austria: Johann
Planck, 1619), 58–59

P. 29
Charles Sheeler
American Interior, 1934
Oil on canvas
33¼ × 30¼
Yale University Art Gallery
Gift of Mrs. Paul Moore

P. 33
Figure 328, a Nassellarian
skeleton, *Callimitra agnesae*,
from D'Arcy Wentworth
Thompson's *On Growth and
Form* (1917; Cambridge:
Cambridge University Press,
1942), 712

Claudia Lonkin
Visitor Experience
Coordinator

Chris Manning
Head of Exhibitions and
Facilities

Caitlin Monachino
Curatorial Assistant

Jamie Pearl
Head of Special Events and
Rentals

Claire Ritz
Digital Media Assistant

Lorena Sferlazza
Education Assistant

Amy Smith-Stewart
Senior Curator

Barbara Toplin
Volunteer Archivist

Jen Wieland
Accountant

Published on the occasion of the exhibition *Frank Stella's Stars, A Survey*, organized by The Aldrich Contemporary Art Museum, September 21, 2020 to May 9, 2021.

Curated by Richard Klein, Exhibitions Director, and Amy Smith-Stewart, Senior Curator

Generous support for *Frank Stella's Stars, A Survey* is provided by the Anne S. Richardson Fund, the Speyer Family Foundation, Martin Margulies, Diana Bowes and James Torrey, Linda and Michael Dugan, and Patricia and Lawrence Kemp.

Copy Editor: Mary Cason
Catalogue design: Gretchen Kraus
Production Coordinator: Caitlin Monachino
Printing: Conti Tipocolor, Florence, Italy

The Aldrich Contemporary Art Museum

The Aldrich Contemporary Art Museum
258 Main Street
Ridgefield, CT 06877
thealdrich.org

GREGORY R. MILLER & CO.

Gregory R. Miller & Co.
62 Cooper Square
New York, NY 10003
grmandco.com

Distributed worldwide by
ARTBOOK | DAP
artbook.com

ISBN: 978-1-941366-29-5

Library of Congress Control Number: 2020948701